HANS KOSMALA

STUDIES, ESSAYS AND REVIEWS

VOLUME I

HANS KOSMALA

STUDIES, ESSAYS AND REVIEWS

VOLUME ONE

OLD TESTAMENT

[redacted]

LEIDEN
E. J. BRILL
1978

[redacted]

ISBN 90 04 05459 6

PRINTED IN THE NETHERLANDS

CONTENTS

Preface VII
Abbreviations IX
Introduction to Volume One XI

The Name of God (YHWH and HU') 1
Annual of the Swedish Theological Institute, II, 1963, 103-106

Agnostos Theos 5
Annual of the Swedish Theological Institute, II, 1963, 106-108

„Anfang, Mitte und Ende" 8
Annual of the Swedish Theological Institute, II, 1963, 108-111

The So-Called Ritual Decalogue 12
Annual of the Swedish Theological Institute, I, 1962, 31-61

Agros Lustrare 43
Annual of the Swedish Theological Institute, II, 1963, 111-114

Mot and the Vine 47
Annual of the Swedish Theological Institute, III, 1964, 147-151

The "Bloody Husband" 52
Vetus Testamentum, XII, 1962, 14-28

J. B. Segal, The Hebrew Passover from the Earliest Times to A.D. 70 67
Vetus Testamentum, XIV, 1964, 504-509

"At the End of the Days" 73
Annual of the Swedish Theological Institute, II, 1963, 27-37

Form and Structure of Ancient Hebrew Poetry, I 84
Vetus Testamentum, XIV, 1964, 423-445

Form and Structure of Ancient Hebrew Poetry, II 107
Vetus Testamentum, XVI, 1966, 152-180

Form and Structure of Isaiah 58 136
Annual of the Swedish Theological Institute, V, 1967, 69-81

Maśkîl 149
Gaster Festschrift (Journal of the Ancient Near Eastern Society of Columbia University, Vol. *5*), 1973, 235-241

A. Dupont-Sommer, Les écrits esséniens découverts près de la Mer Morte 156
Vetus Testamentum, X, 1959, 349-351

H. W. Huppenbauer, Der Mensch zwischen zwei Welten . 159
Vetus Testamentum, XI, 1961, 356-359

Jacob Liver, The House of David 163
Christian News from Israel, X, 3-4, 1959, 36-37

PREFACE

The articles collected here were written and published during four decades up to 1973 in various journals in German or English and are reprinted in their original form. Only a selection can be offered; an almost complete bibliography will be found in ASTI IX, 1974. The studies and essays are divided into three parts and arranged, not chronologically in the sequence of their appearance, but according to their subject matter: (1) Old Testament, (2) New Testament, (3) Judaism. A few book reviews have been added. As the articles cover a wide area, introductions preceding the three parts give a short survey of the material. Friends, including some of my former students, asked me to reissue the articles, but my special thanks must go to Professor P. A. H. de Boer who has often been my mentor and not only encouraged me to prepare this selection of writings but also arranged for their republication by E. J. Brill who kindly accepted and undertook the task.

July 1977
Compton Abdale
Cheltenham, Glos.
England

Hans Kosmala

ABBREVIATIONS

ASTI	Annual of the Swedish Theological Institute
BCIJS	Bulletin of the Christian Institute of Jewish Studies
CJP	The Church and the Jewish People (A Symposium ed. by Göte Hedenquist)
CNI	Christian News from Israel
GF	Gaster Festschrift (Journal of the Ancient Near Eastern Society of Columbia University, Vol. 5)
IRM	International Review of Mission(s)
J	Judaica
JCS	Jews and Christians Series
NT	Novum Testamentum
SH	Saat auf Hoffnung
VT	Vetus Testamentum

INTRODUCTION TO VOLUME ONE

The articles collected in the first part deal with various subjects of the Old Testament or its time and background and were published between 1960 and 1973. The first short study on the name of God (YHWH and HU') discusses the views of Albright and D. N. Friedman as well as Mowinckel's criticism. The second note deals with E. Norden's correct understanding of the idea of God, not as the unknowable but as the unknown God though overlooking the important witness of Is. 45 which presents the *Deus absconditus*. The third article points out that Plato's idea that God holds the beginning, middle, and end of all things is not biblical; but the rabbis accepted it and found it expressed in the word *'emet*, God is truth, which is spelled with the three letters aleph, mem, taw, the first, a middle and the last letter of the Hebrew alphabeth. It may be added that Plato's dictum is echoed in the Moralia of Plutarch (de Iside or Osir. IX) who tells us that the temple of Minerva (originally Isis) at Sais had the inscription: "I am all that was, and is, and will be".

Most Old Testament scholars of name since Wellhausen have regarded the cultic laws in Ex. 34, 14 (or 18) – 26 as a ritual "decalogue", as the "original" decalogue mentioned in verse 28b. The first to conceive the idea was Goethe. The article "The So-Called Ritual Decalogue" shows that it is in reality an ancient feast-calendar (verses 18-24) with an appendix (verses 25f). of four additional injunctions for the feast of Passover. This conclusion is reached after a close comparison of Ex. 34, 18-26 with the parallel edition of these laws in Ex. 23, 14-19. New light on the appended laws on Passover is shed by the Ugaritic and Roman fertility customs in the following article Agros Lustrare. A critical note on the views of G. R. Driver and Th. H. Gaster concerning the time of the Ugaritic fertility rite will be found in the article "Mot and the Vine".

The story of the so-called "Bloody Husband" is not so obscure and difficult to understand as many modern scholars (e.g. Martin

Noth) think, if one leaves the MT as it stands and follows its wording closely and conscientiously.

The book by J. B. Segal, The Hebrew Passover from the Earliest Times to A. D. 70, presenting, as the author himself admits, "highly subjective views" has been critically reviewed. Three further book-reviews follow at the end of part I: Dupont-Sommer, Les écrits esséniens; H. W. Huppenbauer, Der Mensch zwischen zwei Welten; Jacob Liver, The House of David.

"At the End of the Days" is a study on the meaning of the Hebrew expression *b^{e}'ah^{a}rit hayyamim* which has given rise to two different schools of eschatological thought, Gressmann-Volz and Hölscher-Mowinckel. The study also includes a survey of the use of this expression in the Dead Sea Scrolls, the New Testament, and the Targumim.

The following group of three articles on the "Form and Structure of Ancient Hebrew Poetry" opens up a new approach to the problem of Ancient Hebrew metrics showing that not the stressed syllables have to be counted as in Arabic or medieval Hebrew poetry, but the complete notions together with their suffixes have to be taken as the poetic units (*ben*, *banot*, *b^{e}notekem* are all counted as one metrical unit each). For further guide-lines see the first pages of the first article of this group.

The last study of the first part deals with the term *maśkil.* Its meaning lies in its close connection with divine wisdom. This is testified not only in the numerous Biblical passages, but also right down to the use of the term in the Manual of Discipline, the Damascus Document, and in the teaching of the Karaites.

Two substantial articles have not been incorporated in the present collection, as they are within easy reach: one on Jerusalem, together with two short ones on Hinnom and Kidron, in Biblisch-historisches Handwörterbuch, vol. 2, 1964, and one article on the Hebrew root *GBR* and its derivations in Theologisches Wörterbuch zum Alten Testament, Vol. 1 (also in the English version of the Dictionary prepared by Wm. B. Eerdmans Publishing Co.).

The Name of God (YHWH and HU')

1. In a recent article, "The Name of the God of Moses" (*HUCA* XXXII, 1961, p. 121-133), S. Mowinckel has criticized Albright's and D. N. Freedman's view, that the Tetragrammaton should be explained as the Hiphil impf. 3rd p.m. sg. of the verb *hyh*, meaning "he who causes to be, who brings into existence". A few remarks may be added here.

The name of YHWH is ancient, and we have no reason to doubt the Biblical record that it already belongs to the time of the exodus from Egypt, i.e., to the beginnings of Israel's history. In Ex. 3 (verses 6, 13, 15, and 16) and, similarly, in Ex. 6 (verses 2f.) YHWH is introduced as "the God of their fathers", who is now to become their God, the God of the Bne Israel. He is not introduced as the Creator who made heaven and earth. The identification of YHWH with the universal God, the God of Heaven, the Creator of the human race (which would have to include the Egyptians and all the other enemies of the Bne Israel) would not have been very helpful to Moses in his mission to the people. At this early stage YHWH was presented as a family god, a tribal god, who cared for his particular people in the face of, and against, other peoples and their gods. Any other god, however important or mighty, would have been of little interest to the Bne Israel in Egypt.

But be that as it may, the author of Ex. 3 certainly did not think of Israel's God as the one who brought heaven and earth and mankind into being, but of a god, who is, who is there, who exists, who is "alive". The ever-recurring main thought in the Bible is that Israel's God is a Living God:, אל (אלהים) חי, אלהים חיים, חי־יהוה (־אל, ־האלהים, ־אני). Life manifests itself in action. A god that is not active, shows no sign of life, he is dead (Is. 44, 6-23; cf. Dt. 4, 28; Ps. 115, 1-9; 135, 15-18). With other words, the God of Israel is in existence, he is active, and will act—for Israel.

It is true, the אהיה אשר אהיה of Ex. 3, 14 is not the name YHWH itself by which the people of Israel talked about their God or addressed him; but it is certainly meant to be an explanation of the name, and it is the only one we have. As such it is in complete accord with the main characteristic of the god of Israel. It is clear that the explanation in Ex 3 understands the name of YHWH as Qal impf. of *hyh*; only it renders the name in the first person instead of in the third. We must not overlook the fact that, in the frame-work of the story in Ex. 3—we never hear of it again—the expression emphasizes an important point in the mission of Moses to the people. YHWH is the name of the God as thought and pronounced by man: „He is (existent)". When this god speaks of himself (implying the statement contained in YHWH), he can say: "I am . . .". When Moses, therefore, is asked to say: " 'I am' has sent me to you", it means that he should not speak of this god in the third person, as people might speak of him in his absence, but in such a way that it became obvious to them that God had personally appeared and presented himself to Moses as existing and active and speaking in the first person. The question put in verse 13b is thus sufficiently and effectively answered—at least for the time being, for in Ex. 4, 1 Moses continues in the same vein, going back again to the third person: "The people will not believe me . . . and will say: 'YHWH has not appeared to you' "; in other words: There is no "He-Is", your whole message from him is a lie, and we do not listen to you.

In any case, as far as the meaning of YHWH's name is concerned, Ex. 3 sees in it the expression of God's active existence. No other explanation is given here or elsewhere. The ancient concept of God's existence implies also his presence (as can also be seen in the story related in Ex. 33), for God's existence alone without his continued presence with, and action for, Israel would be irrelevant.

We must, however, admit that, formally, the vocalisation *Yahweh* makes the word look like a Hiphil form; but from that alone we cannot simply conclude that it must be or ever was understood as a Hiphil. The *a* vowel in the first syllable is well attested not only by several Church fathers, but also by the Masoretic tradition of the two shorter forms *Yah* and *Yahu.* It is certain that this reading with an *a* in the first syllable goes back to the most ancient times of Israel. Although we are by no means certain of the early Hebrew vocalisation, we do know that the first vowel of Qal impf. was originally *a* (still preserved in the P Guttural verbs), which would make it quite possible to understand the name YHWH as the Imperfect of Qal, especially when we consider that the reading *Yahweh* is very old and that names tend to preserve their ancient reading.

We have seen that the author of Ex. 3 understood the name YHWH as the Imperfect of Qal, and it is more than likely that this understanding is correct. It must be added that no Hiphil form of *hyh* has ever existed (although we have a few examples of the Piel in later Hebrew, meaning "to bring into existence"; see JASTROW, p. 338; J. LEVY does not register a single example of that meaning). For concrete acts of bringing something into being, of creating, making, producing something, etc., ancient Hebrew had plenty of other verbs at its disposal, and the Creator is, therefore, called: *bore'*, *yoṣer*, *'ośeh*, *qoneh* (usually with the object).

We find no trace in the Hebrew Bible which might suggest ALBRIGHT's and D. N. FREEDMAN's explanation of the Tetragrammaton. That the tribal god of Israel became also the Creator God and the God of the Universe is the result of later reflections, which have originally nothing to do with the name of YHWH, although we can see that it lent itself to this amplification of the scope of his action. It was a long-drawn-out development. On the one hand, the Decalogue, for instance, or the Covenant document, still admits of the existence of other gods, the gods of other nations, after which Israel might walk. On the other hand, the new idea can still be seen *in statu nascendi* in many passages in Deutero-Isaiah, beginning with 40, 12-18. Only a supreme Lord, a master of the Universe and ruler of all nations, the Creator of everything and *spiritus rector* of all forces was able to move Cyrus to re-establish the Exiles in their former country. At the same time, in spite of his universal power, he keeps his first and special function as the guardian of his people (cf. Is. 44, 23-45, 7; Jer. 32, 17-22; Ps. 115, 15; 124, 1 and 8; 134, 3).

Later the LXX did much to introduce the God of Israel to the non-Jewish world as the Kyrios and Pantocrator.

2. MOWINCKEL connects the suggestion that YHWH's name expresses God's active existence (and presence) with the pronoun *hu'*, which "is very close to a sort of divine 'name' " (see his article p. 128). He quotes the formula *ki 'ani hu'* (Is. 43, 10), which describes God as "the only really active and creative God" (cf. 41, 4 and 48, 12). There are more such passages. One of the most significant will be found in the Song of Moses (Dt. 32, 39-43): "I, I am He: there is no (other) god with me . . . I am alive for ever". Here *hu'* is really as good as a proper name.

Another interesting example is Is. 52,6. It is possible to think that *hu'* is here only the copula: "I am he that speaks" (as A.V.). It is, however, more likely that *hu'* stands for the divine name, especially when we consider the context: "Therefore my people shall know my name, therefore (namely, or specifically) on that day, that I am He, the speaker; here I am". The sentence seems to point out that God's, the Speaker's, name is *hu'*; he is not only present as the speaker, but he will also act in favour of his people. *'ᵃni hu'* corresponds in every respect to the formula *'ᵃni YHWH* (*'ᵉloheykem*). *Hayyom hahu'* is always the *yom YHWH. Hayyom hahu'* is here intimately connected with *'ᵃni hu'*.

In the address *'attah hu'* of Ps. 102, 28 *hu'* can stand as a divine name, but it can also express the continued existence: "You are", "you are (and remain) the same", for the parallel line runs: "Thy years have no end". In this verse *hu'* implies the same never-ceasing active existence as in the traditional interpretation of the name YHWH: He is (existent) and will be (existent); he is, is alive and acts, and will act (cf. Is. 52, 6, where *hu'* is the speaker who will act). Cf. also the rabbinical explanation of Ex. 3, 14 on p. 111 of this Annual.

MOWINCKEL reminds us that *hu'* replaces the Tetragrammaton also in the Manual of Discipline (S VIII, 13). There are a few more passages which may be included (III, 17. 25; IV, 25) where *hw'h* is used as substitute for *'El* (the divine name YHWH is avoided by the Sect).

To this we add that the Rabbis also used *hu'* in a similar way; cf. the speculations on Ex. 15, 2 ("This is my God—I will praise him"). The word *'anwehu* is divided into *'ᵃni* und *wᵉhu*, "I and He" (mSuk 4, 5). Cf. also G. KLEIN, *Schem ha-mephorasch*, Stockholm 1912. BShab 104a says about *hu'* "ה״ו (to be pronounced *hu'*) is the name of the Holy One, blessed be he".

Since these notes were written, A. MACLAURIN published a valuable study on the Tetragrammaton in *VT* XII 4, pp. 439-463, but he does not mention MOWINCKEL's article.

Agnostos Theos

Eduard Norden kommt in seinem Buch *Agnostos Theos* (letzter Neudruck 1956), S. 87, bei seiner lexikographischen Untersuchung über den Begriff Agnostos Theos zu dem Ergebnis, daß nach allen gnostischen Zeugnissen die Menschen diesen Gott nicht von sich aus zu erkennen vermögen, sondern daß er sich ihnen durch Offenbarung zu erkennen gibt. Der Begriff Agnostos Theos setze die Möglichkeit der Gnosis voraus.

Nach Norden ist der A. Th. keine griechische Idee (S. 83 ff., 109), sondern eine orientalische (113ff.), die durch die Theokrasie auch ins westliche Denken eingedrungen ist (109). Insbesondere—und dies ist ein für uns wichtiger Hinweis Nordens (58-62)—bezeichnet Laurentius Lydos den Gott der Juden als ἄγνωστος θεός. In einem Scholion zu Statius wird diese Vorstellung auf die persischen Magier zurückgeführt (114). Auch dies ist ein uns willkommener Hinweis. Ebendort sagt Norden auch, sich auf Cumont und Bousset berufend, daß die Vorstellung eines höchsten Himmelsgottes auf den Orient weise, „Ohne daß . . . gerade die Unerkennbarkeit dieses Gottes hervorgehoben würde". Für die Herkunft des Gedankens von den „persischen" Magiern bringt Norden aber nur ein Beispiel aus einem babylonischen Gebet für eine Pluralität von Göttern (114f.).

Es ist merkwürdig, daß Norden trotz seiner beiden Hauptbelege, die uns sowohl auf die Juden als auch auf die Perser verweisen, das wichtige Zeugnis von Jes. 45 übersehen hat. Was dort von JHWH ausgesagt wird, erfüllt fast alle Bedingungen Nordens für den Agnostos Theos. (Wir zitieren hier nur Stellen aus Kap. 45, sowie aus dem letzten Abschnitt von 44).

Es handelt sich bei JHWH um einen einzelnen und bestimmten Gott, der, obzwar er in erster Linie der Gott Israels ist, Himmel und Erde geschaffen hat (45,7. 8. 11. 12. 18). Neben diesem Gott gibt es keinen (andern) Gott, was mehrfach refrainartig durch die Formel אני יהוה ואין עוד betont wird (45, 5.6.18.21. mit אל: 22; vgl. a. 14b). JHWH spricht und schafft צדק (45, 8.13.19.23.24.25). Er ist (45, 15) der *Deus absconditus*, den Völkern nicht bekannt. Zu Israel jedoch „spricht er nicht im Verborgenen an einem Ort des Landes der Finsternis" (45, 19; vgl. a. Vers 3). Nun aber offenbart er sich dem Kyros (44, 24-28; 45, 1-3a), damit er den erkenne (3b), den er vorher nicht gekannt hat (2 mal: Verse 4 u. 5). Auch die Völker sollen ihn jetzt daran erkennen (Vers 6; vgl. 20-22), daß er sich in des Kyros Machtentfaltung offenbart.

Hier wird also ausdrücklich der Gott Israels „unbekannter" und „verborgener Gott" genannt, der sich dem Kyros und den Völkern (außerhalb Israels) durch seine Geschichts- und Heilstaten offenbart und sich damit ihnen zu erkennen gibt. Als Schöpfergott ist er auch der universale Gott, der Gott für alle Menschen, von denen er auch erkannt werden soll (45, 22f.).

Es ist darum vielleicht auch richtiger, nicht von der „Unerkennbarkeit" Gottes zu sprechen (Norden S. 114), sondern von seiner (bisherigen) „Unerkanntheit".

Es sei hier noch darauf hingewiesen, daß Jes. 45, 14b (vgl. a.

Vers 23) in 1. Kor. 14, 25 herangezogen wird. Hier handelt es sich um eine Offenbarungsversammlung (vgl. *Hebräer-Essener-Christen*, S. 361), in der ein Außenstehender zur Erkenntnis Gottes gebracht wird.

„Anfang, Mitte und Ende"

Der Spruch, daß Gott Anfang, Mitte und Ende aller Dinge hält, wird schon bei Plato als παλαιὸς λόγος zitiert (s. S. 52f.). Der darin ausgedrückte Gedanke ist, wie man auf den ersten Blick sieht, das Ergebnis theologischer Spekulation. Er ist nicht biblisch. Dennoch enthielt er eine Aussage über Gott, die auch den Rabbinen gut und wertvoll erschien, und auf die sie von sich aus eine Antwort zu geben hatten. Sie verknüpften den Gedanken mit einem Wort der Schrift. Nach der Schrift ist das Wesen Gottes אמת, und es gibt in der Tat kaum ein hebräisches Wort, welches Gottes Wirken besser ausdrücken kann als dieses, da es ja nicht nur Wahrheit, und schon längst nicht nur theoretische Wahrheit, Wahrheit als Prinzip bedeutet, sondern gleichzeitig auch Bestand, Beständigkeit, Echtheit, Sicherheit, Treue, Verläßlichkeit, Wahrhaftigkeit usw., und dies meist in einem ganz konkreten Sinne. Das gleiche Wort diente aber auch zur Bekräftigung oder Bestätigung eines Urteils oder einer Entscheidung (vgl. Jes. 43, 9), und darum, so meinten die Rabbinen, muß das Siegel, das Gott unter seine Entscheidungen setzt, das Wort אמת sein (s. hierzu die Diskussion in pSanh 18a, Z. 13 v.u.). „Was bedeutet aber אמת?" Die erste Antwort ist, daß Gott „der lebendige Gott und der König der Welt "ist. Resch Laqisch aber gibt eine andere. Das Wort besteht aus den drei Buchstaben Aleph, Mem und Taw. „Aleph ist der erste des Alphabeths, Mem steht in der Mitte und Taw am Schluß" (dieser Satz auch in GenR 81, 2 zu Gen. 35, 1). Das Wort אמת fungiert hier also als eine Art Abkürzung des Alphabeths, durch welches alle Dinge sprachlichen Ausdruck finden können, und es steht damit als Symbol für Gottes Wesen und Urheberschaft aller Dinge nach seiner Entscheidung. Dem Ausspruch folgt eine Schriftstelle, durch die er auch biblisch begründet werden soll. Es heißt nämlich (Jes. 44, 6) in der üblichen, jedoch nicht ganz zutreffenden Übersetzung: „Ich bin der Erste, und ich bin der Letzte, und außer mir ist kein Gott". Dies wird dahin erklärt: „Ich, JHWH, bin der Erste, weil ich von einem anderen (hier: vorhergehenden) nicht empfangen habe; und außer mir ist kein Gott, weil ich keinen Sozius habe (zweckgemäß ist hier die Reihenfolge geändert); und was die Letzten betrifft (hier springt der Erklärer auf die Parallelstelle Jes. 41, 4 über), so bin ich es (auch), weil ich in Zukunft sie (d.h. meine Souveränität) nicht einem andern (hier: mir nachfolgenden) weitergeben werde. (Der Erklärer benutzt hier die beiden in der jüdischen Tradition geläufigen Ausdrücke für das Empfangen und Weitergeben, קבל und מסר). In der Sicht des Propheten handelt es sich jedoch darum, daß Gott selbst und allein der Autor aller Geschehnisse ist, sowohl derer, die sich früher ereignet haben, als auch aller, die nun kommen werden (vgl. a. Jes. 42, 9 und 48, 12-16)—und zwar mit besonderer Beziehung auf das Geschick Israels. Der Prophet ist nationalgeschichtlich orientiert. Der griechische Gedanke hingegen, als Ergebnis theologischen Nachdenkens, ist absolut gefaßt und trägt einen ganz und gar universalen und allgemein-menschlichen Charakter (ohne Bevorzugung einer bestimmten Nation). Hier ist wirklich der Uranfang aller Dinge gemeint, die Mitte bezeichnet das Werden und Sichentfalten, und das Ende ist wirkliches Ende, Vergehen und Aufgehen. Etwas anderes hat der Prophet im Sinn: die Dinge, die der Gott Israels getan hat und tun wird—die sogenannten „ersten" und „letzten"—sind die „früheren" Geschehniss und die nunmehr, d.h. nach der Jetztzeit, „folgenden" (Jes. 41, 22), die „neuen" Dinge (42, 9). Die Septuaginta hat die Situation überall richtig verstanden und dies auch in einer sinngemäßen Übersetzung der Gottesaussage in 44, 6 zum Ausdruck gebracht (vgl. a. LXX zu 41, 4). Der Prophet denkt nicht wie die griechischen Philosophen an den Ablauf des Werdens von einem absoluten Anfang bis zum absoluten Ende, sondern ganz un-„eschatologisch" an das Vorher und Nachher in Bezug auf die Gegenwart, in welcher Gott sich dem Volke durch den Propheten als immerwährenden und auch gegenwärtig existierenden und für Israel wirksamen Gott offenbart (vgl. Jes. 43, 10b u. 13). Die rabbinische Buchstabendeutung des Wortes אמת, wenn man sie für sich und ohne den Schrift„beweis" nimmt, steht dem griechischen Denken näher als das prophetische Interesse an Gottes Wirken im Vorher und Nachher des Exils, im Früheren und nunmehr Kommenden und Neuen. Daß das Volk Israel, um das es dem Propheten in erster Linie, ja fast einzig und allein geht, ein Ende haben sollte, ist eine im biblischen Denken ganz unmögliche Idee; denn das Volk hat sein neues Leben erst vor sich und zwar als ewiges Volk (Jes. 44, 7—dieser Vers folgt auf Vers 6!—; 60, 15. 20-23; vgl. 1. Kön. 9, 5) es ist ein Volk von dauerndem Bestand und unvergänglich. Ebensowenig sollen ja auch die Erde und das Menschengeschlecht vergehen (Gen. 8, 21f.). Die Buchstabendeutung von אמת, wenn man sie ernst nehmen sollte, läßt keinen Raum für die Zukunftshoffnung Israels, einen der wichtigsten Leitgedanken des Alten Testaments, sondern sie gibt eben nur die altgriechische Spekulation über Gott wieder. Die aus der Schrift geholte Stütze hilft nicht, denn der Prophet denkt nicht an Entstehen, Werden und Vergehen, am allerwenigsten des Volkes Israel. Die Buchstabenerklärung setzt hingegen die Betrachtung von Anfang, Mitte und Ende der Dinge voraus, ohne welche sie unverständlich ist.

Zu diesen inhaltlichen Erwägungen kommen aber noch zwei weitere Beobachtungen hinzu. Mem ist gar nicht der mittelste der 22 Buchstaben des hebräischen Alphabets, sondern der 13. Es gibt auch keinen mittelsten Buchstaben, denn die Mitte wird von Kaph und Lamed geteilt. Die rabbinische Deutung des Wortes אמת ist also keine ursprüngliche und auf dem Hebräischen beruhende. Weiterhin fällt auf, daß die hebräischen Buchstaben Aleph, Mem und Taw den griechischen Alpha, My und Tau entsprechen, d. h. den Buchstaben, mit welchen die drei entscheidenden Worte des griechischen Spruches, ἀρχή, μέσον und τελευτή, beginnen. Das konnte einem des Griechischen kundigen Juden, der auf das griechische Theologoumenon stieß, kaum entgehen. Zwar dient das hebräische Taw oft als Wiedergabe des Theta, während das griechische Tau im Hebräischen gewöhnlich als Tet erscheint, aber so genau hat man das nie genommen; Regeln für die Umschrift aus dem Griechischen ins Hebräische und umgekehrt lassen sich nicht aufstellen. Alphabethgeschichtlich entspricht das Theta dem Tet und das Tau dem Taw (vgl. hierzu David DIRINGER, *The Alphabeth*, London 1953², S. 449ff.). Sowohl ἀρχή als auch μέσον sind als Fremdwörter (ארכי, מיסון) noch lange in der Mischsprache der palästinischen Rabbinen im Gebrauch gewesen. Für τελευτή läßt sich allerdings kein Beispiel finden; für τέλος hingegen, das in ähnlichen Zusammenhängen anstatt τελευτή im Neuen Testament steht (s. weiter unten), haben wir nur ein indirektes: Apok, 22, 13 als judenchristlich-eschatologische Auslegung von Jes. 44, 6.

Abschließend läßt sich sagen, daß der rabbinische Spruch, der uns aus dem 3. nachchristl. Jahrh. überliefert ist, einen ursprünglich griechischen Gedanken zum Inhalt hat. Er stellt einen Versuch dar, auf einen guten und ansprechenden heidnischen Gedanken die jüdische Antwort zu geben. Die Antwort ist, daß die heidnische Weisheit bereits geheimnisvoll in der biblischen und jüdischen Aussage enthalten ist, nach welcher Gott seinem Wesen nach אמת ist. Später hat man die Entstehung dieser Deutung von אמת vergessen, aber die Deutung selbst ist geblieben, und der Gedanke wurde ins jüdisch-religiöse Denken auf genommen. Was die Begründung betrifft, so will weder die hebräische Buchstabenmystik recht passen, noch der Schriftbeweis aus Jesaja, eben weil der Grundgedanke nicht jüdisch ist. Darüber hinaus muß ausdrücklich vermerkt werden, daß auch nach der griechischen Vorstellung eine der Haupteigenschaften Gottes die Wahrhaftigkeit ist, die darum auch in der Nachfolge Gottes eine wichtige Rolle spielt (vgl. S. 55 f. u. Anmerkungen).

Inwieweit der hiermit verwandte Gedanke, welchen die Erklärung des Gottesnamens JHWH als der, „der da war, ist und sein wird' ausdrückt, kann hier nicht mehr kurz beantwortet werden. In jedem Falle wird man auch die jüdisch-hellenistische Denkweise (LXX, Philo) zur Erklärung heranziehen müssen; vgl. hierzu die kurze Notiz bei C. H. Dodd, *The Bible and the Greeks*, London, 1935 (Neudruck 1954), S. 4. In seiner christlichen Form findet er sich in Apok. 1, 8b (vgl. Hebr. 13, 8). In Apok. 1, 8a (vgl. 1, 4.11.17; 2,8; 21, 6 u. 22, 13) wird ihm der auf Jes. 44, 6 zurückgehende Gedanke zur Seite gestellt, aber hier nicht mit dem Wort אמת verknüpft (mit dem es auch, wie wir gesehen haben, nichts zu tun hat), sondern mit dem ersten und letzten Buchstaben des Alphabets. Die „Mitte" ist hier natürlich ausgelassen, denn die Gegenwart ist nicht mehr die Mitte, sie ist im eschatologischen Leben bereits der Anbruch des Endes.

Das Diktum Apoc. 1, 8b findet sich übrigens wörtlich auch in der rabbinischen Literatur, aber erst als Ausspruch des R. Jiṣhaq (um 300 n. Chr.). Er benützt es, um die Deutung des Gottesnamens in Ex. 3, 14 in einer Weise auszudrücken, die den Zeitgenossen offenbar vertrauter war: „Der Heilige, gepriesen sei er, sagte zu Mose: ‚Sage ihnen: ich bin der, der ich war, und ich bin der, der jetzt ist, und ich bin derselbe für die Zukunft (wörtlich: לעתיד לבא)" (ExR 3). Es kann sein, daß das Griechische von Apoc. 1, 8b die wörtliche Übersetzung des ursprünglich hebräisch gefaßten Satzes ist. Zu beachten ist nur, daß das frühe Christentum und im besonderen die Apokalypse (22, 20) gerade vom „Kommen" des Herrn Jesu spricht. Auch der rabbinische Ausdruck steht häufig synonym für „die kommende Welt".

THE SO-CALLED RITUAL DECALOGUE

The theory that the cultic laws contained in Ex. xxxiv 14 (or 18)-26 form a "decalogue", the original "ten words (=commandments)" as mentioned in verse 28bß, was introduced into modern Old Testament criticism by Julius WELLHAUSEN [1]). It found support in the supposition now widely and perhaps rightly accepted as a fact, that the predominantly ethical laws of our traditional Decalogue (Ex. xx 1-17) were originally not part of the Book of Exodus but inserted later in their present place. WELLHAUSEN found many followers in the 20th century (K. BUDDE, B. STADE, A. KLOSTERMANN, C. STEUERNAGEL, G. WILDEBOER, C. F. KENT, H. HOLZINGER, G. BEER, and many others). Indeed, most Old Testament scholars of name advocated this view.

There is here no need to enlarge upon the history of the various attempts to establish this "original decalogue". The English reader will find a survey in James FRAZER's *Folk-Lore in the Old Testament*, 1919, III, pp. 111ff.; the German reader may be referred to B. D. EERDMANS, *Alttestamentliche Studien III*, *Das Buch Exodus*, 1910, pp. 85ff. or to a more recent summary by E. KUTSCH in *ZThK* 55, 1, 1958, pp. 5ff. ("Erwägungen zur Geschichte der Passafeier und des Massotfestes"). In the latest introduction to the Old Testament the theory is taken for granted without any further investigation [2]).

On the other hand there have been notable Old Testament scholars who were reluctant to accept the idea of a "Ritual Decalogue" (W. v. BAUDISSIN, B. D. EERDMANS, K. MARTI, W. RUDOLPH, and others). A. ALT regarded Ex. xxxiv 10-26 as a "sekundäres Mischgebilde", the basis of which were "priesterlich formulierte Bestimmungen über die kultischen Pflichten der Laien"; M. NOTH, his pupil, is even less distinct and calls them only "kultische Anweisungen" [3]).

The main difficulty in setting up a decalogue lies in the choice of the laws. All are agreed about the last four laws (vv. 25 and 26); but as regards the other six no agreement has ever been reached.

Some include the two commandments in vv. 14 and 17 in the decalogue and leave out laws from the paragraph beginning with verse 18, such as the Sabbath observance (21a), or the three feasts (18a, 22a, 22b), either considering them as interpolations (!) in the decalogue [4]), or counting them as one law, or taking only the first and omitting the other two. Others again disregard verses 14 and 17 and choose their decalogue laws only from verses 18-26. All these methods of selection are completely arbitrary.

There is another difficulty which, however, seems to have disturbed the scholars very little, although it should have been noticed and taken into consideration. If Ex. xxxiv embodies a code of ten ritual laws, whatever the choice of verses may be, it is striking that it should be such a mixed and unsystematic collection. We ought to be able to detect some kind of order in a decalogue. But there is none in the "Ritual Decalogue".

One of its last defenders, R. H. Pfeiffer, was aware of the difficulty and "reconstructed the oldest form of the decalogue" from the "disarranged text" [5]). He invented a new order and grouped the material under two headings with five laws each:(1) the Festivals, (2) the Sacrifices and Offerings.

1.	Ex. xxxiv 21a	6.	Ex. xxxiv 19-20bα
2.	18a (in part)	7.	25a
3.	22a	8.	25b
4.	22b	9.	26a
5.	23	10.	26b.

However, we cannot deal with texts in that way. We cannot think out a system first and then break the text up into fragments and arrange them according to our own concept of order. Our first task should be to consider the text as it is, for it is the only real thing given to us. We have to allow ourselves to be guided by it instead of indulging in our fancies and imposing on it preconceived ideas which may have nothing to do with it. We should rather endeaver to find out whether the text does not follow a system of its own. And this, indeed, is the case with the cultic laws of Ex. xxxiv.

I

Before we proceed to the literary analysis of this text, we must examine the context in which it stands, for the study of contexts is an essential part of all exegesis [6]).

Within its frame-work the text appears to be a self-contained unit. It is of a legal nature, and it is inserted in a non-legal context, namely in an account of the negotiations of Moses with God over the future of the people who were now to go up to the Promised Land after their flagrant apostasy. The story is obviously pieced together [7]), but it forms a continuous whole. At the end of it (xxxiv 10a) God is ready to make a covenant "vis-à-vis" the people on condition that they observe (*š^{e}mor-l^{e}ka*), what he commands them to-day [8]): more precisely, God will drive out the inhabitants of the land before them on condition that they take heed (*hiššamer l^{e}ka pen-*) not to make a covenant with the inhabitants (twice: vv. 12 and 15), but to destroy their altars and their idols, not to join them at their sacrificial meals and not to intermarry with them, as all this would inevitably induce them to worship their gods—and this they must not (v. 14), for according to the covenant they owe allegiance to YHWH Jealous [9]) exclusively [10]).

These are the basic and vital terms of the covenant, no more and no less, to be observed by the people of Israel in their impending conquest of the Promised Land.

Verse 17 is a later addition and belongs to the preceding paragraph (10-16), not to the following (18-26). Its wording makes it clear that it is not a reference to Ex. xx 5, one of the traditional Decalogue commandments, although it agrees with xx 23, which is outside the actual Decalogue. Its literary function is to establish the connection with the story related in ch. xxxii; for the Golden Calf was such a "molten god" (cp. xxxiv 17 with xxxii 8 and note the plural in both cases), and the making of it resulted in God's refusal to go up among them (xxxiii 3).

This (xxxiv 10-16), then, is the original and unamplified text of the covenant in view of the *Landnahme* (cf. xxxiii 1-3 and 12!-17). It did not originally contain any specific moral or ritual laws. The fundamental condition, on which this covenant is based, is the complete separation of Israel from the other nations, but this separation is, as Moses argues, entirely bound up with God's election, and this can manifest itself only in God's continued presence (xxxiii 13b-16). This is Moses' main concern in his negotiations with God.

Leaving out the cultic laws which follow after verse 17, we note that verses 27 and 28b bring the story of the covenant to a conclusion. YHWH said to Moses: "Write down these words (in German: Schreib dir diese Worte auf), for in accordance with these words I have made a covenant with you and with Israel....And he wrote on the tables the words of the covenant". Here ends the story of the covenant. It is made by God for a specific purpose after the episode of the "molten calf".

However, somebody added two words to v. 28b: "the ten words (= commandments)" [11]). They were intended as a comment: the words of the covenant are the Ten Commandments. We do not know who made this unapt comment. Although it must have been added very early, it was certainly not in the original text of the agreement, for it has nothing to do with it, and, what is worse, it spoils the gist of the agreement. The conditions had been communicated to Moses (vv. 10-16), and they contained nothing about the ten commandments. All he was told to do, was to write down the words of the agreement.

The expression "the ten words" does not occur elsewhere in the Book of Exodus. There is not a single reference in Exodus to the traditional Decalogue or any other short code consisting of "ten words". The expression belongs to the thought and language of Dt, where it occurs twice and in its appropriate usage, namely applied to the ("ethical") Decalogue (iv 13 and x 4).

Ex. xxiii 20-33 gives us another text of the covenant, which is more detailed and more ambitious so far as God's promise is concerned, but it contains substantially the same fundamental agreement as xxxiv 10-16 and no more. It is true, the word "covenant" (that is YHWH's) does not occur in the actual text of the document, except that Israel is warned (xxiv 32) against "making a covenant with them (i.e., the inhabitants of the land) and their gods" (!); but when Moses had put down all the words in writing, the document, when read to the people, is called the "Book of the Covenant" (v. 7; on the addition "and all the ordinances" in v. 3 see note 12). Thus the paragraph Ex. xxxiv 10-16, which contains the conditions of the covenant, and which, as we see now, is only the revival or repetition of an earlier agreement, helps us to understand the expression "Book of the Covenant" and to apply it to the right thing, the covenant agreement.

For a considerable time in the past the "Book of the Covenant" has been identified with the portion Ex. xx 1 - xxiii 19 and not with xxiii 20-33, which has never been seen in its own full light, but has always been regarded as, at the most, an appendix to the preceding law code. According to Eissfeldt (*Einleitung*, p. 254f.) it holds out reward and punishment, but that is not its theme; in fact, very little, if anything at all, is said about punishment, except in verse 33b, which contains a general warning. However, EISSFELDT is not very happy about the current identification of the "Book of the Covenant" with xxi-xxiii 19; he prefers to apply the expression to the Decalogue xx 2-17 (*Einleitung*, p. 253), but his arguments are not convincing. R. H. PFEIFFER (*Introduction*, p. 211) thinks, that the original nucleus of the "Book of the Covenant" was the "ancient ritual decalogue", which "was supplemented at various times by editorial additions and laws". He, therefore, calls it the "Covenant Code" irrespective of its Biblical name, which is "Book of the Covenant", *sefer habbᵉrit. Sefer* is not neccesarily a written collection of laws; it can be any written document, short or long, a letter, an agreement, etc., and the word is often used in this sense in the Bible.

In both covenant texts, as we may conveniently call them now, it is Moses himself who writes down "these words", or "all the words of YHWH" (xxxiv 27; xxiv 4). The sentence xxxiv 28b, which has at the end the misleading comment ("the ten words"), then states that Moses wrote "the words of the covenant" on the tables, evidently—and this seems to be the only possible conclusion—on the second pair of tables mentioned in xxxiv 1. But these ought to have contained "the law and the commandment" "like the first tables" (xxiv 12) and, like the first tables, ought to have been written by God himself!

This means that xxxiv 28 fails to distinguish between the "Book of the Covenant" and the tables with "the law and the commandment", which are, indeed, two different things.

A clear picture of the situation can be obtained from ch. xxiv. We give a recapitulation of the events. After the words of the covenant had been communicated to Moses (xxiii 20-23)—the narrative follows the chronological sequence of events—and after he had also been told to come up again with representatives of the people (xxiv 1f.), he went down and told the people "all the words of JHWH" (verse 3) [12]) and wrote them down (the "Covenant Book"), built an altar on the following day early in the morning for the sacrifice to accompany the solemn ceremony of the conclusion of the covenant of YHWH with the people. The sacrifice was prepared and Moses threw half the blood against the altar (for YHWH) and read the Covenant Book publicly. The people agreed to act accordingly and Moses threw or sprinkled the other half of the blood on the people with the words: "This is the blood of the covenant which YHWH has made with you in accordance with all these words" (xxiv 3-8). After having done this Moses went up with the representatives of the people and "they saw YHWH and they ate and drank". With this sacrificial meal (verses 9-11) the ceremony of the conclusion of the covenant was completed. Not until after that, according to this record of events, was Moses asked to come up to YHWH once more to receive the tables of stone, that is, "the law (*torah*) and the commandment (*miṣwah*)", which YHWH had written for the instruction of the people (*l^ehorotam*).

So, whereas in ch. xxiv the two different documents, the Covenant Book and the Tables with the Law are clearly distinguished from each other (with an unsuccessful attempt at a harmonization with the Deuteronomic tradition; see note 12), ch. xxxiv combines them and confuses the point at issue—and the Old Testament scholars. It is obvious that something went wrong with verse 28. Its last two words were already suspect of being of Deuteronomistic origin. We see now that the whole verse appears to be an adaptation to the ideas put forward by Dt: (1) that the two tables of stone, both the first and the second pair, were written by God himself; (2) they contained the "ten words" (Dt iv 13; v 19 (22); x 1-5); (3) these ten words or commandments were God's covenant which he demanded them to do (iv 13); (4) and finally, the tables were therefore called "the tables of the covenant" (ix 9, 11, 15). This combination of ideas is peculiar to Dt [13]) and, with the qualifications mentioned above, is not shared by the Book of Exodus.

The literary analysis shows that the "Book of the Covenant", mentioned in Ex. xxiv 7, is neither the ethical decalogue, as EISSFELDT thinks, nor any collection of ritual laws, as PFEIFFER suggests, nor, as many other scholars take for granted, the code of laws in the section Ex. xx-xxiii 19, but a document containing the agreement, that YHWH will be the God of Israel, lead them into the Promised Land, and give their enemies into their hands; but this he will do only if he is accepted by them as their one and only God to the exclusion of all others.

This tradition of the covenant treaty has always been alive. Even the Book of Dt, which, as we have seen, introduces a new aspect, cannot do without the basic demand of the original agreement, namely, that Israel must not forget YHWH's covenant (*hiššam^eru lakem pen- ...*) and make themselves idols (iv 23) when they take possession of the land. This demand is preceded (in Dt. iv 15-22) by an elaborate argument in typical deuteronomic fashion and followed (vv. 25-31) by the warning that they will have to go into exile if they or their children make such idols. This passage as well as the following sermon (vv. 32-40), which brings us to the Decalogue in ch. v [14]), is also typical for the Deuteronomist, who addresses the people of his time (!). The threat of punishment (exile; cf. iv 26-28) did not figure in the original agreement (Ex. xxxiv 10-16), except that God made it clear to Moses in the preceding conversation, that he was going to discontinue his association with Israel after their apostasy (xxxiii 3bα). The following sentence which says that God would devour them on the way, is an addition, which is taken up again abruptly and explained in verse 5a. This alternative is *not* mentioned in the actual agreement. The present text of Dt knows God as a "devouring fire" and a "jealous God" in the independent verse iv 24 (cf. also the inserted comment in Ex. xxxiv 14), but we must admit that it is inconsistent with the deuteronomic concept of God's mercy as described in iv 29-31 [15]).

It is a noteworthy fact that the "first" of the "ten words", which demands the recognition of YHWH and prohibits the worship of other gods (Dt. v 6-10), forms the fundamental preamble to the Decalogue. It contains the following familiar points: (1) I am YHWH who brought you out of Egypt; therefore (2) you shall have no other gods before me; (3) you shall not make yourself a graven image or likeness of anything; (4) you shall not bow down to them; (5) you shall not serve them; for (6) I, YHWH, your God, am a jealous God. The preamble is a substantial repetition and reminder of the covenant agreement (cf. verse 2!). This is probably the reason why the Decalogue could be described by the Deuteronomist as "Tables of the Covenant". Without the preamble it would not have been possible!

There is yet another passage in which the Book of Dt has made extensive use of the original agreement for a special exhortation: ch. vii (note expecially vv. 9 and 12). Other direct references are: Dt. viii 18f.; xvii 2ff.; xxviii 69, introducing ch. xxix (!, see esp. vv. 8-17); also xxx 1-3 and 17f.; xxxi 16-20.

It cannot be our object here to investigate further into the various versions of the covenant agreement (the text of the "Book of the Covenant"), their interrelationship and the uses that were made of them.

Suffice it to say that the collection of cultic laws in Ex. xxxiv 18-26 is originally not part of the covenant agreement. It has been worked into it, but it is still recognizable as a unit in itself. The parallel section in Ex. xxiii 14-19 is even more distinct from its context, but it is followed by another version of the agreement. From the integration of the short code in the context of the agreement in the one case (xxxiv) and the juxtaposition of the two items in the other (xxiii), we may safely conclude that there must be some inner connection or affinity between them. We shall see later wherein this relationship consists.

II

Most scholars in the past have ascribed Ex. xxxiv and in particular its "ritual code" to J (or JE) [16]), whilst others more recently have come to the conclusion, that "the section Ex. xxxiv 11-26 is on the whole deuteronomistic" [17])—whatever that may mean.

It is true, we have noted certain "deuteronomistic" adaptations in ch. xxxiv, but the general ascription of passages to the various sources, such as J, E, P. D, etc., does not help us any further, because they are still largely based on formal criteria. Certainly, there may be different sources, but the present method of classifying texts is rather artificial and highly hypothetical. The sources which seemed to have been established, had to be subdivided, and no two classifications agree with each other. As regards individual text-sections we do not really gain much for their understanding by this kind of pigeon-holing [18]). We must therefore try another method of analysis.

We are, indeed, very fortunate in having two parallel texts: Ex. xxxiv 18-24 (26) and xxiii 14-17 (19). Already the first glance reveals that these cultic regulations deal with the feasts which Israel had to celebrate after their entry into the country. The two texts are not just two copies of the same code which has been inserted in two different places of the same book, they are no simple repetitions, of which we have several examples in the Bible, but two different editions of the same set of laws. We also notice that the edition in Ex. xxxiv has been considerably amplified, and that, what both editions have in common, show only minor differences in phrasing and in the use of terms, but, as will be seen, these differences are by no means insignificant.

The two editions demand a comparison, and it is quite legitimate to draw conclusions from such a comparison. The reader will find the text of the two versions in parallel columns on pages 40f. For convenience's sake we will call xxiii 14ff. the A-text and xxxiv 18ff.

the B-text. As there are certain amplifications which A has in common with B, we can reduce the actual feast calendar even further to a shorter basic form. The comparison also shows that the following two verses (xxiii 18f. and xxxiv 25f.), practically the same in both A and B and containing four more specific directions, are an appendix to the calendar.

Text A has an introductory sentence (line 1), which is missing in B: "Three times in the year you shall keep a feast to me". It may have been added in A, but it is more likely that it is the original headline of A, which has been omitted in B, because here the text has been more closely worked into the story of the covenant agreement and the line would have disturbed the transition. In ch. xxiii the feast laws appear as a far more independent unit; but there may be also another reason why the A-text has a headline (see further below). Line 1, which is more fully repeated at the end of the text in line 8 (also in B), explains its character and its purpose: it is the annual feast calendar.

The three feasts are named in lines 2, 6, and 7: the Feast of Unleavened Bread in the month of Aviv, the Feast of Harvest or Feast of Weeks (its later name) at the time of the wheat harvest, and the Feast of Ingathering at the end or the turn of the year. The second and third feasts are clearly agricultural feasts and not feasts of desert Bedouins. The same applies to the first feast, as the eating of unleavened bread shows, for bread is the product of cultivated land, not of the desert. Even the dough for the unleavened bread which the Israelites ate in the desert was brought out from Egypt (Ex. xii 34, 39). The idea behind the biblical tradition is that the commandment to celebrate these three feasts was given to the Israelites in anticipation of the conquest of the Land of Canaan and their settlement in that country. We must conclude this from the fact that the list of feasts was inserted in the story of the covenant agreement or, in the other case, placed closely beside it.

We also note that the first feast, which enjoins the eating of *maṣṣot* for seven days in the month of Aviv, is intimately connected with the exodus from Egypt, which is YHWH's feast. The text (line 2) is the same in both editions (except for two unimportant variants). The originally agricultural feast is transformed into an historical feast commemorating the most decisive event for the existence of Israel, the saving of the people in Egypt ("Passover") and its deliverance (exodus) from Egypt. History is the dealing of YHWH with his

TEXT B

Text	Ex xxxiv	line
את חג המצות תשמר·	18a	2a
שבעת ימים תאכל מצות, אשר צויתך למועד חדש האביב;		b
כי בחדש האביב יצאת ממצרים·	b	c
כל פטר רחם לי·	19a	3a
וכל מקנך תזכר, פטר שור ושה·	b	b
ופטר חמור תפדה בשה, ואם לא תפדה וערפתו·	20a	c
כל בכור בניך תפדה·	b	d
ולא יראו פני ריקם·		4
ששת ימים תעבד, וביום השביעי תשבת :	21a	5a
בחריש ובקציר תשבת·	b	b
וחג שבעת תעשה לך,	22a	6a
בכורי קציר חטים·		b
וחג האסיף	b	7a
תקופת השנה·		b
שלש פעמים בשנה יראה כל זכורך את פני האדן יהוה אלהי ישראל·	23ab	8
כי אוריש גוים מפניך והרחבתי את גבלך,	24a	9a
ולא יחמד איש את ארצך בעלתך לראות את פני יהוה אלהיך שלש פעמים בשנה·	b	b

APPENDIX

Text	Ex xxxiv	Law No.
לא תשחט על חמץ דם זבחי,	25a	1
ולא ילין לבקר זבח חג הפסח·	b	2
ראשית בכורי אדמתך תביא בית יהוח אלהיך·	26a	3
לא תבשל גדי בחלב אמו·	b	4

people. The Mazzot-Feast with the Passover-night at its beginning is therefore the YHWH-Feast κατ' ἐξοχήν. The remembrance of this historical fact overshadowed the original meaning of the agricultural feast so completely that hardly any trace of its agricultural character is left in the two calendars in Ex. except that the eating of a certain kind of bread plays an important rôle in the celebration, and even that has been linked up by early tradition with the exodus itself (Ex. xii 39).

TEXT A

	Ex xxiii	line
שלש רגלים תחג לי בשנה·	14	1
את חג המצות תשמר·	15a	2a
שבעת ימים תאכל מצות, כאשר צויתך למועד חדש האביב;		b
כי בו יצאת ממצרים·		c
ולא יראו פני ריקם·	b	4
וחג הקציר	16a	6a
בכורי מעשיך אשר תזרע בשדה·		b
וחג האסף	b	7a
בצאת השנה, באספך את מעשיך מן השדה·		b
שלש פעמים בשנה יראה כל זכורך אל פני האדן יהוה·	17ab	8

APPENDIX		Law No.
לא תזבח על חמץ דם זבחי,	18a	1
ולא ילין חלב חגי עד בקר·	b	2
ראשית בכורי אדמתך תביא בית יהוה אלהיך·	19a	3
לא תבשל גדי בחלב אמו·	b	4

It is different with the other two feasts. Let us look into the B-text first. Whilst the Mazzot-Feast (line 2) is here enjoined in a direct way with the word *tišmor*, "you shall observe [19]) .... as I have commanded you", the corresponding verb for the second and third feasts (lines 6a and 7a; they share the same verb!) is *taʿaśeh lᵉka*, literally: "you shall make (for yourself) the Feast of Weeks [20]).... and the Feast of Ingathering". The difference in treatment between the first and the two other feasts is noteworthy.

The A-text, on the other hand, has undergone some remarkable editorial work, for all three feasts (see lines 2a, 6a, and 7a) are here made dependent on the same command *tišmor*: "you shall observe the Feast of Mazzot......and the Feast of Harvest.... and the Feast of Ingathering". The intention in this wording is clear: all three feasts are introduced in the direct way as divine commandments. In order to impress on the minds of the people this new aspect that all three feasts are YHWH feasts, the commandment was preceded by an introductory formula (line 1): "Three times in the year you shall celebrate a feast to (for) me". The formula in B (line 6a), "you shall make yourself...." for the second and third feast is suppressed in A, as it would contradict line 1 (not in B). But A did not suppress entirely the fact that the two feasts are really agricultural feasts and that man brings his offering from his *maʿaśeh*, his work on the field (lines 6b and 7c). The same fact, although not expressly mentioned, underlies line 6 (in connection with line 7) in B, according to which man shall make himself a feast, evidently in order to celebrate the successful conclusion of his work and to enjoy the fruit of his labour.

Whilst A brings the result of man's labour into close connection with YHWH, the deuteronomic edition of the feast calendar (Dt. xvi 1-17) takes us another step further and stresses more God's blessing than man's labour (verses 15b and 17) ; see below p. 47.

Immediately after the commandment to observe the Feast of Unleavened Bread the A-text has the injunction: "They shall not see my face empty-handed" (line 4) [21]). Does this apply only to the first of the three feasts? Why is this demand not repeated after the other two feasts, or mentioned at the end of the feast calendar with reference to all feasts, where there was an excellent opportunity in the summary which concludes the calendar in both forms A and B, and uses the same expression (line 8): "Three times in the year every male shall see the face of the Lord..." ? The latter has been done in the final summary of the deuteronomic edition of the calendar, where this demand was omitted after the rules for the Mazzot-Feast (Dt. xvi 1-8) and placed at the end of the calendar with reference to all feasts (verse 16b) [22]). We have to find an explanation for the curious place given to the demand in the A-text and also to answer the question, what kind of offering the Israelite has to bring when he appears before the Lord at Passover time, for the eating of the Passover animal is not an offering to YHWH, but a sacrificial meal.

The B-text contains the same demand after the law to celebrate the Mazzot-Feast, but it is separated from it by a special injunction saying that "all firstborn belong to me (YHWH)" (lines 3a-d), that is, the male ox and sheep and the donkey (which can be redeemed by a sheep), and in principle even the firstborn son (who, however, must be redeemed). It may be that we have here in the B-text the answer to the question, what man must bring as the offering demanded in line 4, but we are not sure about it. The insertion of the law concerning the offering of the male firstborn in B may have quite a different reason and may have no reference to the gift mentioned in line 4. One thing, however, is certain; the offering cannot be connected with the Passover animal (which must be a male, but not a firstborn animal), for it is eaten and not presented to God. On the other hand, we must realise that the killing of the firstborn of the Egyptians—YHWH himself smites the firstborn not only of man but also of the cattle (Ex. xii 13, 23, 27, and 29)—and the saving of the firstborn of Israel, just as Israel is already YHWH's firstborn son (iv 22), are inseparably linked up with the exodus from Egypt. The rules regarding the offering of the firstborn, inserted in B after the Mazzot-Feast, were certainly connected with the commemoration and grateful recognition of YHWH's historic feat. Just this is specially pointed out in the parallel passage Ex. xiii 11-16, after this same law of the consecration of all firstborn, both of man and of beast (xiii 2), had already been mentioned immediately after the story of the exodus (xii) and before the commandment to celebrate the event (xiii 3ff.) [23]). It is quite possible that the rite of the consecration or offering of the firstborn (or the redemption and substitution by something else) may have taken place during the festive season of the Passover-Mazzot celebration, or near it, and not necessarily as part of the actual feast. We do not know. But undoubtedly there was a connection between the two. The whole problem of the offering of the firstborn, animal or man, is certainly far more complicated than we imagine, for we have also to take into account the wide-spread custom of the sacrifice of the firstborn as a propitiatory rite to ensure the success of an undertaking or of one's labour, including the labour on the field. The Bible records it several times.. It may well be that Israel's tradition shared or had adopted the heathen rite of consecrating the firstborn—reminiscences of this kind will be found also in Gen. xxii—but Israel's law transformed it into a more humane custom. Only a closer study of the whole complex of ideas concerning the firstborn would help us to get beyond mere suppositions and conjectures [24]).

The law about observing the Sabbath during the time of ploughing (before the Mazzot-Feast) and the time of harvesting (after the Mazzot-Feast) is also placed in B (line 5) between the first two feasts. Many scholars, in fact most defenders of the "Ritual Decalogue" (including PFEIFFER, l.c., p. 221), saw in it the general commandment of Sabbath observance (leaving out verse 21b!) as in the "ethical" Decalogue. This is a complete misunderstanding of the purpose of this line. If we leave the text as it is, omitting nothing, it is clear that the commandment, repeated in the first part of vers 21, is taken for granted as a general commandment; but what is new here is that Sabbath observance is enjoined also for the two main seasons of labour during the agricultural year, tilling the ground and bringing in the crops [25]). The fact that the line (5) was inserted here, is an indication that the inserter thought this to be the proper place, for he conceived the whole paragraph as an agricultural feast-calendar!

Line 8 concludes the calendar in both editions and calls on every male Israelite to see the face of the Lord on these three festive occasions in the year. The "Adon", the Lord, is now no longer the local Canaanite divinity, but "the Adon YHWH" (in A and B), to which B adds: "the God of Israel". This qualification should not be omitted, as some seem to suggest [26]), for the three feasts are now YHWH's feasts.

B has a further addition in line 9 which gives the assurance that no one "will desire your land, when you go up to see the face of YHWH, your God, three times in the year" (not in A). This, then, is the end of the calendar.

III

The introduction of a new calendar, even though it may be based on an old one, is an act of legislation. The calendar plays an important rôle in the organised life of a community. It becomes law which has to be observed. If in any code of laws new or more detailed regulations are needed after its promulgation, such additions can be and have been made in two ways: either the new rule was inserted in the existing code at the appropriate place, or it was appended at the end of the original laws. Both methods of adding new provisions have been employed in our calendar. Edition B of the calendar, which is rich in insertions compared with edition A, is a model of the first kind, and both editions are excellent examples for the second kind of additions. It is also evident, at least in the case before us, that the method of appending new regulations instead of inserting them is the older of the two.

D. DAUBE has an instructive chapter on "Codes and Codas" in his book *Studies in Biblical Law* [27]), from which the present writer has learned much, although he found afterwards, that Samuel BOCHART, a French scholar of the 17th century, had already a clear notion of the character of the four special rules contained in Ex. xxiii 18f. and xxxiv 25f. He regarded them as additional to the law of the three feasts, although we may perhaps not agree with his distribution of the appended laws among the three feasts [28]). We may go back even further and mention that 500 years before him Maimonides connected the fourth rule, and with it, it seems, also the first three, with the pilgrimage feasts [29]) (see also further below).

There is no need here to discuss the first two laws of this group in detail (see the commentaries). That they belong to the Mazzot-Passover Feast, nobody has ever doubted. It is more difficult to decide to which feast the third law belongs. There has been a general consensus amongst the exegetes from the Middle Ages down to our day [30]), that, as it deals with *bikkurim*, it must be relegated to the Feast of Harvest (or Weeks), the time of the wheat harvest, when the first-fruits of that harvest had to be brought to the sanctuary. As this was an agricultural feast, it was only natural that the first of the seasonal agricultural produce played its part in the celebration itself during which the divinity, first the local Canaanite god and later JHWH, the God of Israel, should receive a gift of this kind as a token of gratitude for his blessings. The offering consisted according to a later edition of the calendar (Lev. xxiii 17) of two loaves of special wheat bread: "You shall bring (them.....as) *bikkurim* for JHWH". As these *bikkurim* are already mentioned in both the original calendar texts (Ex. xxiii 16 and xxxiv 22), it is surprising that they should be mentioned once more in the appendix which is expected to bring additional regulations in regarding the feasts. This is the case with laws 1, 2, and 4, whilst law 3 would, then, contain nothing new. This is hardly likely. We cannot take for granted that the third regulation belongs to the Feast of Harvest merely because of the occurrence of the same word *bikkurim*; we must leave the possibility open that this regulation is really a new one and implies something else than the *bikkurim* offered at the feast of the wheat harvest. Moreover, there is a decisive difference in the wording, which must not be overlooked. Whereas the B-text makes it quite clear (xxxiv 22) that it understands by *bikkurim* expressly the first-fruits of the wheat harvest, the A-text is perhaps a little less distinct (xxiii 16): "the first-fruits of your labour, (of that) which you sow (or: have sown) on the field"; but it is clearly the first-fruits of the grain-harvest, may be of both, barley and wheat [31]), of which the latter is the more important. We see that the kind of *bikkurim* which are to be offered is carefully stated. The wording of the appended regulation is strikingly different. No reference is made in it to any grain, nor to sowing or any labour on the field. The reference here is simply to the earth, the soil, apart from any labour, as if to stress that the soil brings forth fruit by itself. What, then, are the *bikkurim* of the *’*^{a}*damah*?

We are accustomed to understand the word *bikkurim* as "first-fruits of the grain harvest", but the more general meaning of the root *bkr* is "break forth", "be early", pi. "bring forth", "produce"; cf. Ez. xlvii 12: "month by month they will bring forth (fruit)"; also in Aramaic: Targ Yer I Dt. xxxiii 14, **דמבכרי ארעיה**, "which his land produces". It is, however, true that the root very often also implies the element of newness, freshness, earliness, and first occurrence, which is predominant in many applications of the verb and its derivations. In the expression *bikkurey ’admat*^{e}*ka* the element of earliness or first occurrence is expressed by the preceding word *re’šit*; and the meaning of the whole expression is: "the first(lings) of the produce (or fruit) of your soil", as it can hardly be pleonastic. In order to avoid any pleonasm in the translation, it has also been rendered as follows: "the best of the first-fruits of the soil", as the word *re’šit* can sometimes mean "the best", "the choice part". But this is rather an attempt to get out of the dilemma than a solution of the problem. The expression is unique. Nevertheless, there is a close parallel in Dt where not only a very similar expression is used, but also the same act seems to be described (Dt xxvi 1-10). We compare Ex. xxiii 19a (xxxiv 26a) with Dt. xxvi 10 (cf. also verse 2):

תביא בית יהוה ...	אדמתך	בכורי	ראשית	
...... לפני יהוה ...	האדמה	פרי	ראשית	הבאתי את

We find that the difference between the two lines is only slight. The passage in Dt. has the word *p*^{e}*ri* instead of *bikkurim*, but considering that the latter word is also used in a wider sense, the meaning remains the same: "the first(lings) of the fruit (produce) of your soil". It was this first produce which the Israelites were to bring before JHWH, or to his House (cf. Dt. xxvi 2b, or to the priest, verses 3f.), exactly as he was told in the two Exodus texts.

According to Dt. xxvi the various samples of the produce of the soil were to be put into a basket. The use of a basket as a container would exclude whole sheaves, but it is possible that the ears of young soft grain, which could be parched and eaten as *qaluy*, were included in this offering of the fruit of the earth. It must have taken place at the time of Passover, that is, earlier in the year and not after the actual harvest of the ripe grain [32]). The things offered have consisted of "the first of all kinds of fruit of the earth" (Dt. xxvi 2; cf. also Ez. xliv 30, see note 35). There were no restrictions. The expression "fruit of the earth" does not apply to tree fruits. The distinction between these two kinds of fruit is ancient (cf. Gen. i 29; Ex. x 15; Lev. xxvii 30). Still to-day the pious Jew distinguishes between the benedictions over "fruit of the tree" and "fruit of the earth" [33]). Of these two different kinds of fruit, the more important for the sustenance of men as well as of the animals is undoubtedly the fruit of the earth. This is stressed throughout in the Bible: Gen. i 29f.; iii 18; iv 3; ix 3; Ex. ix 22; x 12; Jer. xii 4; Ps. civ 14 (!); Prov. xv 17; etc. The Book of Dt. especially praises the land (unlike Egypt) as a natural "vegetable garden", "a land for which JHWH cares. . . from the beginning (*re'šit*) of the year to the end of the year" (xi 10-12). By God's care, who gives the necessary rains, the land brings forth its fruit by itself, so to speak, without man's hard labour (unlike Egypt, "which you watered with your foot", a reference to the tread-mill).

The season for the fruit of the earth to grow is, of course, the time of the rains, that is, the early part of the year till about Passover. This is the time for all fresh vegetables, cabbage, lettuce, leek, etc., fresh onions, garlic, celery, parsley, all sweet, bitter, and aromatic herbs, as well as all edible roots, such as radish, horse-radish, turnip, etc., in fact for everything, over which the benediction is said: ". . . . who createst the fruit of the earth" [34]).

Dt. xxvi 1 defines the date for the offering of the "fresh fruit of the earth" as the time "when you enter the land which JHWH gives you as inheritance. . .". This is a distinct date which we cannot overlook. The same date is mentioned in Lev. xxiii 10 for the offering of the Omer at the Passover-Feast, and we learn from that passage how the date was interpreted. For there is an ancient tradition according to which the Israelites came into the land at the time, when

Passover was to be celebrated, and they began to eat of the produce of the land, including *qaluy* (Jos. v 10f.). It was known to the writer of Lev. xxiii 9ff. (s. verse 14); it must have been known also to the author of Dt. xxvi 1ff.

Was the ceremony to be performed only on that one occasion? It could certainly be repeated every year at about the same time in commemoration of the gift of God[35]), just as the exodus from Egypt was remembered every year at the Passover-Mazzot-Feast. The Deuteronomist adds: "...and when you settle in it". This is a definite hint, that the offering of fresh fruit of the earth was laid down by him as a rule to be followed every year at Passover time. It also seems that he meant it to be a special ceremony, as he did not incorporate it in his calender (ch. xvi), but put it at the end of his book before the blessings and the curses as if to impress once more on the people his concept of the history between God and his people as expressed in the profession of faith (xxvi 5-10); see further below.

It is possible that this act of faith as provided in Dt. was never performed in Israel. Not even Passover was duly observed as a YHWH-feast for hundreds of years (2 Kings xxiiii 21-23; 2 Chr. xxx 5, 26; xxxv 18). It is, however, a noteworthy fact that the deuteronomic avowal of faith retained its original connection with Passover and found its place in the Passover Haggadah, in which it forms the basic text since times immemorial[36]) (the verses 9-10 were later omitted, probably after the destruction of Jerusalem and the loss of the land; but that they were also an integral part of the Haggadah can still be seen in the final benediction). Also the association of the "fruit of the earth" with Passover has survived since antiquity. Still to-day the Jew eats (symbolically) a small quantity of some "fruit of the earth" on Passover night before he begins with the recital of the traditional Haggadah and praises God with the benediction: "....who creates the fruit of the earth". Why is this done? Jewish tradition gives no answer to this question, although it proffers many explanations. The real reason for this custom was early forgotten. The motive for this ancient custom can only be sought in the even more ancient connection of "fruit of the earth" with Passover. We have discussed the meaning and the origin of the eating of *karpas* (= καρπὸς τῆς γῆς, the usual LXX translation of *p^{e}ri ha-$^{\prime a}$damah*), in *Judaica* XIV (2), 1960, pp. 91-102 („Warum ißt man Karpas am Sederabend?"), and we must refer the reader to this article, which is a necessary complement to the present observations.

As the identity of the two formulas Ex. xxiii 19a (xxxiv 26a) and Dt. xxvi 10 cannot be denied, it is more than likely that they concern the same offering of the first produce of the land at Passover time, only that the passage in Dt. prescribes a definite ceremony for it. The third regulation of the ancient calendar appendix would, therefore, have to be connected with the Passover-Mazzot-Feast rather than with the Feast of Weeks.

This conclusion throws new light on the injunction which follows after the commandment to celebrate the Mazzot-(Passover-) Feast: "You shall not see my face empty-handed". According to an old tradition, which is older than the Book of Dt., the Israelites were taught that the good land, into which they were moving, was a gift of their God who had promised it to their fathers. Therefore they were expected to offer samples of the produce of the good land to show their gratitude to their God, on whom they were utterly dependent, not only in the past but also in the future when he would continue to bless the land and the people. This is the basic theme of the Book of Dt. The gratitude for the gifts of God is expressed in many psalms and finally in the benedictions after the meal, which are largely based on Dt. It is in the deuteronomic edition of the calendar that very little emphasis, if any, is put on the labour of man (which is underlined in the older forms of the calender in Ex. xxiii and xxxiv); what is important is the blessing which God has given him (Dt. xvi 17; cf. 1 Chr. xxix 14).

The Canaanites evidently had a different attitude to their gods. They had to invoke their favour, whilst JHWH blessed his people freely (provided that they observed the Covenant). The Canaanites tried to prevail on their gods by propitiatory rites to make their land fertile. YHWH however was no fertility god. He could not be induced by magical rites to show his favour and grace. He was a very different God, as the story of the negotiations between Moses and YHWH shows (esp. Ex. xxxiii 16-19, which led to the conclusion of the Covenant with Moses and the people, xxxiv 27). He was distinct from the other gods, both in his essence and in his demands vis-à-vis his people. Therefore, his people also were "distinct from all the people on the face of the earth" (xxxiii 16b). In seeking to appreciate YHWH's laws concerning his feasts we must have due regard for the main tenor of the context in which they are embedded.

This would also explain the placing of the demand, not to see the face of JHWH empty-handed, immediately after the instruction for the Passover-Mazzot-Feast. This feast was celebrated early in the agricultural year, about the Spring equinox (as most scholars agree), evidently before any harvesting. It was natural to offer something at the actual harvest-feasts, the second and third feasts, which were celebrated later in the year, but not during the season of ploughing and sowing, that is, during the time of the rains, when there was nothing to offer, at least nothing from man's labour in the field[37]). This would be the time when in pre-Israelite Canaan fertility rites were practiced and the gods entreated for their blessing. The fourth law in the appendix to the Israelitic calendar may therefore be closer to the third law than we imagine.

IV

Much has been written about this particular law, "you shall not boil a kid in its mother's milk", from the early middle ages onward by both Jewish and Christian writers, and yet S. Bochart is obliged to state, that there is hardly any other law in the whole Pentateuch about which we know less than about this. He [38]) and another 17th century scholar, John Spencer [39]), discuss the problem in detail, and we have still something to learn from both. The last to write about it was James Frazer, who after a brief account of the problem gives us a very long list of apparently similar practices among all kinds of people[40]), but they have really very little to do with the Biblical prohibition.

Philo Alexandrinus (De virt. 142-144) and a number of medieval Jewish exegetes, among them Ibn Ezra (Commentary on Ex. xxiii 19), held, that this precept was given for humanitarian reasons. We may discard that idea. Others thought that this prohibition was directed against some idolatrous or magical rite. Maimonides seems to have been the first to express this opinion (Moreh Nebukhim III, 48). He says, that the custom to boil meat in milk[41]) was most likely prohibited, "because there is a trace (literally: a smell) of idolatry in it: perhaps they did it like that in one of their services or at one of their feasts". He finds a support for this view in the fact that the Torah mentions it twice in connection with the commandment to celebrate the three feasts "as if it meant to say: at the time of your feasts, when you come before me, do not cook your food in the manner as the heathen do. This I hold for the most important reason for the prohibition....". John Spencer was in favour of this explanation, which has also been adopted by modern scholars beginning with A. Dillmann, W. Robertson Smith and their successors down to our day. Although it is highly probable that this theory is correct, we still have no absolute proof of it. Boiling a kid in its mother's milk is still to-day a favourite dish offered by Jordanian Arabs (Bedouins) to guests, but the connection with a fertility rite, if there was any among the pre-islamic Arabs, seems to have been lost. Spencer quotes an anonymous Karaite[42]), who makes the following statement: "There was a custom among the ancient nations who, when they had gathered all the crops, used to boil a kid in its mother's milk, and then, as a magical rite (*derek kešep*), sprinkle that milk on trees, fields, gardens, and orchards, believing that in this way they would render them more fruitful in the following year". Frazer, who also adduces this sentence, thinks, that "little or no weight can be given to the unsupported statement of an anonymous medieval writer". The reason for Frazer's censure lies probably in the fact, that no parallel can be found in the immense folkloristic material he had collected. Although we do not know the source from which our Karaite derived his wisdom, we must admit that it is an independent statement and more explicit than the other medieval explanations which are based on suppositions. We cannot, therefore, disregard it so easily. It is clear that our informant sees in the custom a fertility rite, whereas Maimonides regarded the biblical prohibition in the main as a dietary law. In this respect Maimonides was preceded by the Book of Dt., which took this law out of the calendar appendix (Ex. xxiii and xxxiv) and added it to the list of dietary laws (Dt. xiv 21b, *after* the concluding line 21a!). The transference to its present place in Dt., was evidently carried out after the completion of the list. It is quite possible that he who took that step was no longer aware of the original significance of the law, because it passed at that time already for a general dietary prohibition. The Calendar of Ex. xxiii and xxxiv, together with its appendix, makes the impression of great antiquity: it is primitive in form and content, and it has been connected by historical tradition (by its context) with the entry into the land of Canaan. The problem of the biblical prohibition could really only be solved if we could discover in the literary remains of, say, the second half of the second pre-Christian millenium some record of a custom, which the religious law of the ancient Israelites rejected in order to keep them separate from the indigenous heathen population.

Among the clay tablets found in Ugarit (Ras Shamrah), dating from the 14th and 13th century B.C., there is one which contains a certain ritual and a mythical text, the recital of which is evidently meant to accompany or to follow the performance of the ritual [43]). It begins with an invitation to the "good gods" to partake of food and wine and wishing them peace (lines 1-7). It makes reference to some mythical act with parallels taken from the work in the vinyard (8-11), and describes the performance of a sacrificial ritual (12-15). This is followed by an account of the walk of the two (pregnant?) goddesses through the bare fields with an astrological allusion or direction which concerns especially the moon(-god) (lines 16-20). The next few lines (21-27) deal with the two sons to be born who will be sucking the breats of the goddesses, which is paralleled with the growing of the grapes of the vine; a sacrifice for grace is also mentioned. Lines 28f. speak of the return of the goddesses from their walk (cf. lines 16f.). After that follows the long narrative of the procreation and the birth of the two gods Shachar and Shalim. Towards the end we hear, that the "good gods" scour the fields, but now they come to the sown land, the fields yielding the crops, and the story ends up with much eating and drinking (bread, or food in general, and wine).

There is much in this myth which "is rendered obscure by allusions which cannot now be understood" (Driver), but there cannot be any doubt that its main theme is fertility. Two things happen here, or rather, are *expected* to happen: the procreation and birth of the two gods and the growing of the crops in the fields (and vinyards). They happen not only simultaneously, but they are also closely connected with each other: the fruitfulness of the goddesses and the fruitfulness of the fields; and there is also the performance of a rite, which can only be a fertility rite. It is contained in lines 13-15:

wšd . šd ilm . šd aṯrt . wrḫm
ʿl . išt . šbʿd . ǵzrm . ṭb[ḫ g]d . bḥlb . annḫ . bḫmat
wʿl . agn . šbʿdm . dǵ[ ]t.

It is unfortunate, that the important line 14 has a small patch where the script is rubbed off. The text has been completed by Virolleaud in the way indicated above. His suggestion is very likely correct. There is room only for two slender letters in the Ugaritic script, *ḫ* and *g*. The meaning of the word *annḫ* is unknown, but Virolleaud thinks that it is undoubtedly an animal. *ḥlb* and *ḫmat*, which are clearly readable, are parallel words, and so *gd* and *annḫ* are most likely the same. U. CASSUTO adopted VIROLLEAUD's view and compared *annḫ* at once to Hebr. *ṭaleh* and offered the following translation[44]):

טבן[ח ג]די בחלב, טלה בחמאה

"...boil the kid in milk, the lamb in butter",

evidently because the young lamb corresponds to the young of a goat, and sacrifices were commonly taken from both, sheep and goats (cf. Ex. xii 5). GORDON warns against any rash conclusions, as the proposed meaning of *annḫ* depends on the restored and tenuous parallel (*g*)*d*[45]). Even though *gd* is practically the only possible reading here—for what other animal denoted by a short word ending with *d* is there, that could be slaughtered?—*annḫ* may mean something else. DRIVER, following AISTLEITNER, suggests "mint" comparing it to Syriac *nanʿa*, Acc. *nanaḫu*, or Arab. naʿnaʿ[46]). Mint has indeed been widely used in the Orient since ancient times to give flavour to the meat, but it is usually added to or mixed with the meat while it is cooked (not prepared in a separate pot like mint-sauce in England). Line 15 mentions only one seething-vessel. Besides, in line 14, *annḫ* would have to share with *gd* the same verb *ṭbḫ* which necessarily implies "slaughtering" (an animal), apart from preparing the meat for consumption. DRIVER's proposal is hardly acceptable.

We would render the line as follows:

"Over the fire seven times the 'young men'[47]) cook a kid in milk)",
an *annḫ* in butter (or creamy, or curdled, milk)",

leaving *annḫ* untranslated.

The next line (15) contains a gap of several letters towards the end. It has been completed by GINSBERG and DRIVER (dǵ(ṣt . yṣq)t)[48]), who offer the following translation:

"and over the cauldron seven times fresh water is poured".

This is an ingenious conjecture, for any house-wife knows, that meat cannot be cooked in milk alone, as the milk would quickly boil over and the meat would burn, if water is not added from time to time; but whether this conjecture is correct, nobody can say.

Meat cooked in milk is certainly good milk-producing food for pregnant women, and indeed we hear a few lines later (l. 24), that the two sons to be born will be sucking "the nipple of the breast" of the goddesses (cf. also lines 59 and 61, where after their birth they actually do so). This fact probably induced DRIVER to see in line 13 a reference to it. Deriving *šd* from a root *šdy* (cf. Aram. šdy; so far not represented in Ugaritic), meaning "issue", "discharge," he interprets the line as follows: "And the effluence (sc. of milk from the breasts), the effluence of Athirat-and-Raḥmay, is a divine effluence". The word for "effluence" seems far-fetched and its meaning here too sophisticated considering that line 24 uses simple and direct language [49]). Besides, the translation makes only a tautological statement; the effluence of goddesses ought to be divine effluence.

VIROLLEAUD derives the first *šd* from a verb *šdy*, which he compares to Hebr. *śdd* (!), whereas he reads the second and third *šd* as "field" (= Hebr. *śdh*), and translates: "Et laboure (imper.) le champ des dieux, le champ d'Ashérat et du Miséricordieux!" There is much to be said for this rendering of the line, except that the derivation of the first *šd* is rather hypothetical and doubtful. Apart from that we prefer VIROLLEAUD's interpretation of the line, because the paragraph immediately before it (lines 9-11) speaks in terms of the work in the vineyard with reference to the treatment of the god Mot-and-Sar[50]), and immediately afterwords (line 16), the fertility goddesses are roaming about in the *mdbr* (= the still empty fields) and return again (line 28f.). These last lines conclude the first part of the text containing the directions for the actors of the divine ritual. Line 28 is a repetition of line 16, with the omission of the first *šd*, which does not seem to be needed any more. We would, therefore, suggest the following translation of line 15:

"The field is the field of the gods, the field of A. and R.".

The (pregnant) goddesses are to impart fruitfulness to the field whilst they are going to and fro. According to line 15 the field, that is, the field of man, is not really his field, but the field of the goddesses. At the end of the myth (lines 69-73) the gods are received by the "watchman of the sown land" (*nǵr mdr* = Hebr. *noṣer haśśadeh*) Why only by the watchman? Why not by the proprietor? This watchman is not a poor man: he has got plenty of food, and plenty of wine for a party to get drunk! He is the host! He is in possession of the land, he is only called a watchman, because the real proprietors are the gods [51]). That the land belongs to JHWH is ancient belief in Israel (cf. Lev. xxv 23; Dt. xxxii 43; Joel ii 18; 2 Chr. vii 19f.). Perhaps the ancient Israelite belief, that God is the giver of the land, is not so very different from the Canaanite view, according to which the gods are the real proprietors of the soil. YHWH was going to take it over from the gods of Canaan, just as the Israelites, in a parallel action, were obliged to destroy their altars and places of worship as laid down in the Covenant treaty.

On the basis of lines 16 and 28 *šd* must mean "field", not "effluence"; cf. also the juxtaposition of *mdbr*, *šd*, and *mdrʿ* in lines 68f. As lines 14 and 15 are framed by the lines 13 and 16, there must be some closer connection between them. It is true line 16 begins a new act. But why should the goddesses run about in the fields immediately after the cooking of the kid in milk? Has the statement of our anonymous Karaite some foundation after all? Is there any ancient tradition behind it? We are tempted to answer this question in the affirmative. Perhaps the seven additions of water—if DRIVER's conjecture is correct—also served another purpose, namely, to maintain or even to increase the quantity of the liquid which was needed to sprinkle it on the field.

However, we hear nothing in our Ugaritic text, that the liquid was used in that way to render the fields fruitful; but neither do we hear that the meat was eaten. On the other hand, the meat and the watered-down milk must have been put to *some* use. The ancient actors certainly knew what to do with them without being told—only we are left in the dark.

A few points should be noted here. The Ugaritic word for "cauldron" is *agn*. Its Hebrew equivalent is *ʾaggan*, which occurs only once in the Bible in its specific use, namely, in the same ancient story of the Covenant-treaty (Ex. xxiv 6) [52]): the blood is poured into *ʾagganot*, sacrificial vessels, from which it is sprinkled over the people.

DRIVER [53]) thinks that the rite prohibited in the Bible was connected with the Feast of Weeks in June—he gives no reasons for this view—and, following T. M. GASTER [54]), he suggests, that the Ugaritic tablet must, therefore, be connected with a Canaanite feast of first-fruits in early summer. We should be more careful in fixing the season for the performance of this ritual ceremony. Being a fertility-rite it would have to be carried out much earlier in the year; any such ceremony would be quite senseless in June, when the harvest is over. The eating and drinking, mentioned at the end of our text, takes the place of a promise which a fertility pantomine must contain: the gods will participate in a feast made for them by the "watchman", when the time of harvest comes.

It should also be noted, that the lambing season—a kid is required!—

is the early spring. A lamb or a kid would be just ready for such a ritual in spring. The Israelites were to hold a similar feast (and sacrificial meal) at the same time of the year. How easily could it slip into, or be mistaken for, a fertility ritual! The prohibition in the calendar-appendix was clearly designed to avoid this danger. The Passover-animal was not to be boiled in milk and not in water (Ex. xii 9) [55]); both were used in the Canaanite rite (provided DRIVER's translation of line 15 proves correct). It should be eaten "roasted on fire". If cooked in a pot in some liquid, it would have to be cut up first; but the Biblical law prescribes that the animal should be roasted whole. Finally the Israelites should not take a lamb or a kid, but a young male sheep or goat "one year old" (xii 5), that is, an animal that was a lamb or a kid the year before at about Passover-time (!). The Israelites were to be distinct from all other peoples (xxxiii 16) in beliefs, rites, and worship. This applies in a special way to Passover. It was to be different from all similar heathen sacrificial meals (note the stress in this respect in xxxiv 15). It is not for nothing that just with regard to this feast it is said in the first appended law (xxiii 18a and xxxiv 25a), it is "my (=YHWH's) *zebaḥ* (sacrificial meal)", and in the second (xxiii 18b), it is "my feast"; for in that early period of Israel's settlement in Canaan there was still the danger that they might adopt the pagan Spring feast. This also explains the emphasis in later times, that "they prepared the Passover (-animal) in fire according to the ordinance" (2 Chr. xxxv 13) [56]).

From all these observations it becomes clear, that the fourth appended law also, like the other three, is closely connected with Passover or the time of Passover.

Summarizing the results of our investigation, we draw the following conclusions:

The paragraph in Ex xxxiv, which has so far been regarded as a "ritual decalogue" and as the "original decalogue", is in reality an ancient feast-calendar (verses 18-24) with an appendix (verses 25-26) of four additional injunctions relating to the Feast of Passover, the first two for certain, and, in all probability the other two also.

The author of the far more systematic calendar in the Book of Dt. (xvi 1-17) took over the summary of the calendar (Ex. xxxiv 23) in xvi 16 and worked the first two appended laws into the laws for the Mazzot-Feast, xvi 3a and 4a; the third he recorded in the special ceremony described in xxvi 1-11 and most probably to be observed near Passover; and the fourth he attached to the dietary laws, xiv 21b, after the list had been concluded.

The Calendar in Lev. xxiii represents another and later edition, amplified by two more feasts, the New Year's Festival and the Day of Atonement, the inclusion of the law for the observance of the Sabbath at the beginning, and an appendix with further regulations concerning the Feast of Tabernacles. The main interest of this calendar lies in the sacrifices and offerings.

The calendar in Nu. xxviiif. is no longer a calendar proper, but rather a list of the offerings to be offered on the appropriate days of the year.

---

1) *Die Composition des Hexateuchs und der historischen Bücher des Alten Testaments*, 1889², 1899³. WELLHAUSEN had a forerunner, for the first to conceive the idea of a cultic decalogue was Goethe; s. Kurt GALLING in *EvTh* VIII, 1948/49, pp. 529-545 („Goethe als theologischer Schriftsteller").

2) Otto EISSFELDT, *Einleitung in das Alte Testament*, 1956, pp. 80, 84, 185, 221, 254-257, 265.

3) ALT, *Kleine Schriften* I, p. 317, Anm. 1; NOTH, *Gesammelte Studien* zum AT, 1957, p. 16.—It is interesting to note that both seem to take verses 10 (11)-26 as a unit, although the verses 27f. are in reality the continuation and conclusion of the covenant story 10-16(17). They evidently follow the suggestions of WELLHAUSEN and BUDDE. It is the paragraph 18-24(26) which forms a unit; see further below.

4) G. BEER, *Exodus* (*HAT*) 1939, p. 161; cf. the analysis given by M. NOTH in *Überlieferungsgeschichte*, p. 33.—This is the most surprising omission, for the paragraph 18-24 is, as will be demonstrated further below, the ancient feast calendar!

5) *Introduction to the Old Testament*, 1941, 1948², p. 221.

6) The reader will find some notes on the importance of the study of contexts in VT XII (1), 1962, p. 17.

7) M. NOTH says (Überlieferungsgeschichte, p. 33, n. 114) about Ex. xxxiii: „Es handelt sich hier anscheinend um ein Konglomerat von sekundären Wucherungen....". Ex. xxxiv, apart from some amplifications, he ascribes to J (p. 33 and n. 118).

8) For this understanding note the wording in Gen. xvii 10: "This is *my* covenant which *you* shall observe...".

9) This name points to the exclusiveness of YHWH, who does not suffer any other god beside him; cf. the similar name "JHWH Unique" in Dt. vi 4.

10) Verse 14 is a parenthesis; it contains a general comment and separates the two verses 13 and 15, which belong together.

11) EERDMANS, MARTI, and BAENTSCH say, they are a gloss (s. EERDMANS, l.c., p. 87); W. RUDOLPH says, they are not (*BZAW* 68, 1938, p. 59), but his argument is arbitrary.

12) It must be noted, that the conditions laid down in the covenant treaty are referred to throughout as "the words of YHWH" or "the words of the covenant" both in Ex. xxiv and xxxiv. The words in xxiv 3, "and all the ordinances", are an additional comment in order to bring the passage into harmony with the Deuteronomic tradition and evidently refers to Ex. xx 1ff. (the Decalogue, which

was inserted in Ex. between xix 25 and xx 18) and perhaps also to xxi 1ff; but they are contrary to the story of ch. xxiv, continued in verse 12, according to which the promulgation of the laws follows *after* the conclusion of the covenant.

13) The Book was written in the 7th century B.C., in which King Manasseh reigned (696-642). This (see 2 Kings xxi) may explain its strong emphasis on the uniqueness of YHWH, the utter dependence of the people and the land on him alone, and the uniqueness of his law, in which the ethical commandments come first. The author used ancient traditions, but handled his material freely.

14) The passage on the three refuge cities (vv. 41-43) is an insertion.

15) The theme of God's mercy, grace and love has very fittingly been worked into the story of Ex. xxxiv in verses 5-9, in which God consents not to remove his presence from the people.

16) H. L. Strack, Einleitung i.d. AT (1906), p. 45; M. Noth, *Überlieferungsgeschichte*, p. 33; O. Eissfeldt, *Einleitung*, p. 237.

17) E. Kutsch, „Erwägungen....", p. 7. Pfeiffer, *Introduction*, p. 221, calls Ex. xxxiv 10-26 "the old ritual Decalogue, preserved in a late Deuteronomistic edition".—For curiosity's sake we note that, whereas the ritual code of Ex. xxxiv is ascribed to J or the Deuteronomist, the parallel text in Ex. xxiii is supposed to belong to the "Covenant Book" or "Covenant Code" which, it seems, is neither J nor D.

18) s. *VT* XII (1), 1962, p. 19.

19) *šmr* and *mišmeret* are the standard expressions used in direct divine commandments (*ṣiwwah, miṣwah*); cf. Dt. v 12 (in Ex. xx 8: *zakor*) Jos. xxii 3, Gen. xxvi 5; and often.

20) Text A has preserved its older and distinctly agricultural name: Feast of Harvest.

21) *Welo yir'u panay reyqam*; the same also Ex. xxx 20bß, 23 (with *'et*); xxiii 17 (with *'el* for *'et*); Is. i 12; Ps. xlii 3; see the commentaries and cf. Job xxxiii 26. Correct vocalisation in the benediction of the circumcision meal: *weyizkeh lir'ot peney haššekinah* etc.

22) Some scholars decided that the line, "they shall not see my face empty-handed", is in Ex. xxiii and xxxiv in the wrong, but in Dt. xvi in the right place (cf. Eerdmans, l.c., p. 88). It is not as simple as that.

23) E. Kutsch (l.c., pp. 8-10) has reduced the problem of the offering of the firstborn to the question whether the Passover sacrifice (das Passatier) was such an offering of the firstborn. Of course, it was not, and it has nothing to do with it. The inclusion of the firstborn of man in this law should be sufficient to show that we have here to do with something quite different.

24) cf. also the comments on Ex. iv 24-26 in *VT* XII (1), 1962, pp. 20-23.

25) E. Kutsch has interpreted the line correctly (l.c. 16f.).

26) Pfeiffer, l.c., p. 221.

27) Cambridge 1947, pp. 74-101. Unfortunately, D. is somewhat onesided when he discounts the first method of inserting new legal material. "A strictly logical mind", he says (p. 74), "would insert the new rule, in accordance with its contents, between these or those two of the old provisions. As a matter of fact, however, it is not inserted in this manner".

28) See his stupendous work *Hierozoicon*, 1692[3], I, p. 639f. He referred the first two to Passover, the third to the Feast of Weeks, and the fourth, following Abravanel, to the Feast of Tabernacles.

29) Moreh Nebukhim III, 48.

30) e.g. Georg Beer, *Exodus* (*HAT*), 1939, p. 161.

31) cf. Ruth i 22; ii 23.

32) Perhaps we have to connect the ceremony described in Dt. xxvi with the

other one commanded in Lev. xxiii 9-14, the offering of the Omer, or vice versa. This special regulation is obviously modelled on the passage in Dt. (the entry into the land is mentioned, and the first-fruits are called *re'šit*; Lev. ii 14 has *bikkurim* instead, unless this passage refers to the meal-offering of the Feast of Weeks, xxiii 16f., which, however, consisted of two baked loaves, not of parched ears). It follows immediately after the laws on the Passover-Mazzot-Feast. The counting of the fifty Omer-days, the days leading to the Feast of Weeks (Pentecost), begins "the day after the Sabbath, the day that you brought the sheaf of the wave-offering" (verses 15f.), according to Pharisaic tradition the day after the first Passover-day. Lev. connects this firstfruit-offering with the Passover-Feast, and the language used in v. 10 would indicate that also the firstfruit-offering in Dt. xxvi must be relegated to the Passover-Feast, not to the Feast of Weeks. The Mishnah describes the performance of the Omer-offering during the period of the Second Temple in great detail (Men 10). It was then only a token offering; the ears were collected from a field near Jerusalem (10, 2). The Mishnah connects it with Passover, which is in agreement with Lev. xxiii 9ff. Only after the Omer had been brought to the Temple could meal-offerings and *bikkurim* be offered (10, 6f.). The Mishnah makes a clear difference between the wave-offering (first-fruit of the young grain) and the *bikkurim* (first-fruit of the harvest of the ripe grain), which are usually reserved for the Feast of Weeks, but these *bikkurim* were sometimes offered before the Feast of Weeks (as we may conclude from 10, 6, last sentence, but it was not the rule; see mBikk 1, 3). On the offering of the Omer cf. T. Worden, "The Literary Influence of the Ugaritic Fertility Myth on the Old Testament", *VT* III (3), 1953, pp. 292ff. The offering of the *bikkurim* is described in Mishnah Bikkurim ch. 1-3; again it represents the procedure during the time of the Second Temple. They were restricted to the seven kinds mentioned in Dt. viii 8. This is a random list of the products of the land to show its goodness, for which the Israelite should praise God. The passage does not say that the *bikkurim* should be taken only from these seven kinds; that is a later rabbinical injunction. The list includes also fruits from trees, i.e. fruits which ripen later in the year. The Mishnah says that the *bikkurim* were not accepted before *ʿaṣeret*, that is, as Bikk 1, 3 explains, the Day of the Feast of Weeks, not, as in Dt. xvi 8, the seventh day of the Mazzot-Feast. The season for the offering of the *bikkurim* lasted from the Feast of Weeks to the Feast of Tabernacles (Bikk 1, 10). Several changes seem to have been made during the period of the Second Temple. Texts from the Torah were used for purposes for which they were not originally intended. The procedure followed in the offering of the early fruit of the earth (Dt. xxvi 1ff.) was applied to the offering of the *bikkurim* generally from Shavuoth to Sukkoth (cf. mBikk 3, 6), including the profession of faith (vv. 5-10), which was appropriate only for the time or season of the entry into the land (see the further discussion in this article). In Ex. xxiii *ḥaggi*, "my feast", is applied to the Passover-Mazzot-Feast alone; in mishnaic times it is Sukkoth that is simply "the *ḥag*". It is probable that the beginning of the offering of the *bikkurim* was uniformly fixed for the Feast of Weeks (mBikk 1, 3), because the harvest time was different in the various parts and climates of the country (cf. the early eating of parched grain in the Jordan valley, Jos. v 11; Lev. xxiii 14 also admits of an early harvest; further Mishna Men 10, 8; Bikk 1, 3). There is also a tendency in post-exilic times to bring the two feasts, Shavuoth and Passover, nearer together; in Ex. and Dt. they are still carefully separated. See also the remarks by B. Noack in this Annual p. 87.

33) Mishnah Ber 6, 1.

34) Ber 6, 1-3 and the discussion in Babli fol. 38b f. Bread is not reckoned among the fruits of the earth and has a different benediction; cf. Ps. civ 14. Also wine and all other foodstuffs have their benedictions.

[35]) That such offerings were made every year must be concluded from Ez. xliv 30, where we find almost the same expression *re'šit kol-bikkurey kōl*, "the first of all produce of every kind". For the translation of the word *bikkurim* see above (p. 46) on Ez. xlvii 12. It must also be noted that the first of the grain harvest ("groats of barley") is mentioned separately.

[36]) Mishnah Pes 10, 4. The Biblical injunction for the "Haggadah" is Ex. xiii 8.

[37]) The Arabs of to-day do not sow before the rains, even when they come late.

[38]) Samuel Bochart, *Hierozoicon*, Ed. tert. ex rec. Joh. Leusden, Lugduni Batavorum, 1692, pars I, pp. 631-640.

[39]) John Spencer, *De Legibus Hebraeorum Ritualibus et earum rationibus libri tres*, Cantabrigiae, 1685, pp. 270f. and 298-308.

[40]) James G. Frazer, *Folk-Lore in the Old Testament*, 1919, III, pp. 111-164.

[41]) This is the later rabbinical generalisation of the Biblical law (Hull 115b).

[42]) l.c. p. 300. He quotes from Ralph Cudworth, *The True Notion of the Lord's Supper*, 1642.

[43]) Text published by Charles Virolleaud in *Syria* XIV, 1933, pp. 128-151; he also offers a preliminary translation and a commentary. — C. H. Gordon, *Ugaritic Manual*, 1955, p. 144f., text 52 (text only). — G. R. Driver, *Canaanite Myths and Legends*, 1956, pp. 22f. and 120-125 (text and a new attempt at a translation). — We follow here Gordon's transliteration and numbering of lines.

[44]) *Ha'Elah ʿAnat* (Hebr.), 1951, pp. 26 and 40; — *Šemot* (Hebr., Commentary on Exodus), 1952, pp. 212f.; — *Enziqlopedyah miqra'it*, II, 1954, p. 435.

[45]) *UM*, p. 240, nr. 180.

[46]) *Canaanite Myths*, pp. 121 and 135 n. 28.

[47]) Virolleaud does not give a translation of the word *ġzrm* here, but suggests that it possibly means "heroes (gods)". Driver translates it with "sacrificers" or "heroes". *ġzr* denotes normally a "young (strong) man", and this seems to be the correct translation also in the present line. Cf. the ancient story of the covenant sacrifice (Ex. xxiv 5): the animals are slaughtered and prepared for the sacrificial meal and/or the offering on the altar by the *naʿarey bᵉney Jisra'el* (who may have been appointed for this task).

[48]) cf. Arab. *dâġiṣatu*, "pure water"; Driver, l.c., p. 153, n. 28.

[49]) Driver has to explain the meaning in a footnote (here taken into his translation).

[50]) cf. also Worden (s. note), p. 293; John Gray, The Legacry of Canaan, 1957, pp. 56f.

[51]) In Job xxvii 18 (to be read in its context) the wealthy (and wicked) man's house is called "a hut which a watchman has made". Vis-à-vis God he is only a "watchman": to-morrow he may be dismissed and his property given to someone else.

[52]) From the other two occurences, Is. xxii 24 and Cant vii 3, we cannot learn much.

[53]) l.c. p. 23b.

[54]) Thespis, 1950, pp. 225f.

[55]) That it should not be eaten raw either, was enjoined in order to distinguish the Passover-meal from other pagan sacrificial meals, where meat was eaten raw; cf. R. K. Yerkes, *Sacrifice*, 1953 (British edition), pp. 81f.; W. Robertson Smith, *Religion of the Semites*, 1894 (Reprint 1956), pp. 338f.; Th. Nöldeke in Hastings ERE I, 665b; all quote Nilus (Migne LXXIX, 612ff.).

[56]) *bšl* (pi.), used here and in Dt. xvi 7, means originally "to prepare the meat for consumption"; therefore the full expressions: *baššel ba'eš*, *bammayyim*, *bæḥalab*.

Additional notes:

ad [3]) See now also Hans-Joachim Kraus, *Gottesdienst in Israel*, 1962², pp. 42f. He says that Ex. xxxiv 18-26 is a "*Kultkalender*", not a "*jahwistischer Dekalog*".

ad [47]) and [52]) Walter Beyerlin, *Herkunft und Geschichte der ältesten Sinaitraditionen*, 1961, p. 47, sees in the story Ex. xxiv 3-8 an ancient "*Sinaitradition*". True, there is a very ancient tradition behind it, but the Israelites seem to have here much in common with the people of Ugarit.

Agros Lustrare

(Additional note on *ASTI* I, pp. 52-55). Down to our time it has been the custom in Roman Catholic country districts to make processions through the fields sometime between Easter and Whitsuntide, especially during Rogation week, with prayers for a blessing on the fruits of the earth. The custom was abolished by most Churches of the Reformation. The fact that this custom, together with many others, was based on ancient Roman rites has never been denied in the Roman Church. Polydoro VIRGILIO (*De rerum inventoribus*, 1499, V, 1) admits that not a few of the ancient Roman institutions have come down to us, but the Church has made them better and put them to a better use. A large number of such customs were listed in a (Protestant) book which appeared anonymously in 1667 (no place): *Conformitez des cérémonies modernes avec les anciennes*; the author refers the above mentioned practice to the *ambarvalia* (p. 95 f.).

There existed in ancient Rome the company of the *fratres arvales*; the legend connects this institution with Romulus (Gell. VI, 7; Plinius XVIII, 2). They continued to fulfil various public functions in Rome under the emperors until the end of the fourth century. Varro (V, 85) tells us that, originally, as the name indicates (*arva* are the arable, the ploughed, or sown fields), "they were priests who offered sacrifices in order that the fields might be fruitful". We do not know the rite performed by them in detail (cf. Strabo V, 3, 2; Plinius XVIII, 2); but we have two descriptions of the *ambarvalia* which were carried out by the people every year (Virgil G. I, 338-350 and Tibullus II, 1). They were devoted to Ceres-Demeter, the authoress of the earth's fertility (and fertility in general), and were considered to be of great antiquity: *fruges lustramus et agros, ritus a prisco traditus exstat avo* (Tib. line 1f.). *Lustrare agros* (Virg. Ecl. V, 75; Tib. line 1) means *purgare agros* (Tib. line 17), but Manilius informs us that *lustrare* is synonymous with *circumire*, "to go round", by which he explains the name of the sacrificial victim, *hostia ambarvalis*, which is derived *ab ambiendis arvis* (Sat. III, 5). The consecrated lamb (*sacer agnus*, Tib. line 15) was taken three times round the young corn followed by the joyous crowd shouting invitations to Ceres to come and dwell with them. After that the victim was sacrificed on the altar. A mixture of honey, milk, and wine was also offered to Ceres (Virg. G. I, 344-347).

This fertility ritual was observed at the time "when the winter has fallen at last and the spring is serene" (line 340), and no one was allowed to put the sickle to the corn before he had celebrated this feast of Ceres (348). It seems to have been observed a little later in the year than the corresponding feast inUgarit, in the coastlands of the eastern Mediterranean, probably owing to the geographical situation (Ugarit lies 6⁰ further south than Rome) and the different climate. Virgil says: "When the lambs are fat" (341); evidently, they were then no longer "kids".

It is obvious that the fertility ritual in ancient Rome was not the same as that in Ugarit, but it cannot be denied that there are many parallel features: a lamb (that is, an animal of the same year) was sacrificed; there are special functionaries who carried out the rite (*fratres arvales*, comparable to the *ǵẓrm* in the Ugaritic ritual); the going round or across the fields (*arva* = *mdrʿ*); milk played its part in both ceremonies; finally there was also the invitation to the divinity or divinities to join the people in the feast. The Romans were allowed to get drunk on that day (Tib. lines 27-29). The Ugaritic tablet has at the end the description of a similar drinking-bout, to which the gods are invited, with much wine. It is possible, contrary to what has been said in *ASTI* I, 55, that the banquet, mentioned in the Ugaritic fertility myth, took place on the same day; but then so much happens between the rite itself and the feast—the two children are born in the meantime—that a later date for the feast would be more likely.

We have in the Ugaritic myth no injunction that nothing must be reaped or eaten before the ritual had taken place, as in Rome (Virgil, G. line 348 and Plinius XVIII, 2 end), but that may be taken for granted, especially as the Ugaritic rituals seem to have been performed somewhat earlier in the year. The Roman custom corresponds, however, to the Hebrew ordinance in that the offering must be made before anything of the new harvest can be eaten (Lev. 23, 14). There is another parallel between the feast of the *ambarvalia* and the ceremonies at Passover: the day when the Roman feast was celebrated was strictly a day of rest (Tib. lines 5-10): cf. Lev. 23, 7. The celebrants were also obliged to cleanse themselves for the feast; they had to come in clean garments and with clean hands (Tib. lines 13-14). Israel law demanded ritual cleanness for Passover not only for the levites and priests, but also for the ordinary people (2 Chron. 30, 17f.; Is. 30, 29; cf. Nu. 9, 10.13). The Romans also refrained from sexual intercourse the night before the feast. Although the laws for Passover are silent about this, there was the general rule that coition made a person unclean (cf. Ex. 19, 10. 14f.).

Wine does not seem to have played any part in the three most ancient celebrations of Passover, recorded in the Bible (Ex. 12; Nu. 9; Jos. 5); at least we have no scriptural evidence for it. The oldest witness for the drinking of wine at Passover is Jub. 49, 6 (2nd cent B.C.), where this custom is said to have been instituted on the first Passover night. It is, however, highly unlikely that the Israelites drank wine on the night of their hurried flight from Egypt. The custom has probably been introduced only after their settlement in Canaan (cf. Is. 62, 9).

MOT AND THE VINE:

THE TIME OF THE UGARITIC FERTILITY RITE

The following is a further note on *ASTI* I, pp. 52-55 (cf. also II, pp. 111-114).

G. R. Driver maintains (*Canaanite Myths and Legends*, 1956, p. 23b) that viticulture "seems to have begun in June according to the old Hebrew calendar found at Gezer" and that the rite of cooking a kid in the mother's milk is "connected in the Old Testament with the Feast of Weeks in June". That would mean that the performance of the Ugaritic fertility rite took place sometime in June. Driver's first statement is hardly correct; for the second we have no evidence. He bases his view largely on Th. H. Gaster's comments on the text (Thespis, 1950, pp. 225 f.; 2nd ed. 1961, pp 420-422), who, however, is far more cautious in his statements. As regards the fertility rite itself and the Old Testament allusion to it, we may refer the reader to our remarks in *ASTI* I, but a few notes on viticulture in connexion with the poetic piece which was recited seven times at the beginning of the performance may not be amiss here.

In Palestine grapes begin to ripe in June or even earlier. Sometimes they come on the market as early as the second half of May (as in the present and comparatively cold and rainy spring 1964). Grape-gathering continues throughout the summer till September or October for the later grapes. June would be too late for any pruning. It takes place fairly early in the year, though in some districts not before February, because January and the first half of February can be very cold with temperatures below freezing point (cf. Ps. 78, 47).

The vine is cut down to a stock. As a rule "three eyes" are left to it—evidently a very ancient custom. We remember here the dream of the butler of the king of Egypt, who dreamed of a vine, and "in the vine were three branches . . . ." (Gen. 40, 10). After the pruning the stock is fastened to a stout stake. Gaster says that "the vinestalk suggests the *membrum virile*". He who has ever seen a pruned vine in its earliest stage will agree. Gaster gives other Semitic, Greek, and Latin examples in which the vine and its fruit serve as sexual symbols (so does the fruit of other trees in various languages!). But the vine is often used metaphorically without any sexual associations (Jer. 2, 21; 6, 9; Hos. 14,8; Ps. 80, 9; etc.; Joh. 15, 5; Rev. 14, 18). Indeed the sexual imagery, interesting though it may be, does not help us much towards an understanding of the short poem which introduces the directions to the performers of the fertility rite. DRIVER confesses that "the connexion between the poetical pieces and the directions is not always clear" (l.c., p. 22a). In the present case, we think, it is.

The text (Gordon, Ugaritic Manual, 1955, p. 144, no. 52, lines 8-11; Driver, l.c., p. 120a), arranged in its natural lines, runs as follows:

A (8) *mt.wšr.yṯb* ||
B *bdh.ḫṭ.ṯkl* | *bdh* (9) *ḫṭ.ulmn* ||
C *yzbrnn.zbrm.gpn* | (10) *yṣmdnn.ṣmdm.gpn* ||
D *yšql* (11) *šdmth km gpn.*

In this quatrain Mot is compared to a pruned vine. What does that mean? U. CASSUTO wrote an excellent article on Baal and Mot and their relationship to each other as early as 1942 in Hebrew (*BIES* IX, pp. 44-51). *Hebraica non leguntur.* Twenty years later it was translated into English (IEJ XII, pp. 77-86). CASSUTO has shown convincingly that Mot's function was to cut life and cause death in the widest possible meaning. This is what his name, Death, indicates. He is the symbol of the forces opposed to fertility. (His view has been criticized by A. KAPELRUD, IEJ XIII, pp. 127-129; see also M. Loewenstamm's reply following Kapelrud's remarks). Independently of CASSUTO Gordon came to similar conclusions (*Ugaritic Literature*, 1949, pp. 3-5).

Death is often personified in Hebrew, he is the ruler of the Sheol (the nether world, hell); cf. Hos. 13, 14; 1 Kor. 15, 55. Later Death is identified with "Satan", "the Devil" ("Death" and "Hell" Rev. 1, 18; 20, 13 f.; "Devil" and "Hell": Heb. 2, 14); he is also the "enemy" who spoils the sower's crop (Mat. 13, 39)!

Now it is also clear that fertility does not imply any wild and useless growth of vegetation, it refers to the fruitfulness of cultivated land, of tamed and tended nature only. Bearing these two things in mind, we translate the passage as follows:

A Mot-and-Šar sits [1]),
B In his hand[2]) the staff [3]) of bereavement [4])
—in his hand [2]) the staff [3]) of widowhood [4]);
C They (have) prune(d) him [5]) as one prunes [5]) the

vine—they bind (have bound) him [6]) as one
binds [6]) the vine,

D He is felled [7]) in his field like a vine.

NOTES ON THE TRANSLATION

[1]) „sits", not „enthroned and firm ensconced in regal sway" (as GASTER has it), not in glory—quite on the contrary, Mot *sits*, that is, he does not move, he is doomed to inactivity, he cannot follow his usual business, because he is harnessed, fettered to the stake (the „staff"); note the following lines! The verb *yšb* occurs several times in the Bible in the sense of stitting inactive, as for instance in Jes. 30, 7; 47, 5; cf. especially Jer. 8, 14 where inactivity and helplessness is also connected with privation (8, 13): no grapes on the vine; what was given, has been taken away.

[2]) „in his hand ..... in his hand", not, as GASTER translates, „in his either hand a rood", or DRIVER, „having in one hand .... and in the other ....", as if there were two sticks serving as kind of crutches; it is one and the same stick, and we have a simple parallelism before us. Mot is bound to the stake (of bereavement and widowhood) like the vine which is pruned and bound.

[3]) *ḫṭ* is here not a „sceptre" or an „ensign of authority", but the staff of privation, or, if we do take the word in the sense of „screptre", it is definitely meant ironically.

[4]) „bereavement" and „widowhood". Exactly this same pair, „these two things", can be found in Is. 47, 8 and 9 in a similarly figurative sense and also connected with the verb *yšb* (cf. also 47, 5).

[5]) *ẓbr* = prune, still used dialectically in Arabic.

[6]) *šmd* = bind, usually binding animals to their yoke, harnessing them, making natural forces useful. Here the object is vine and, metaphorically, Mot. — AISTLEITNER does not note in his Wörterbuch the meaning „to prune" under *ẓbr*; he takes this word synonymously with *ṣmd*, „anschirren", „anspannen", and translates the line: „Seiler befestigen das Geschirr, Sattler legen das Geschirr an" —but this is a bit out of the way.

[7]) *šql*, from the root *ql(l)* which is used a few times in connexion with Mot: cf. GORDON, text 49, VI, 21: „Mot is down"; 31 f.: „M. is aroused from his prostration". The Š would mean: Mot is felled in his field, in his realm of activity, he is reduced to silence and inactivity, he sits (line A), he cannot damage, spoil, or annihilate the crop. Mot is bound. The binding of Satan as Death is mentioned as late as in Rev. 20, 2 f.! The reverse action where Satan binds a woman will be found in Luk. 13, 16. As regards *šdmth* see LEHMANN, *VT* III (1953), 361 ff.

We should also note the structure of this little poem. It is symmetrical with the dividing line going between lines B and C. The first part of the poem (lines A and B) gives a general description of Mot's present state, in the second part (lines C and D) his humiliation is compared to the pruning and binding of the vine. As lines B and C are clearly parallel to each other, we realise that also lines A and D correspond to each other: Mot sits inactive—he is humbled (pruned and bound) like a vine.

The comparison may not be near to our modern way of thinking but it is in accordance with the ancient understanding of nature. To the ancients death and resurrection (rejuvenation, regeneration, any new life) were very close to each other. There is no life, no fertility, unless preceded by death (cf. John 12, 24), but death, on the other hand, must be bound, overcome in one way or another (1 Cor. 15, 55-57). The Ugaritic poem expresses this idea very well indeed.

Can we now say something more definite about the time of the performance of the Ugaritic fertility rite? As the pruning and binding of the vine is done in the winter after the coldest days are over, the time for the ritual would, then, be in the early spring, at or before the spring equinox, for Mot is being bound or has just been bound.

One or two points must be cleared up here. GASTER says (l.c., p. 422) that "pruning need not necessarily refer to the real pruning, but rather to the preliminary trimming of superfluous branches earlier in the year". He reminds us that the term *zmr* in the Gezer calendar is assigned to May-June. The comparison between Mot and the vine in the Ugaritic poem, however, makes sense only if we think of the "real" pruning. The pruned vine makes a very sorry impression indeed, and it is this picture only which can adequately describe or express the miserable state of Mot.

After being pruned and bound to a stake the vine begins to grow branches and much foliage apart from the branches carrying fruit. As soon as the clusters begin to appear many of the barren branches with their superfluous leaves are removed (John 15, 2) in order to allow all the sap to rise into the grapes and also to expose them a little more to the sun and the air. This is a lengthy and important, but nevertheless minor operation and not to be compared with the actual pruning.

The reading *zmr* in the Gezer calendar is certain, but what does it mean there? The verb *zmr* occurs twice in the Bible: Lev. 25, 3 f. where it evidently describes the whole work in the vineyard, and Is. 5, 6 where *zmr*, together with the digging up, refers again to the tilling of the vineyard. So in the only two or three occurrances the verb *zmr* is used in a rather general sense. As regaids the meaning of *zamir* in Cant. 2, 12 we are not certain enough to draw any valid conclusions.

From the root *zmr* is derived the noun *z^emorah*, "branch", not so much the one which has been cut off, but rather one with a cluster of grapes (Nu. 13, 23) or one which is going to bear grapes (Nah. 2,3; figuratively also Is. 17, 10). The word *zmr* in the Gezer calendar must be a noun, evidently the masculine form of *z^emorah* (cp. the form in Nah. 2, 3: זְמֹרֵיהֶם), the "fruit(-branch)". In the Gezer calendar *zmr* comes before *qayiṣ*, the "summer fruit". Jeremiah (40, 10 and 12) observes the same order: (grape-)wine, summer fruit, oil. Indeed, June is no longer the month when the vine is pruned, for the vine is already full of grapes, the vintage starts and continues throughout the summer months. Therefore, we sometimes get, quite correctly, also the reverse order: *qayiṣ w^eqaṣir* (Is. 16, 9 f.), *qaṣir ubaṣir* (Jer. 48, 32; Mi. 7, 1 even mentions the late grapes!). The Gezer calendar cannot be adduced as proof for any pruning or trimming in June; even the trimming of superfluous branches must be done before June, as that month is already a month of grape-gathering.

The season for the Ugaritic fertility rite was, therefore, much earlier in the year. The likeliest time was the time round about the spring equinox, for in the introductory poem Mot appears to have just been bound and the kids could then still be called kids.

THE "BLOODY HUSBAND" [1])

The circumcision story Ex iv 24-26 is one of the strangest stories in the Old Testament and one of the most difficult to explain. For this very reason it has always attracted the attention of scholars. The explanations offered in more recent times [2]) do not differ fundamentally from each other, for most of them follow the traditional Rabbinic understanding of the text, which found its expression already in the Targum Onkelos. With the exception of the interpretation offered by one particular school of thought the modern approach concerns itself mainly with details of the text, but for the story as a whole no satisfactory explanation has so far been found. Martin Noth in a recent commentary on the book of Exodus [3]) raises a number of questions, answers them in part or tentatively and sums up his findings with the words: "but these are only vague conjectures, for the passage, because of its extreme brevity, is very obscure". His conclusion, coming as it does after the varied attempts of the past at solving the riddle, sounds almost like a final *non liquet*.

However, it must be pointed out that the Hebrew of the three verses appears grammatically simple and clear, nothing is wrong with it, nothing is wanting. The actual difficulties come from the

---

[1]) Based on a paper read to Bible students of the H.U. in Bet Hillel, Jerusalem, February 18, 1960.

[2]) Select bibliography: Ad. Reinach, „La lutte de Yahvé avec Jacob et Moïse et l'origine de la circoncision", *REES* 1908, 338-362. — Ed. Meyer, *Die Israeliten und ihre Nachbarstämme*, 1906, 59. — J. Hehn, „Der Blutbräutigam", *ZAW* 50, 1932, 1-8. — J. Coppens, „La prétendue aggression nocturne de Jahvé contre Moïse, Sephorah et leur fils", *Eph. Theol. Lov.* 1941, 68ff. — J. de Groot, "The Story of the Bloody Husband", *OTS II*, 1943, 10-17. — R. Junker, „Der Blutbräutigam", *Nötscher Festschr.*, 1951, 120-128. — F. Sierksma, „Quelques remarques sur la circoncision en Israël", *OTS IX*, 1951, 143ff. — E. Auerbach, *Moses*, 1953, 54-56. — S. Talmon, „Ḥatan-Damim" (Hebr.), *Eretz Israel III*, 1954, 93-96. — Th. H. Gaster, *The Holy and the Profane*, 1955, 45-65. — R. Patai, *Sex and Family in the Bible and the Middle East*, 1959, 199-201.

[3]) 1959 (*Das Alte Testament Deutsch*), 35f.

context in which the verses are embedded. Most interpreters, even the earliest, therefore felt obliged to read or translate the text differently in order to fit it in with its context, adding or altering a word here or there, thus introducing new points or ideas. Others again approached the text from some preconceived idea of their own. It is quite evident that the circumcision story is a story by itself from whatever source it was taken and that it ought to be judged on its own merits, but that for some reason or other, which must be found out, it came to be inserted after verse 23. According to the context in which it now stands God attacks Moses in the night with the intention of killing him. It is true we can compare the story to another likewise obscure story in which Jacob is attacked in the latter half of the night by "a man" who turns out to be God (Gen xxxii 24ff.). In fact the two stories have a number of elements in common. But whilst the narrator of the Jacob story explains its meaning in his own allegorizing way (28ff.), which may perhaps not be very satisfactory, no explanation is given to us in the circumcision story, nor can we easily imagine any motive for JHWH's action. The pious Jewish mind had difficulty in understanding why God himself should want to kill his servant. In order to mitigate the harshness of the story, the Targumist slightly shifted the accent and made the aggressor a *mal'ak*, a divine messenger. The Greek translators had previously done the same, but possibly for different reasons.

Theological interference never does a text any good, for, after all, it may have a plain and straightforward meaning of its own. Another theological consideration led the late Chief Rabbi HERTZ to weaken the purport of the words, "and God sought to kill him", and to create a situation which is in no way indicated in the story. The words, he says [1]), are an anthropomorphic way of saying that Moses fell suddenly into a serious illness, because he had forgotten or postponed the circumcision of his son. This helps him to explain another curious point of the story. There is no reason why Zipporah should circumcise her son. But she performed the ceremony in the place of Moses, because he was disabled by his illness and therefore could not do it.

The *ERE* has in vol. III an article of over forty columns on circumcision, perhaps the most easily accessible discussion of the

---

[1]) *The Pentateuch and Haftorahs*, 1938, 221.

subject in general. It also mentions our story, but it seems to have perplexed the authors of the article so much, that in one column we read, that Moses had failed to circumcise his son (p. 662a below; that is the traditional view) and in another we are informed, that Moses himself had not been circumcised and that the circumcision of his son was performed vicariously (p. 679b above). According to this view Moses had not been circumcised all his life—a very strange idea, for when a baby he had been adopted by the daughter of the Pharaoh of Egypt where circumcision was an ancient custom.

Nevertheless, the view that Moses was not circumcised at the moment of the nocturnal incident recorded in Ex iv 24ff. is held by a number of scholars. Even Martin NOTH seems to prefer it to others especially because the expression *ḥatan-damim* must indicate a close connexion between circumcision and marriage, and, indeed there is sufficient ethnological evidence from Africa and South-Western Asia for such a connexion. He is, therefore, tempted to think that the appearance of the son on the scene is a later accretion and that, originally, the story dealt with Moses and Zipporah only (l.c., see p. 14 n. 3). However, he makes no attempt to alter the text.

A different line of approach was opened up over fifty years ago by Eduard MEYER. It has been adopted by a number of scholars including Georg BEER in his commentary on Exodus [1]) and Elias AUERBACH in his book on Moses (s.p. 14 n. 2). This, too, begins from the expression *ḥatan-damim*, but takes it in the meaning of "bloody bridegroom". When does the bridegroom become "bloody"? In the night when he goes in to his bride. In other words, the story deals with the *ius primae noctis*, for which the god or demon or whoever conceals himself behind the letters JHWH contends with Moses, and therefore is about to kill him. Zipporah very quickly grasps the precarious situation, circumcises her son and touches with the foreskin the privy parts of the god in order to make him believe that the mark of blood on him is the blood of his first night with Zipporah. This interpretation of the story is so phantastic, not to say ridiculous, if one tries to picture to oneself the actual circumstances demanded by this interpretation, that it can be dismissed at once. He must be a very silly god who can be cheated so easily. He must also have seen that Zipporah had had a son already before this pretended first night. Some logicality must be ascribed even

---

[1]) 1939 (*HAT*), 38f.

to demons. Besides, the interpretation is completely divorced from the text and it does not explain why the story should have been inserted just here.

Most attempts to explain the story are remarkable for their lack of respect for the Hebrew wording. The student of a biblical text must consider it in the first place as it has been transmitted to us. The transmission of texts has been done, on the whole, with considerable care. He has to ask himself whether a text does not follow a line of its own. He has to give full attention to it and must allow himself to be guided by it, taking the text as he finds it instead of altering it or imposing on it his own ideas or, maybe, his misled imagination. The text is the only thing that is given and it should be sacred to us. But even if we fail to understand its meaning at once, it will be advisable to leave the text untouched so long as we have no definite proof that it is defective or faulty. Sometimes we can prove that, but not as often as we assume a text to be corrupt.

One more point must be considered here. The biblical books consist of composite texts. That means that a narrative, for instance, is interrupted and something else is inserted into the text, which the writer, or a commentator, or a redactor or whoever gave the text its present form, felt obliged to mention. We do not always know for certain why this was done, but we ought always to try and find out the motive for his insertion, for this is part of our exegesis of the inserted passage. Our next step should be to discover the source or tradition whence an inserted piece was taken. There is another common type of insertions the purpose of which is clearly to explain by way of a comment or midrash some unusual term, some name which the text contains, or some particular idea the text expresses. We still lack an adequate study of all the types of insertions in and additions to the original text, of the methods which were applied in making such additions together with the reasons which occasioned them. A study such as this would be an invaluable contribution to the understanding of biblical texts [1]).

Let us return to our story and its context. The narrative in Ex iii and iv of how God finally succeeded in persuading Moses to go to Pharaoh — itself by no means a unit — is broken off after iv 17. God had just told Moses that he would meet Aaron, who would be his

---

1) It must be noted that in recent years FOHRER, SEELIGMANN, TALMON, a.o. have taken up related problems in some of their studies.

mouthpiece. The logical sequence of the narrative demands that Aaron should now come to meet Moses, after God had also appeared to Aaron and told him to do so. But the narrative is not taken up again till verse 27, where we find God talking to Aaron and putting him on the way to meet Moses. A whole paragraph (verses 18-26) containing more information about Moses and his family and relatives interrups the narrative. We must perhaps except verse 20b, but only perhaps, for the staff or rod with which he is to do the signs (17b) is no longer his private property (vers 2), but is now the "rod of God". The narrator or someone after him probably saw that the tale was not complete. A few important things were missing. There was first of all the human element. Moses was a married man: he had a wife and two children and a father-in-law who had been very good to him. He could not just leave his family behind. He went home, bade his father-in-law farewell and took his wife and two sons with him to Egypt after God had appeared to him again and had told him once more to go as all the men who had sought his life were now dead.

But the most important point had not been mentioned at all in the main narrative. Moses had only been told to do certain signs that the people might believe him and to go to Pharaoh and to announce that they wished to leave Egypt (iii 10, 18). What he was to say to the unwilling Pharaoh, he had not been told. So God had to appear to him once more and give him further directions. This is done in iv 21-23. Verse 21 resumes the thread of the narrative at the point where verse 17 broke off: Moses is once more told to work the miracles (note the different word), further that Pharaoh's heart would be hardened and that, if he would not let them go, Moses should tell him that his firstborn would be slain. No mention is made of the other plagues. The two ideas, the concern for the family and the charge respecting the slaying of the firstborn, are two different items and independent of each other. They were brought together, formally connected with each other and inserted into the text at the most suitable moment, namely when God had left Moses (in verse 17) in order to talk to Aaron. The fact that God had to appear to Moses twice again, does not greatly disturb the modern reader who is used to reading his Bible, and probably did not disturb the ancient reader either, because good narrative form has been maintained throughout. Nor is there any doubt who is acting or who is talking to whom. Every one of the four short paragraphs mentions the names of the persons concerned. Verse 18: "Moses went... to Jethro"; verse 19: "JHWH said to Moses"; verse 20: "Moses took his wife..."; verses 21-23: "JHWH said to Moses". We know exactly where we are.

What follows next — the circumcision story — has no connection with the original narrative or with the insertions which it follows, neither in contents, nor in form, nor in atmosphere. The acting person in verse 24 is named, it is JHWH; in verse 25 it is Zipporah, and in verse 26a it is JHWH again. JHWH, we are told, is about to kill somebody who is on a journey and now resting in an inn for the night. That somebody is together with Zipporah. That is — to be exact — all we can say. In the preceding pieces every person is carefully mentioned by name, sometimes even where the name might have been replaced by the pronoun, or is otherwise clearly distinguished. The extreme care that has been taken in inserting the various pieces is remarkable, and just here, where the person to be killed should have been named or unmistakably indicated, we are left in the dark. Modern text criticism does not help us either, for the verses 18-26 — excepting a half-verse here and there according to choice — are lumped together and assigned to J[1]) or J_1 [2]) = L[3]), the latter being a general receptacle for various kinds of traditional material which cannot be referred to J (=J_2), E, or P [4]). But as the circumcision story has nothing in common with the main narrative of Ex iv nor with the insertions 18-23, it must come from a different stock of traditions.

The name of Moses' wife is not mentioned anywhere in the whole chapter except here. It is true, she appears in the inserted verse 20, but without mention of her name: "Moses took his wife and his sons, and set them on the ass, and returned to the land of Egypt" This is a surprising statement as one should have thought that the presence of his family was bound to become a burden for him during the execution of his dangerous mission. The main narrative does not give the impression that any such move was envisaged, and ch. xviii, indeed, finds them all in the house of Jethro in Midian. Evidently they had not followed him into Egypt and the inserted record iv 20 had to be reconciled by another insertion in xviii 2: "after she

---

1) Martin NOTH, *Überlieferungsgeschichte des Pentateuch*, 1948, p. 31.
2) G. BEER, *Exodus* (s. p. 16 n. 1), 12.
3) O. EISSFELDT, *Einleitung i.d. AT*, 1956², 231.
4) EISSFELDT, *l.c.*, 200.

had been sent back". Besides we have to note that in iv 20 Moses has already at least two sons (cf. xviii 3-4), whilst five verses later, in the appended circumcision story, we hear that Zipporah, who is given here the same name as in ii 21 and xviii 2a, has only one. The story we may conveniently call a "Zipporah" story. Moses' name is not mentioned in it; there is reference only to "her son", though not by name. We are really sure only of three persons who figure in the story: Zipporah, her son, and JHWH.

At the time of the incident Zipporah evidently had only this one son. He was thus her firstborn son. So far as the sequence of events is concerned, the story of the circumcision of her firstborn son is wrongly placed, where we find it now. As regards time it belongs to an earlier period in the life of Moses, and as regards the locality, it belongs to Midian, the homeland of Zipporah. It is a Midianite story and has, therefore, most likely also a Midianite background. The right place for the circumcision story would be fairly immediately after Ex ii 15-22, where we are told that Moses had fled to Midian, found refuge in the house of Jethro and took his daughter Zipporah to wife who bore him "a son". Moses spent a long time, *jamim rabbim*, in Midian (ii 23). It was during that time in the land of Midian that Moses came to know the God of his forefathers who would lead his people out of Egypt (iii 1ff.). We cannot escape the conclusion from the story told to us in ch. xviii, that Jethro had some kind of faith in the god (xviii 1, 9, 10f.) who had revealed himself to the *ger* Moses in the land of Midian (ii 22, iii 1ff.). In xviii 19ff. Jethro gives Moses important instructions with regard to the administration of justice. Moses followed his advice. Naturally we know next to nothing of the earlier beliefs which Jethro, his family and his tribe held, but the story in xviii leaves no doubt, that Jethro identified his own god, the god of his district, of whom he was the priest, with the god who had revealed himself to Moses. Perhaps the ideas Jethro had inherited or formed of this divinity may have been in many respects somewhat cruder or at least different from the beliefs which Moses came to hold during the long and uninterrupted experience with that god. Some of those older beliefs may have been preserved in the Midianite tradition for some time, for, after all, the Midianites were not Israelites who had a distinct and unique historic experience with the god whom they had accepted. Zipporah was brought up in her father's house and it is natural to presume that she may have retained some of the older beliefs to which she was accustomed since her early youth. Besides she did not participate in the great work of liberation (xviii 1f.). Customs, beliefs, "superstitions" do not easily die out. The story of Rachel who had stolen her father's Teraphim in order to take them with her into her new homeland is a good illustration. In other words we cannot easily dismiss Zipporah's Midianite origin and upbringing. We have to take her past into account when reading the story of the circumcision of her son. In spite of the fact that the divinity in this story bears the name of the God of Israel, he was the divinity of the Midianite desert lands. As we have pointed out, the Midianite conception of God must not necessarily be the same as that of the later Moses or the prophets of Israel. This reflexion would account for the "strange" and "un-Israelite" behaviour of God in our story, although it may not explain it, since we know too little, if anything at all, of Zipporah's background. We can only imagine that her beliefs must have been different from Israelite ideas (as we know them) in many a detail.

According to Hebrew tradition the Midianites were an Arab people or tribe. Midian was a descendent of Abraham by Ketura who had born him five other sons (Gen xxv 1ff.). All of them were sent eastwards. The Ishmaelites and Edomites who lived in the lands south of Cannaan descend from the same father Abraham (xxv 12ff. and xxxvi 1ff). There must have been a good deal of inter-marriage between these tribes (cf. xxviii 9, apart from many other instances of inter-marriage related in the historical books of the Bible), and it seems that they also merged into one another (cf. the example Judg i 16) or disappeared in other ways. On one occasion (viii 24) the Midianites are counted among the Ishmaelites. In the course of centuries even the names of some of them were no longer remembered — except in the literary remains of the Hebrew Bible. Their successors and heirs are the northern Arabs. The story recorded in Ex iv shows indeed traces of a civilisation which reminds us of the Arab world. The least we can say at this point is that it has an ideological background different from that of the Israelites.

Why has this story been inserted after Ex iv 23? Finding it here in a series of Moses stories we quite naturally presume that it is a continuation of the conversations and dealings between JHWH and Moses. Nevertheless there is no intelligible reason in the Moses stories before us why JHWH should all of a sudden kill the man whom he had just entrusted with a most important mission concerning the lives of thousands of people. Nor does the inserted story itself offer any reason why Moses should now lose his life. His name is not mentioned, he is not necessarily one of the dramatis personae. Only the Syriac version has added his name at the beginning of the paragraph and says: "and Moses was on the way in a resting-place...". The LXX did not find the name of Moses in the Hebrew text. Besides we should not forget that the Hebrew text can also be translated "and it happened, or it came to pass on the way in an (the) inn that..".

We must reject the traditional view that Moses is the *ḥatan-damim*, although we acknowledge the good taste of the ancient Rabbis in attempting to provide an acceptable meaning for the story. We must also reject the view which sees in the story an aetiological description of the custom of circumcision, a view which is shared to-day by very many scholars including NOTH and ALBRIGHT, evidently for want of a better explanation. Naturally we have to discard the sexological interpretation also, which has become a fashion in some circles. None of these explanations answers the question why the story found its place just here after iv 23. To answer such a question is an important part of Biblical exegesis.

Why, then, has it been attached to verse 23? Apparently an obvious link is missing — or is it?

The two verses preceding our story make two important statements. JHWH says: "my son, my firstborn is Israel", and he says: "I will slay thy son, thy firstborn". Both statements concern "the son, the firstborn". In the first the firstborn is God's: he is to live and to become his personal property and holy people. In the second the firstborn is Pharaoh's and Egypt's, who will lose their life. As Moses does not play any rôle in the story following immediately afterwards, he cannot be the link which connects verse 24 with verse 23. It is "the son, the firstborn" that does this. He figures both in our story and in the preceding two verses.

Texts which have been transmitted from generation to generation — in oral or in written form, that is here of no importance — have in the course of time undergone certain changes, very often they have been "completed". One of the methods of completing texts makes use of key-words or key-ideas. It is true this method is not so often applied in the older Hebrew literature, but it is very common in later times. The rabbinic as well as the New Testament literature is full of such additions, where a word, an expression, or an idea was sufficient for someone who felt the need for "completion" to commit to writing all he knew about the subject in question. But we have also examples in the Old Testament for which the Qumran manuscript Is[a] is a good witness.

The study of the association of ideas has been sadly neglected in our exegesis of Biblical texts. This is true also with regard to the problem of Ex iv 24-26. We have so far looked at it from the more formal side; but there is also another point less readily appearant which our story has in common with the narrative in which it is inserted, the narrative of the exodus from Egypt. The culminating events in the preparation for the exodus are, as we have seen, the preservation of the firstborn of Israel and the slaying of the firstborn of Egypt. The decisive sign on which the execution of the divine plan is made dependent, is a visible sign of blood.

The circumcision story deals with the same theme of the killing and the preservation of the firstborn son, not with Moses. In order to save him, Zipporah acted at once. Verse 25 describes the sequence of her acts vis-à-vis the threatening divinity: she took a flint, she cut off the foreskin of her son, *wattaggaʿ lᵉraglajw*, and then she said something after she had finished. The translation of the Hebrew words just mentioned seems to be difficult. Most expositors and translaters, both Jewish and Christian, render the word *haggiᵃʿ* with "to cast" or "to throw": "she cast the foreskin.....". But there is not a single case in the whole Bible, in which the verb has this meaning. It always signifies "to touch", "to reach", or "to make touch", "to make reach" (this applies also to the forms in the *qal*, even where God inflicts pain on some one: it is by his touch). *Lᵉraglajw* is usually translated "at his feet": "she cast it at his feet"; but then one would expect the prepositions *ʾel* or *ʿal*. The only possible literal translation is: "she made it touch (with regard to) his feet", meaning "she touched with it his feet or legs".

For many scholars the favourite translation of *regel* in this passage is "sexual organs", because the word is sometimes used euphemistically in that sense. According to their respective theories Zipporah cast her son's foreskin at the privy parts of Moses who is thought to be standing by and looking on, or at those of the god who wanted to embrace Zipporah, as it seems, in the presence of Moses. The one or the other of the two must have been half naked in order to enable Zipporah to hit the mark. One does not need much imagination in order to realise that the whole scene is in either case utterly impossible.

The meaning of the grammatically simple text is: "Zipporah touched with the foreskin the legs of *her son*". She would hardly touch with it that part on which she had just performed the operation with the flint, so as not to cause unnecessary pain to the child, but she would touch the place near it, the upper part of the legs. For *regel* sometimes also means just the leg. Why should she do that? The foreskin still contains fresh blood. With it she touches the thighs of the child and smears the drop of blood on them. She makes with the blood of circumcision a visible sign on the child in order to demonstrate that the required circumcision was performed on him and completed. Had she thrown the foreskin away without making this mark of blood on him, hardly anything would have been seen, for the blood from the fresh wound, a drop or two, would have fallen on the earth. It is important, therefore, to make the sign on the child *visible*. It must be *seen*. That is necessary for any blood-rite. When God commanded the Israelites to smear the blood of the slaughtered animal on the lintel and the door posts, it was done in order that it might be seen: "When I *see* the blood, I will pass over you . . . and not smite you" (Ex xii 13 and 23).

Blood rites often serve as a prophylactic, especially among the Arab peoples. The *ʿaqiqah* is a ceremony with a sacrifice designed to avert evil from the child. On that occasion the blood of the animal is smeared on the forehead of the child [1]), that is on that part of his body where it can be seen. The Samaritans have a similar custom at their Passover. They take blood from the Passover lamb and draw with it a line on the forehead of the children down to the point of the nose. The custom has been noted by many visitors in the past. DALMAN records the view of the Priest Jizhaq saying that this custom is of Arab origin [2]). This information is undoubtedly correct, but the custom may also have some indirect connexion with the command in xii 7 and 22f. to mark the houses with the blood of the animal, although the Samaritans keep this commandment at the same time, also literally, and still mark their tents with the blood in memory of the ancient injunction [3]). The purpose of the blood rite is clear in both cases: it is to preserve the life of the inmates and the life of the child.

There is further material in pre-Islamic Arab traditions which

---

[1]) E. WESTERMARCK, *Ritual and Belief in Morocco*, 1926, II, 414.
[2]) *PJ VIII*, 1912, 124.
[3]) Joachim JEREMIAS, *Die Passahfeier der Samaritaner*, 1932, 91f.

helps us to understand other traits of our story, such as the belief that "mother and child can be attacked by one of the Ginn", some divinity or demon, especially by night [1]).

Now we come to the last difficulty in our story. After Zipporah had made the sign of blood on her son so that the divinity might see the mark, she had actually completed her work. But to the visible sign an audible sign is added, evidently to make quite sure that the divinity will now let the child go unharmed. Zipporah says: "*ḥatan-damim 'attah li*". To whom is she talking? The usual translation is: "a bloody bridegroom (a bridegroom of blood) art thou to me". It is understood that she says that to Moses. It is difficult to understand how she can say that to Moses — even if he is present. *Ḥatan* in Biblical Hebrew is the bridegroom, usually a young man about to marry or just being married and going in to his bride. *Ḥatunnah* is the wedding. In some cases a *ḥatan* is a prospective son-in-law or a just newly married son-in-law. Moses is no longer a bridegroom, he is Zipporah's husband. He had been her lawful husband for some time, for she had a son by him (ii 21f.). The word *ḥatan* is definitely no longer applicable to Moses.

S. TALMON (s. p. 14, n. 2) has seen this difficulty and although he applies the expression *ḥatan* to Moses, he realises that he cannot be anymore Zipporah's *ḥatan*. He explains the passage in that way that Moses has now become the *ḥatan-damim* to JHWH, and he suggests that the Jod in the word *li* is an abbreviation of the Tetragrammaton. But this explanation is possible only if we accept an alteration of the Hebrew text which has never been noted by the Rabbis. Nor does the LXX draw any such conclusions from the Hebrew text. Besides the idea itself, "bridegroom of blood to JHWH" — and what should it mean? — is foreign to Israelite thought as it would imply a definitely feminine quality in JHWH's personality. JHWH is a masculine god. That he betrothes Israel unto himself (Hos ii 18ff.) is a more congenial metaphor.

Eduard MEYER and his followers think, of course, that Zipporah is talking to the demon in order to make him believe that he has just spent the wedding night with his virginal bride. We can dismiss that view.

Another solution was suggested by the late Chief Rabbi HERTZ [2]).

---

[1]) E. WESTERMARCK, *l.c.*, I, 303; J. WELLHAUSEN, *Reste arabischen Heidentums*, 1897², 148ff.

[2]) see p. 15, n. 1.

According to his view Zipporah is addressing herself to the child telling him, that he is now a "bridegroom-of-blood", i.e., a "Bridegroom of the Covenant", for by the circumcision the child is received into the Covenant. He compares the expression *ḥ*ᵉ*tan-damim* to the expression *ḥ*ᵃ*tan-torah* of the feast Simḥat Tora, but that expression was not formed until the Middle Ages. Moreover this explanation would presuppose all the later development of Jewish thought on the Covenant of circumcision. It must also be pointed out that the expression *ḥ*ᵃ*tan-damim* has never been used as a theological term in that sense, simply because Moses was always thought to be the *ḥ*ᵃ*tan-damim*.

Zipporah indeed addresses her child and applies the words to him, but she is not really talking tò him alone — she is saying them in front of the divinity so that the divinity may hear them. The words she utters are a statement, a declaration, introduced by the simple *wattomer* and the particle *ki*: they are the ritual formula which must accompany the ritual act. After the divinity had heard this declaration, he let him (the son) go. Here ends the sequence of events described in simple and clear language in verses 25 and 26a.

What does this expression *ḥ*ᵃ*tan-damim* mean? It is unique in Hebrew usage, it does not occur elsewhere. We know, of course, that the word *ḥ*ᵃ*tan* — by itself — has been applied metaphorically to an infant fit for circumcision (Babli BB 98b), but the expression *ḥ*ᵃ*tan-damim* is never used to denote the "*rak hannimol lišmonah*", the child (immediately) after the circumcision. What, then, is the *ḥ*ᵃ*tan-damim*? Is he a bridegroom after all, or, if not, how shall we understand that double expression?

We are in a fortunate position, for the person who inserted the story, or someone after him added a comment to it and by doing so supplied us also with the key to the understanding of the story. If a friend gave you the key to his house that you may open it and enter in, he would expect you to use the key as it is. But if you, instead of using it, went to have it altered, you would not succeed in opening the door. But this is what many commentators do with the key offered to us in verse 26b: *'aẓ 'am*ᵉ*rah ḥ*ᵃ*tan damim lammulot*. They did not like the word *'am*ᵉ*rah*; they changed it into *'am*ᵉ*ru* (EHRLICH, GRESSMANN, BEER a.o.) and translated the line: "at that time they called the circumcised bridegroom of blood", suggesting that the expression *ḥ*ᵃ*tan-damim* was at that time used among the Hebrew-speaking people. But that is not what the MT suggests. It says: *'am*ᵉ-

rah, and we must therefore translate: "at that time she, i.e., Zipporah, used the expression *ḥatan-damim* with regard to the circumcised" [1]). Zipporah was a Midianite woman. If our text says, "she used the expression. . .", it is clear that the author of the line intends to point out that *she* used this expression, an expression to which she was accustomed in her home-land. It was not a term of the Hebrew-speaking Israelites, and we must take the hint the author gives us.

As the Midianites must be classed as Arabs we have to turn to the Arabic language for enlightenment. It has long been noted by the lexicographers of the Hebrew language, that *ḫatana* in Arabic means "circumcise". The expression which Zipporah used can only be a connotation for the circumcised with a strong emphasis on blood which plays so important a part in our story, for the sign of blood is made in order to avert the evil intention of the divinity. We do not know the vocalisation of the word in Zipporah's language. In the Hebrew text, with Hebrew vocalisation, it became a Hebrew word meaning "bridegroom". The Arabic word for "circumcise" has been compared with the Akkadic word *ḫatânu*, "to guard", "to protect". Perhaps there was, in very ancient times, a closer connexion between the two roots. This would suit our archaic story very well. Zipporah says the ritual formula: "A blood-circumcised one art thou with regard to me" [2]), and the divinity, seeing the blood of circumcision and hearing Zipporah's declaration, disappears. The (firstborn) son is saved.

The interpretation of Ex iv 24-26 offered here relies entirely on the transmitted Hebrew text, which needs no emendation. The text which the Greek translators had before them was evidently the same as the MT, but it is interesting to note what they did with it. They translated verse 25 from *wattaggaʿ leraglajw* onward as follows: "she fell at his feet", as if to implore (the angel of) God to have mercy on her son, "and she said: ἔστη τὸ αἷμα τῆς περιτομῆς τοῦ παιδίου μοῦ". The English translation of THOMSON-MUSES [3]) renders the sentence thus: "The blood of the circumcision of my son has stopped me". This translation (as well as that of the following verse) is wrong. The translation given in BAGSTER's edition of the LXX text has:

---

[1]) For this translation of *mulot* see U. CASSUTO, *The Book of Exodus*, 1951, 39 (Hebr.).

[2]) For the rendering of the particle *le* cf. Judg. xvii 2b.

[3]) *The Septuagint Bible in the Translation of* Charles THOMSON, as edited by C. A. MUSES (The Falcon's Wing Press), 1954.

"The blood of the circumcision of my son is staunched". This is a possible translation (cf. the clearer wording in Lk viii 44: "the flow of blood ceased"), but it makes no sense here, for the expression *ḥᵃtan-damim* rather indicates the presence of blood, not the cessation, which the Greek translators must have understood. The verb ἱστάναι "to stand" (basic meaning), is frequently used as a more emphatic word for εἶναι, "to exist", "to be present", "to be there", and very often presupposes visual perception. Many such examples can be found in the LXX (e.g. Num xxii 24; Jos ii 11; — Ex xiv 19f.; Num xii 5; Deut xxxi 15, compare with MT). Ἔστη normally describes an event of the past, but occasionally the statement remains valid for the present and the (immediate) future (LXX Jer xxxi 11 = MT xlviii 11). This is the rule in gnomic and formulary sentences, curses, etc. (cf. II Sam v 6). The Greek version of Ex iv 25b, therefore, simply says: "The blood of the circumcision of my son was or is there (the result of the circumcision being still visible)". The last line (verse 26b) in the Hebrew text containing the explanation of an unusual term could hardly be rendered in Greek at all. The LXX simply repeats Zipporah's declaration as given in verse 25b, but connects it this time closely with 26a: "and he (the divine messenger) departed from him (the son) *because she said* (διότι εἶπεν): the blood of the circumcision of my son was (and is) there". By this ingenious resumption of the important words the Greek translator shows that he understood their intrinsic function as the necessary and effective formula which completed the ritual act.

Although the LXX handles the Hebrew text in its own way, it nevertheless confirms the MT and bears out our interpretation of it.

J. B. SEGAL, *The Hebrew Passover from the Earliest Times to A.D. 70.* (London Oriental Series Volume 12). Oxford University Press 1963. XVI + 294 pp. Price: 42 sh.

The present work is divided into two parts. In the first one (3 chapters) the author discusses all the available historical Passover texts from the Bible, the Elephantine ostraca and papyri, the book of Jubilees, down to New Testament times (ch. 1) and those from the Pentateuch (ch. 2). The biblical as well as some later texts are presented in full in translation. Chapter 3 deals with the modern theories on the origins and development of the festival. There are two groups of theories: 1) BEER, MCNEILE, STEUERNAGEL, ARNOLD, GUTHE, G. B. GRAY, MAY, PFEIFFER, WINNETT base their views on the Source Hypothesis whilst 2) MOWINCKEL, NICOLSKY, PEDERSEN, ENGNELL follow "a rational line of approach" analysing the texts within the framework of the Near Eastern pattern. In the second part of the book (4 chapters) the author develops his own theory on Passover as a New Year Festival (see below) and deals with its various phases: Primitive P., P. in Canaan, and the Last Phase. The last chapter ends (p. 266 ff., not marked as a conclusion) with a recapitulation of the author's arguments. The book has a select bibliography; but quite a few relevant books and articles have appeared since 1959 which might have been included. There is also a general index but, unfortunately, no index of passages.

The author's main contention is that "to the Hebrews the Passover was primarily a New Year festival" (p. 117). After the word "Passover" he adds "(and Tabernacles)"; the brackets indicate that he does not care much about the year beginning at the time of the autumn equinox. This is a pity, for he should have investigated into the problem of the "Hebrew" New Year before identifying the Passover feast with it. Norman SNAITH's *The Jewish New Year Festival* (1947) is mentioned in his bibliography, but he does not raise the issue of the book. H.-J. KRAUSS' *Gottesdienst in Israel* (1962) was probably not yet available to him. Professor SEGAL follows closely the "myth and ritual" line (p. 114) and its "patternism". The first to postulate that the Passover is "first of all a New Year Feast" was Professor HOOKE (1935). I. ENGNELL continued along this path (1951), but admitted a year later that the problem of Passover probably will never find its definite solution. The present book makes a new attempt to approach the problem from the point of view of Near Eastern Patternism. It is a pity that the author has ignored M. NOTH's cautionary methodological remarks in his article "Gott, König, Volk im Alten Testament" (1950, not registered in the bibliography) to which all too little attention has so far been paid in the field of Old Testament Study (cf. also H. FRANKFORT on ENGNELL in *Kingship and the Gods*, 1948, p. 405; further Ruth BENEDICT, *Patterns of*

Culture, Mentor Paperback, p. 47). The author might have profited more from a closer study of the Hebrew texts w i t h i n their contexts. It is regrettable that he quotes, and deals with, passages on Passover-Maṣṣoth out of their contexts (e.g., Ex. xxiii and xxxiv). We cannot look for "patterns" unless we have first a clear picture of the Hebrew concept.

It is not possible in this review to deal with all the problems and arguments of the book. Only a few shall be discussed. The author says (p. 134) that the name Pesaḥ and the term *ḥag* are invariably associated with the Lord of Israel with the notable exception of the *ḥag* which Jeroboam made for the people (1 Kings xii 32 f.); evidently this was not a Passover feast, as it was to correspond to the Feast of Tabernacles in Judah. It should be noted, however, that the oldest cultic calendar has the simple wording: "The Feast of Unleavened Bread you shall observe . . . . the Feast of Weeks you shall make for (to) yourself (!) . . . . and the Feast of Ingathering" (Ex. xxxiv 18a, 22). There is no reference to the God of Israel in the actual calendar (without the insertions), except in the appended laws (xxiii 18a-19a; 34, 25a and 26a) and in the additional headline (xxiii 14, missing in ch. xxxiv) which refers to all three feasts transforming the originally agricultural feasts into feasts devoted to YHWH.

On pages 116 and 136 the author seems to have misunderstood DALMAN's remarks. The common lambing season in Palestine is indeed the rainiest (and coldest) period of the year. He makes Passover-time, his New Year Festival, the beginning of the fiscal year, but the traditional date for the tithe of cattle was the 1st of Elul or the 1st of Tishri. He says (pp. 135 f. and 258) that in the Near East (evidently also in Israel) spring was the normal season for numbering the people and mustering the young men; he gives (p. 136. n. 3) as an example that "the Babylonian army was summoned . . . from Ayar to Teshrit" (!). There is a curious tradition in the Mishnah (RH i 2) according to which on the 1st of Tishri (not in spring) all that come into the world pass before God like legions of soldiers.

On page 116 we find the statement that "wherever the Passover and Tabernacles are both mentioned in a single passage of the Bible, it is the former that is mentioned first". The author points out that "it is said to occur in the first month, Tabernacles in the seventh". This seems to be a reference to the famous institution of the Passover in Ex. xii, where God says to Moses and Aaron, before he institutes anything about Passover, that "this month is to you the foremost of the months, the first to you with regard to the months of the year" (verse 1 f.). From the point of view of literary criticism verse 2 is clearly an insertion, for this note on the calendar has nothing whatever to do with what follows. As it stands it is addressed to Moses and Aaron—not to the people. Whenever God calls on Moses (and Aaron) to give the people a message, that message is always introduced by words such as these: "Speak to the people of Israel . . ." (numerous examples in Ex., Lev., and Num.). In Ex. xii this formula appears only after verse 2 introducing the Passover laws. It is evident that verse 2 contains an innovation in the calendar; the editor found it necessary to insert this note already here in order to explain the date given in verse 18. The announcement in this form and in this place makes sense only if it was to replace an earlier and different counting of the months and beginning of the year. The new counting was adopted from the Babylonians. The change is here vindicated by the fact that in this month the most decisive event in the history of Israel took place: their exodus from Egypt and their emergence as an independent people. The adoption of the Babylonian counting of the months was thus referred back to antiquity and passed for an early commandment of the God of Israel. However, it does not say anything about a New Year F e s t i v a l.

The ancient Canaanite year which the Israelites accepted after the *Landnahme* began round about the autumn equinox. This ancient year is clearly observed in Ex. xxiii and xxxiv. It is throughout, even in one of its additions (xxxiv 21), a year based entirely on the agricultural life in the land of Canaan. Although the (Passover-)Maṣṣoth Feast is mentioned first in this list, the end or turn of the year falls near the autumnal Feast of Ingathering which is mentioned as the last agricultural feast in the Bible. It is true, in the Gezer Calendar the month of Ingathering heads the list of the agricultural year, but it should not be forgotten that fruit is still being gathered right through the first part of *ḥorep* (the root *ḥrp* means "to pluck", "to gather"). The early rains are still much needed for the ripening of certain fruit which also applies to the late grapes.

What the author seems to be aiming at in saying that Passover is always mentioned first and Tabernacles last is to connect Passover with the New Year. But even if we take the biblical texts (Ex. xxiii and xxxiv), and not the Gezer Calendar, as the standard of the sequence of the feasts, we should still not be in a position to combine Passover with the New Year, for it would remain the first feast in the agricultural year which begins with the rainy season, with ploughing and sowing (used as a metaphor in Hos. x 12 and Jer. iv 3!).

The time when the crops are green and the corn begins to ear, roughly about the spring equinox or perhaps before, was in the Orient the time of fertility rites, the time for the invocation of the gods to bless the crops. This was the first agricultural feast in the year beginning with the autumn season. Professor SEGAL did not investigate into the relationship between the Passover-Maṣṣoth Feast and pagan fertility feasts, although he seems to admit such a connexion, for he touches on such a Babylonian rite (p. 122) and "Near East" rites generally (p. 151); the word "fertility" does not occur in the Index. The pagan feasts were celebrated at about the same time of the year as Passover. A connexion undoubtedly existed, although with a decisive difference: Passover was a feast dedicated entirely to YHWH who had freed them from the bondage of Egypt at this time of the year (Ex. xxiii 15 and xxxiv 18) and had also given them a goodly land (Josh. v 10 f.; main theme of Deuteronomy). God blessed the crops of this land (cf. Deut. xvi 17) without having to be induced by fertility magic.

From the moment of the entry of the Israelites into Canaan their God became closely bound up with the land, its seasons and vegetation, its corn and fruit crops. The preponderance of the agricultural seasons (and feasts) in ancient Israel is so striking that God became quite naturally their institutor or guarantor (Gen. viii 22): "sowing and harvesting", "(winter) cold and (summer) heat" will not cease (the other two pairs are in reverse order: day and night instead of night and day!). The word *qayiṣ* sometimes symbolizes the "end" (see Amos viii 1; Mic. vii 1; Jer. viii 20); it never applies to the time of the spring equinox, otherwise it would never have come to mean "summerfruit".

There is nowhere in the Hebrew Bible any mention of a specific New Year Festival. We have only the brief and casual indication of "the end of the year" in Ex. xxiii and xxxiv (*haššanah* is the current, not the oncoming year!), but this reference is so vague that some scholars have declared that the ancient Israelite calendar does not know of any New Year Festival (E. AUERBACH, *VT* VIII, 1958, p. 337; H.-J. KRAUS, *Gottesdienst in Israel*, 1962, p. 85).

In the Mishnaic tradition we cannot find the slightest trace that Passover or even Tabernacles were called New Year Festivals. Both were full-moon feasts, whilst the months and, therefore, also the New Year, were always beginning with the New Moon. A day actually called *Rosh Hashanah* does not occur until we come to Mishnaic times. The tractate RH (i 1) mentions four kinds of New Years none of which is connected with any of the three *Regalim*, as all of them begin on the first day of a month (Nisan, Elul, Tishri, Shebat—for the last, the New Year for trees, the School of Hillel fixed the date from the first to the fifteenth day of Shebat; the first half of Shebat would be too early for the planting of trees). The New Year *kat' exochen* is the one dated round about the autumn equinox as in ancient Canaan-Israel, i.e., on the first of the seventh Babylonian month (Tishri means "beginning", "opening" of the year).

Even in this late document (RH i 2) the ancient association of the three great feasts with agriculture and vegetation is retained and clearly expressed. Palestine is a land where life depends entirely on the seasons, the rains and the sun, and the Hebrew Bible makes no secret of it. The statement of Professor SEGAL on p. 117 is, therefore, all the more surprising. Although he agrees that there is some connexion between Passover and Tabernacles on the one hand and the agricultural seasons on the other, he declares: ". . . . their relationship to the calendar is constant. The date of each is not fixed by the processes of vegetation, but by the calendar". True, the calendar (with moon-months and intercalation) was and still is based on, or rather adapted to, the sun-year; but are not the seasons governed by the same course of the sun? H. FRANKFORT is certainly right when he points to the dependence of the calendar on nature. He quotes (*Kingship and the Gods*, ch. 22, n. 1, p. 408) A. J. WENSINCK: "The New Year rites and conceptions go back to the direct dependence of primitive man upon nature . . . . they have their roots in the ancient, purely religious conception of nature . . .". With other words, if the agricultural feasts are fixed by the calendar, the calendar follows the sun-year and its seasons with the equinoxes and solstices as the only fixed points (we disregard here the calendars based on the pure moonyear). The fixing of the feasts within the calendar has been a long process. In the Jewish calendar the feasts are celebrated on fixed days; the last to be fixed on a certain calendar day was Shavuoth.

The calendar problem is extremely complicated, and the author refrains from dealing with its intricacies as his mind is entirely set to make Passover at all costs a New Year Festival after the Near Eastern pattern. The Jewish tradition has never considered Passover (or even Tabernacles) as a New Year Festival, and we cannot easily dispense with that tradition.

Israel inherited the agricultural traditions of Canaan. The names of the ancient Hebrew months—so far as we know them: *Abib*, *Ziw*, *Ṣaḥ* (from an inscription recently found in Arad; cf. Is. xviii 4), *Ethanim*, *Bul*—refer all to the seasons of the year (weather and vegetation). The identification of *Ziw*, *Ethanim*, and *Bul* with the second, seventh, and eighth months of the Babylonian counting will be found in later comments which had been added to the text when the names were no longer current.

A note on the author's treatment of the record of the Last Supper in the Synoptic Gospels must be added here. Although his findings are of no particular importance for his main thesis, his procedure is characteristic of his approach to texts: he does not listen to them attentively enough. The author says (pp. 243 and 245) that the Synoptic Gospels do not mention the slaughter of the Pesaḥ victim in the Temple and the eating of its meat and, therefore, concludes that this omission is "a clear indication that the identification of the Last Supper as a Pesaḥ meal is an artificial device". This conclusion is all the more surprising as he gives practically all Synoptic references of the various stages of "doing" the Pesaḥ in connexion with the Last Supper, "slaughtering", "preparing", and "eating" on p. 34, n. 1; see also his reference on p. 243, n. 2. The author overlooks completely that it is not the intention of the Synoptics to describe a Passover meal in all its details or to identify Christ with the Passover lamb that is being slaughtered and eaten, but to point out that Christ compares himself to the bread which is broken (!) and to "the cup after the meal". Luke especially (in the so-called long text) follows the order of the Passover Night celebration, and it is from that very fact that we must try to understand the meaning and significance of the Eucharistic Words.

This leads us to the Passover Haggadah which the author does not take into consideration for his study, as he is dealing with the Passover only so far as it is connected with the Temple, that is, so long as the eating of the Pesaḥ forms "the most important component of it". However, the participants were not only eating the meat all the time, they also were to relate the historical Passover event. This was an old and important biblical injunction (Ex. xiii 8) which the author mentions on pp. 150 and 260 but never comes back to this important point which, after all, explains why Passover should be a YHWH feast. He drops this point, because it would certainly have weakened his main argument that Passover was a New Year Festival and not so much a feast to remember YHWH's great deed for Israel (Exodus and the Promised Land). Naturally he knows that Pesaḥ is "invariably associated with the Lord of Israel" (p. 134), but to explain why this is so should have been part of his job in this book.

That the story of the Exodus and the Promised Land does not figure in the Synoptic record of the Last Supper is quite a different matter: Jesus transformed the traditional Passover meal with its *zeker yeṣi'at miṣrayim* into something entirely new and different, so much so that the Johannine Gospel could easily ignore any connexion of the Last Supper with a Passover meal and yet bring out fully the new significance of the last gathering as recorded by the Synoptics (see the reviewer's book *Hebräer-Essener-Christen*, pp. 174-191).

It is a pity that the author has not included the Jewish Passover with its Haggadah in his study since it certainly contains many elements belonging to pre-Christian and even pre-Maccabean times (see his note 3 on p. 241).

In a letter to the reviewer the author admitted that his views are "highly subjective". The accumulation of such expressions as "perhaps", "probably", "it may be", "it seems", "it is possible" in his most important chapter (for instance pp. 148-151 and then again in his recapitulation pp. 266 ff.) weaken his arguments considerably and even the most well-meaning reader is left with a "it may be—it may not be".

Nevertheless, in spite of its shortcomings and defects, this is an important and valuable work, and we cannot afford to ignore it in future studies of the Passover.

"AT THE END OF THE DAYS"

I

Much has been written on the "eschatology" of the Old Testament prophets in the last 30 or 40 years, but little agreement seems to have been achieved. Statements resulting from these studies range from one extreme to the other, from: "all prophets of the Old Testament, including the pre-exilic prophets, are eschatologists" to "there is no pre-exilic or prophetic eschatology" [1]). On the following pages we shall not discuss the various aspects of the eschatological problems of the Old Testament, but concentrate on the Hebrew expression which seems to be the cause of the confusion: באחרית הימים. It occurs a number of times in various books of the Old Testament, and by no means only in those of the prophets. It appears always in the same form and with the same preposition as a fixed form of speech: Gen. 49, 1; Nu. 24, 14; Dt. 4, 30; 31, 29; Is. 2, 2 (Mi. 4, 1); Jer. 23, 20 (30,24); 48, 47; 49, 39; Ez. 38, 16; Hos. 3, 5; for the occurrences in the book of Daniel see further below. The traditional translations vary slightly. The AV has: "in the latter days", but twice "in the last days"; the RV has throughout "in the latter days"; the RSV: "in the latter days", but twice "in (the) days to come"; the most common modern rendering is: "at the end of the days".

This interpretation of the formula has given rise to two schools of thought:

1) Hugo GRESSMANN, *Der Messias*, 1929, pp. 74-77 and 82-87, says: There are eschatological oracles in the books of the OT, and there is even an older "popular (volkstümliche) eschatology" (*l.c.*, p. 75). Cf. also Paul VOLZ, *Jesaja II*, übersetzt und erklärt, 1932.

2) The literary critics maintain that there is no pre-prophetic or prophetic eschatology. See G. HÖLSCHER, *Die Ursprünge der jüdischen Eschatology*, 1925, and, after him, S. MOWINCKEL, *He That Cometh*, 1956, chapter V, especially pp. 126--133; survey on pp. 126ff.

Both schools take for granted that *b*^{e}*'aḫ*^{a}*rit hayyamim* means "in the last days" or "at the end of the days" tacitly implying the *finis* of this world or at least of this world epoch. They take the expression as an eschatological concept. The first school, therefore, concludes that we find eschatological thought in the books where this and similar expressions (see the list which GRESSMANN gives, *l.c.*, pp. 83f.) are used. The other school, however, feels compelled to postulate that the expression *beʾaḥarit hayyamim* "occurs only in late passages, or late editorial links" (MOWINCKEL, *l.c.*, p. 131, note 2). In other words, "there is no eschatology in the pre-prophetic age" (p. 130), "and the eschatological sayings in the prophetic books belong to the later strata, and come from the age of post-exilic Judaism" (p. 132). HÖLSCHER, therefore, deletes all "eschatological formulas" from the pre-exilic prophets, especially the most suspect of all: "am Ende der Tage" (GRESSMANN, p. 84).

As we see, both views are dependent on the same (traditional) understanding of the formula *beʾaḥarit hayyamim*. But this is not quite what the Hebrew expression conveys. The traditional interpretation of the formula was suggested by the Septuagint which translates it by: ἐπ' ἐσχάτου (ἐσχάτων) τ. ἡμερῶν, ἔσχατον τ.ἡ., ἐν ταῖς ἐσχάταις ἡμέραις —ἔσχατον, of course, meaning simply "the end". However, it should be noted that ἔσχατον does not necessarily denote the "abrupt end", but rather the "furthest", the "utmost", the "extreme", "what comes last". Nevertheless, it is this Greek expression in the commonly accepted sense of "end", which has come to signify in Christian theology "the end of the days", i.e., "the end of the universe as it at present exists". We need not wonder, then, that the quarrel in all discussions on eschatology in the Old Testament turns on the proper definition of the term "eschatology". As it is the creation of Christian theologians, we should realise that it is a *stark belastetes Wort*, tainted by later ideas, which should not be summarily applied to the much earlier and far more primitive Old Testament concept *beʾaḥarit hayyamim* [2]).

II

What is the original meaning of that expression?

The root *ʾḥr* points out that something is "behind" or that something (else) "follows". The derivations from this root are applied to both, space and time. *ʾaḥarit* has never lost the original element of the root. Here are two examples: "(the land or lands) which lie behind (or beyond) the sea" (Ps 139, 9); ". . . that which will happen: tell us what the earlier things were . . . that we may know what followed after them, or let us hear the coming things" (Is. 41, 22). There are a few cases in which *'aḫᵃrit* is used in a loose way in the sense of "end", as for instance in Dt. 11, 12, where the beginning and the end of the ever-recurring agricultural year are described (*re'šit* and *'aḫᵃrit*), where each end is followed by a new beginning; cf. however Job 8, 7, where the two words are used succinctly. The expression *'aḫᵃrit 'adam* does not necessarily imply the final "end", the death of man, but rather his future time or fate which follows the present situation or circumstances, as in Nu. 23.10; Prov. 19, 20; Job. 8, 7, etc.; cf. here also Sir. 11, 25-28, which deals with the period before and after man's death.

The translation "end" in the expression *bᵉ'aḫᵃrit hayyamim* is in every respect inadequate and can be misleading. *Hayyamim* is never used in the absolute sense for "time" [3]). In *hayyom* the article has a demonstrative meaning: *hayyom* is the "present day", "to-day" — the fuller expression being (*'ad*) *hayyom hazzeh*, in contradistinction to *hayyom hahu'*, a (definite) day of the time to come. Likewise *hayyamim* are the (days of the) present time, the present period, and, correspondingly, the fuller, but possibly later expression is *hayyamim ha'elleh*; cf. Zach. 8, 9. 15; Qoh. 7, 10. *'Aḫᵃrit hayyamim*, therefore, signifies "the day, or days, or the time which will follow or come after a certain period, usually the present period" [4]). It equals the expressions *hayyamim hahem*, or *ba'et hahu'*, or (*hinneh*) *yamim ba'im*, all of which point to a time which is not yet, but will come after the present period has come to an end.

This definition of *bᵉ'aḫᵃrit hayyamim* is borne out by Hos. 3,4f: "Many days the Israelites will (shall) dwell without a king ... Afterwards they will (shall) return and seek the Lord ... and come in fear to the Lord and his goodness *bᵉ'aḫᵃrit hayyamim*". The word *'aḫar* which introduces the first part of verse 5 makes it quite clear that the parallel expression *bᵉ'aḫᵃrit hayyamim* refers to the "many days" at the beginning of verse 4, describing the period which will have to pass; "afterwards" the events foreseen in verse 5 will take place.

No passage in the Old Testament which has *bᵉ'aḫᵃrit hayyamim* is eschatological in the sense in which we use the word. There is an oracle, Joel 3, 1, which does not contain this expression, but employs the adverb *'aḫᵃrey-ken* instead, in the same sense: "Und es wird sein nach diesem ..." [5]). Even in so late a passage as Dan. 2, 28f. the expression *bᵉ'aḫᵃrit yomayya'* is still idiomatically used and clearly defined as the time *'aḫrey dnah*, the days or time which will come "after this", that is, "after these days". Also in the other places of the Book of Daniel, *'aḫrit* must be so understood: 8, 19; 8, 23; 10, 14 *b'aḫrit hayyamim*; 12, 8 *'aḫrit 'elleh*. Both the LXX and Theodotion render it as usual by ἐπ' ἐσχάτου (ἐσχάτων) τῶν ἡμερῶν, with the exception of the last passage, which Theodotion translates τὰ ἔσχατα τούτων, and the LXX ἡ λύσις τοῦ λόγου τούτου, that is, the "interpretation of this word" [6]).

III

When the Book of Daniel really means the "end", the "conclusion of the final period", or the "final, decisive period" itself, it says so and uses the proper Hebrew word for "end", "finish": *qeṣ* [7]). This word is derived from the root *qṣṣ*, "cut off". All passages containing the word *qeṣ* are in the Hebrew chapters. Their Greek renderings are interesting. *Qeṣ hayyamim* we find in 12, 13 (LXX and Theodotion: συντέλεια ἡμερῶν); *'et qeṣ*, the "period of the end", in 8, 17; 11, 35; 11, 40 (LXX: ὥρα καιροῦ, καιρὸς συντελείας, ὥρα συντελείας; Theodotion: πέρας καιροῦ); similarly *'ad qeṣ* in 9, 26 or *'ad 'et qeṣ*, in 11, 35 and 12, 9: or just *qeṣ* in 12, 13 (also more in the sense of *'et qeṣ*). In three places *qeṣ* is connected with *mo'ed*: 8, 19; 11, 27, 35, with special reference to the "appointed time" of the end. The Greek translations of *qeṣ* vary to some extent. The LXX renders the word by συντέλεια and καιρός, Theodotion by καιρός mostly together with πέρας (with the exception of 12, 13; see above). Sometimes καιρός stands for *mo'ed* (in connection with *qeṣ*). A complete list of the Greek translations would show that καιρός became the predominant word for the "end" or the "time of the end", the "appointed time (of the end)". The LXX, it is true, gives some preference to συντέλεια, whilst Theodotion, who lived in the latter part of the sub-apostolic age, evidently found the word καιρός, as applied to eschatological time, already in use and preferred it to συντέλεια. It had already been widely employed as an eschatological term in the New Testament writings. Matthew uses συντέλεια (see further below); there is only one clear example for the eschatological use of the word καιρός, Mat. 8,29; but cf. also 13,30; 16,3; 21,34. 41 and 26,18 with eschatological implications (otherwise he uses καιρός as a general word for time).

The Book of Daniel which knows and uses the old Hebraic expression *b'aḫrit hayyamim* (even in the Aramaic passage 2, 28) still idiomatically, has a fully developed eschatology in the strict sense. The "end" of the days is a real end. To express this, it uses the word *qeṣ*, which is not used in this sense in the older Biblical texts [8]). The "days of the end" are literally numbered. The end is one of "Heil" and "Unheil", of salvation and doom, and it is the doom by which the days come to an end: the "wrath of God" (8, 19) is bound to come, the doom had been determined (9, 26.27; 11, 36; cf. a. Is. 10, 23; 28, 22).

IV

In spite of the correct use of the term *beʾaḫarit hayyamim* in the Book of Daniel, it was only natural that this expression also came under the spell of eschatology, for it presupposes that the present time or period of days will come to some kind of end, before the things that shall happen will happen.

Although the older translations still distinguish between *ʾaḫarit* and *qeṣ*:

Greek: ἔσχατος—συντέλεια, πέρας, καιρός
Latin: *in novissimis temporibus—finis dierum*
Luther: künftige Zeiten, hernach—Ende der Tage
AV: the latter days—the end of the days
(about the Aramaic translation see last chapter),

modern scholars seem to take no notice of this distinction. They translate *beʾaḫarit hayyamim*: "am Ende der Tage" (GRESSMANN, l.c., p. 84), die "Endzeit" (GES.-BUHL, p. 27a), "at the end of the days" (KOEHLER-BAUMGARTNER, p. 33b; MOWINCKEL, p. 131, n. 2). Modern translations should, therefore, be used cautiously, for *ʾaḫarit* and *qeṣ* should be distinguished from each other.

It is on the identification of *ʾaḫarit* with *qeṣ* that the two modern schools base their different conclusions. Because the expression *beʾaḫarit hayyamim* is interpreted as meaning "at the end of the days", the one school says, there is a pre-exilic eschatology, whilst the other school, which says there is none, has to declare that all the passages containing that expression are not original but belong to the age of post-exilic Judaism. As already pointed out, the "eschatological" interpretation of the old-Biblical expression *beʾaḫarit hayyamim* goes back to the Greek translation in its modern understanding, but we should keep in mind that ἔσχατος is originally not quite the same as συντέλεια, τέλος, or πέρας (see the dictionaries).

We do not know when the identification of *'aḫ^{a}rit* (*hayyamim*) with *qeṣ* (*hayyamim*) took place, but we do know that this development was practically completed in New Testament times. Two or three reasons for this trend may be given.

1) There are prophecies of doom in the prophetic writings of the Old Testament. Doom together with salvation forms a necessary and integral part of the (later) eschatological view (cf., for instance, the Biblical quotations in the Damascus document).

2) Some of the OT prophecies had never come true: Is. 2, 2ff., (cf. Jub. 1, 29), Hos. 3, 4f., Joel 3 (cf. Acts 2, 16-25) and 4, and many others. There are a number of references and allusions to Isaiah already in the Book of Daniel.

3) Important events had happened during the exilic and post-exilic period, such as the return to the land of the fathers, the re-erection of the Temple, and we may even include its re-dedication under the Maccabeans. All of them could be understood as fulfilment of former prophecies and evidently they were so understood. However, the dissatisfaction with the priestly kingship of the Hasmoneans, which bore so little resemblance to the prophetic ideals, and the ensuing Roman rule, gave rise to serious doubts. This could not be what the prophets had in mind. The new world-period with a new victorious life of the Jewish people as visualized by the prophets was still to come and to come soon. They conceived it as something utterly different from the present era of spiritual dearth and political subjection.

The authority of the Scriptures was never doubted. God was faithful and the word of his prophets true. The fact that the prophecies had not come true in the past made a new interpretation for the present time of longing and hope necessary. The task was vigorously taken up by the Essenic movement and, after it, together with new aspects, by Early Christianity. The new interpretation became the mainspring of their theologies. "The time of the end", "the end of the time(s)", when all the prophecies of doom and salvation would be fulfilled, was n o w.

It is true that Jewish apocalyptic thought, especially in its earlier representations, did not always conceive the end as a world catastrophe, cf. for instance the new creation according to Jub. 1, 29; 5, 12; 23, 26 ff.), but the "last" days or times (Test. Levi 14, 1; TIs 6, 1; TZ 8, 2; TD 5, 4; TG 8, 2; TJOs 19, 10) are seen as a real end, a completion, or consummation: τελείωσις χρόνων (TR 6, 8);

συντέλεια τῶν αἰώνων (TL 10, 2; TB 11, 3); καιρὸς συντελείας (TZ 9, 9); *finis saeculi* (4 Ezra 6, 25); *finis temporis*, *temporum* (2 Bar. 27, 15; 29, 8; 30, 3); *consummatio* (4 Ezra 9, 5); *c. mundi* (2 Bar. 56, 2); *c. saeculi* (83, 7); *c. exitus dierum* (Ass. Mos. 1, 18); (*tempora* ?) *consummentur* (10,13).

V

A few notes on the eschatological expressions in the literature of Qumran and the New Testament may follow here in order to give an idea of the further development of eschatological thought and to show the affinity between its two main trends.

In the Dead Sea Scrolls both expressions (1) *ʾaḫ*^{a}*rit* and (2) *qeṣ* are in use and to some extent still distinguished from each other.

1a) *B*^{e}*ʾaḫ*^{a}*rit hayyamim*. In Sa I, 1 the expression is clearly applied to the "Messianic" time, as the Messiah is already thought to be present in the congregation. It is not quite clear whether this refers to the time of the *qeṣ* or the time after the *qeṣ*. There are two more passages in the Damascus document. D IV, 4 says, that "the elect of Israel . . . shall stand *b*^{e}*ʾaḫ*^{a}*rit hayyamim*", that is, evidently, during (IV, 8f.) and after (IV, 10) the "completion of the *qeṣ*". According to D VI, 10f. "the Teacher of Righteousness arises *b*^{e}*ʾaḫ*^{a}*rit hayyamim*", that is, after the "*qeṣ* of wickedness".

(1b) *L*^{e}*ʾaḫ*^{a}*rit hayyamim* occurs only in pHab II, 5f. and IX, 6. It should be noted that in these two examples the preposition *b*^{e} has been replaced by the particle *l*^{e}. The difference may not be great, but all translators including the latest (DUPONT-SOMMER and Johann MAIER) render both passages in the same way as those with *b*^{e}: "at the end of the days". It seems that pHab employs the term only in a loose way indicating that the event will take place sometime during the last period. The period thus described begins practically with the day(s) of judgment (cf. also V, 3-6).

(2) *Qeṣ* is definitely, as in the Book of Daniel, "the time of the end", during which the wicked people reign, those who do not believe in the message of the Teacher of Righteousness, "whom God had given . . . to interpret all the words of his servants, the prophets, through whom God had announced all the things that would come over his people . . ." (pHab II, 8-10). The *qeṣ* is, therefore, sometimes described as the *qeṣ riš*^{ʿa}*h*, the end-period of wickedness (D VI, 10.14; XII, 23; XV, 7.10; pHab VII, 7.12). The very last part of the end-time is called *qeṣ ʾaḫ*^{a}*ron* (S IV, 16f.; pHab VII, 7.12). The NT equivalent

is καιρὸς ἔσχατος (1 P. 1,5), which is here already the beginning of the new aeon. *Qeṣ* is sometimes itself the end-period, sometimes the conclusion of this period (S III, 23; or with special reference to the fact that it is fixed by God, *qeṣ neḥeraṣah*, S IV, 20.25 and H III, 36 with allusion to Dan. 9, 26f. and 11, 36 and the corresponding passages in Isaiah). S III, 13-15 (*qiṣṣim*), evidently referring to decisive periods of the past, seems to admit periods of visitation ("Heil" and/or "Unheil").

Summarizing the results of this brief examination of the Scrolls, we may say that the idea of the end is rendered by the word *qeṣ* with a special emphasis on its wickedness, on judgment, and doom; more generally, however, by *'aḥarit hayyamim* perhaps with a greater stress on salvation.

VI

Both expressions appear in their Greek form in the New Testament. For *be'aḥarit hayyamim* see the translations of the LXX. *Qeṣ* is usually rendered by καιρός as in the Greek translations of the Book of Daniel. Both expressions are here even more closely connected with each other: sometimes they are practically identified (cf. 2 Tim. 3, 1).

All passages in John have the singular, "on the last day (ἐν τῇ ἐσχάτῃ ἡμέρᾳ), with reference to the last judgment (12, 48) or the resurrection (6, 39.40.44.54; 11, 24). The plural, "in the last days" (ἐν ταῖς ἐσχάταις ἡμέραις) is used in Acts 2, 17 (quotation of Joel 3, 1ff., which has not *be'aḥarit hayyamim*; see note 5), James 5, 3, and 2 Tim. 3, 1; with ἐπί in 2 P. 3, 3; ἐπ' ἐσχάτου τῶν χρόνων in 1 P. 1,20.

As the present time of the New Testament is "end-time", the word καιρός is very frequent here. Many passages in the New Testament, in which καιρός is usually translated with "time" or, occasionally, "appointed time", actually refer to the present, or almost present, time of the end. It is quite impossible to deal with the concept καιρός without having due regard to the eschatological mood of the context [9]), in which we find it. Admittedly, there are cases where καιρός is used in a more general sense like χρόνος, but there are also other cases where χρόνος is used synonymously with καιρός [10]). About the plural καιροί see examples below.

Here is a list of passages in which the word καιρός can best be studied in its eschatological aspect. The list is not complete.

Mt. 8, 29.
Mk. 1, 15: 10, 30; 13, 33.

Lk. 1, 20; 19, 44; 21, 8.24. 36 (= E 6, 18).
Rom. 3, 26; 12, 11 (*v. l.*); 13, 11.
1. Cor. 4, 5.
Gal. 6, 9.
Eph. 1, 10; 5, 16 (= Col. 4, 5).
1. Thess. 5, 1.
2. Thess. 2, 6.
1. Tim. 2, 6; 4, 1; 6, 15.
2. Tim. 3.1.
Heb. 9, 9 f.
1. P. 1, 11; 4, 17; 5, 6.
Rev. 1, 3; 11, 18; 12, 12. 14; 22, 10.

A number of expressions with *qeṣ*, common in the Scrolls, have their Greek equivalents in the New Testament, although they are not always indentical in meaning.

ad Mk. 1, 15 and Lk. 21, 24 cf. D IV, 10: בשלים קץ (cf. a. LXX Dan. 12, 13 a. Dan. Theodot. 5, 26).

ad Lk. 21, 36 and Eph. 6, 18 cf. D VI, 10; XV, 7.10: בכל קץ

ad Eph. 5, 16, Col. 4, 5; 2 Tim. 3, 1 (Test. Dan. 6, 6) cf. D VI, 10. 14; XII, 23; XV, 7.10; pHab V, 7f.: קץ הרשע(ה)

ad 1 P. 1, 5 (ἐν καιρῷ ἐσχάτῳ) and 1 Tim. 4, 1 (ἐν ὑστέροις καιροῖς) cf. S IV, 16f.; pHab VII, 7.12: (ה)קץ (ה)אחרון.

ad Mat. 16, 3. Lk. 21, 24, Acts 1, 7 and 17, 26 (καιροί) cf. S III, 14f: קצים.
(ad Rom. 13, 11, καιρός + ὥρα, cf. LXX Dan. 8, 17; 11, 35.40).
(ad Lk. 19, 43 cf. D VII, 11).

The word συντέλεια used in the sense of *qeṣ* is peculiar to Matthew: 13, 39.40.49; 24, 3; 28 ,20 (cf. also Heb. 9, 26). It is taken from LXX Dan. 11, 27.35.40; 12, 13; (not in Theodotion).

VII

A few remarks on the Targumim may conclude our observations. All Targumim render *bᵉ'aḇᵃrit hayyamim* by *bᵉsop yomayya'*, although the Aramaic passage in Dan. 2, 28 has *bᵉ'aḇᵃrit yomayya'* (Hebraism?). We see that the Targumists did not follow this precedent, but conceived the Hebrew *'aḇᵃrit hayyamim* as "the end of the days". There is no exception. The Aramaic *sop* corresponds to Hebrew *qeṣ*, not to Hebrew *'aḇᵃrit*. The common Semitic root means "to take an end", "to be no more", "to cease to exist", "to perish". *Sop*, therefore, denotes the "absolute end". In Hebrew the word *sop* is used as an

Aramaism in a few late passages (s. Ges.-Buhl p. 539 b). In Aramaic it is the common word for "end", the "absolute finish".

The Targumim (together with the literature of Qumran and the New Testament) stand at the end of the development of eschatological thought. For them the *'aḥªrit* is the *sop*. But in spite of the use of the term *sop yomayya'*, the genuine eschatological mood (from Daniel to the NT) seems to be missing in the Targumim; the eschatological expectation has lost much of its urgency, for we do not get the impression that "the end" is really very near.

---

1) See Joh. LINDBLOM, "Gibt es eine Eschatologie bei den alttestamentlichen Propheten?" (*StTh* VI, 2, 1953, pp. 79-114), p. 79, and his bibliographical notes He himself takes a middle course, especially in his latest work *Prophecy in Ancient Israel*, Oxford 1962. pp. 360-375, where he employs the term "eschatology in the wider sense".

2) In LINDBLOM's article (see note 1), p. 80 n. 3, is a reference to an article by A. W. ARGYLE in *The Hibbert Journal* 51, 1953, pp. 385 ff., who seems to have come to a similar conclusion, namely, that the notion *eschaton* is inappropriate when one speaks of eschatology in the Old Testament.

3) Even the word *ʿolam* (which comes nearest to this notion of "time", especially in such expressions as *meʿolam weʿad ʿolam*, or *ʿolamim*) very often only means a "long time", a "life-time", or a similar period of some length. For practical purposes we translate the term *leʿolam* with "for ever", although it refers in each case only to the period in view (cf. Dt. 15, 17; 1 Sam. 1, 22; Is. 42, 14; etc.). The fact that *ʿolam* denotes a long, but actually limited period made it possible that in post-Biblical Hebrew *ʿolam* came to mean "world-period" and "world" (αἰών, κόσμος.

The present article does not deal with "time" in the Bible, but rather with the "end" of (the) time(s), that is, with certain limitations of time. It may not be inopportune here to say a few words about the most recent study by James BARR, *Biblical Words for Time*, 1962, as one of the words for time, καιρός, stands in its centre. One cannot come to a full understanding of "time" in the Bible without taking into account these various limitations which are so often connected with Biblical time or times. I can find only two examples in his book (pp. 38 and 40), where he refers Greek καιρός to Hebrew *qeṣ*, and that only *en passant*. The Greek expressions, especially in the NT, must be studied in close connection with their older equivalents in the Bible and now also with those in the Essenic literature. What the author says on p. 118 is so little that it becomes irrelevant. In spite of some pertinent remarks which this book contains, it must be said, that the philosophical approach as the author demonstrates it—he calls it "theological-philosophical"—is insufficient, and it obscures rather than elucidates the meaning of καιρός in many important passages of the NT (see, for instance, his treatment of 1 Cor. 7, 29 on p. 43), where its content cannot be divorced from the ever-present eschatological thought or mood. This is not the place to review his statements in detail. It seems that we shall have to turn back again to some of the results of older Biblical studies which the author so violently criticizes.

4) Cf. here Akkadian *ina aḫrat umi*, which is simply "in future"; the f. pl. *aḫriat* also means "future"; likewise other derivations from the root *aḫr* refer to the (sometimes immediate) future; see BEZOLD, *Bab.-Ass. Glossar*, p. 24b. The

note in Koehler-Baumgartner, p. 33b, s.v., that the Akk. expression is an "eschatological term", is incorrect; see now also the brief remarks by Arvid Kapelrud in his article "Eschatology in the Book of Micah", *VT* XI, 1961, No. 4., p. 395f.—In Ugaritic texts so far no expression corresponding to the Hebrew and Akkadian has been found; but *baḫr* is here also "afterwards"; *uḫryt* (*mt*) (only occurence in 2 Aqht VI, 35) is the time after man has spent his present life, i.e., man's future or fate; cp. the Hebrew expression *ʾaḥarit ʾadam* mentioned above.

[5]) It is interesting to note that Luke, when quoting this verse in Acts 2, 17, renders the adverbial expression by ἐν ταῖς ἐσχάταις ἡμέραις. The LXX translation is literal.

[6]) The word λύσις sometimes stands for *pešer*; see Kosmala, *Hebräer—Essener—Christen*, p. 275, n. 13; p. 350, n.l.

[7]) Th. C. Vriezen, "Prophecy and Eschatology" in *VT Supplement* I, 1953, pp. 199-229, says: "For *future* and *end*, for *later* and *last* Hebrew thought has only one word, *ʾaḥarit* . . ." (p. 223 bottom). He does not seem to know the word *qeṣ*, which is the proper word for "end" in the OT, and the Book of Daniel uses it with reference to time.

[8]) A few words should be said here about Amos 8, 2, where *qeṣ* is not a distinct concept of time. For Amos the present time is a time of "sins" (1, 3.6.9.11.13; 2, 1.4.6) especially with regard to Israel, so that God cannot let them go on in that way any longer (cf. 3, 1f.). In other words: "the end (*qeṣ*) is coming to my people Israel" (8, 2; 9, 8), that is, to Israel in its present state, for "days will come" (9, 13), when everything will be repaired (!) (9, 11-15). J. H. Grönbaek ("Zur Frage der Eschatologie in der Verkündigung der Gerichtspropheten", *SEÅ* 24, 1959, pp. 5-21) is right, when he hesitates to call this *Verkündigung* of Amos eschatological (l.c., p. 11).

[9]) Like James Barr; see note 3, second part.

[10]) Even Barr quotes a few such cases, *l.c.*, p. 42.

FORM AND STRUCTURE IN ANCIENT HEBREW POETRY[1])

(A NEW APPROACH)

When I began to study theology and to read the Hebrew Bible forty years ago, it was a great shock to me when I discovered that the prophets communicated God's word in poetical form instead of using plain language, and that even God himself occasionally expressed his will in poems. Earlier I had gained the impression that writing poetry was not a serious occupation, that poets were dreamers and spent their time on versifying their thoughts that might have been expressed more clearly in ordinary speech, provided they had to say something really worth while. I fully agreed with Plato who was not much in favour of poetry. With these ideas at the back of my mind, it took me some time to recover from the shock and to become familiar with the fact that the word of God was imparted to us very often, though not always, in poetic form.

In my student years metrical studies in the Hebrew Bible were much *en vogue* in Germany, and there were few lectures on the books of the prophets in which texts were not examined metrically. Sometimes it was like this: one line was considered to be too short, so a word or two had to be added, whilst another line seemed to be too long, so a word or two had to be removed. The actual text as handed down seemed to be a minor concern. DUHM's commentary on Isaiah which appeared in its third and last edition in 1914 can serve as an illustration of that method of scanning Hebrew poetry. This method could not possibly lead to any sound results. Not what the prophet meant to express and indeed had expressed in the text preserved to us, but rather what he ought to have said and how the text, therefore, ought to be emended, seemed to have become the all-important object of critical scholarship.

---

[1]) The following is a paper read at the meeting of the Society for Old Testament Study at Bangor (Wales) on July 23, 1964.

In another respect also the modern efforts in finding out the principles of Hebrew "metre" were doomed to failure. We looked upon Hebrew poetry in the same way as we approached Greek and Latin poetry: we scanned the verses, we counted the syllables judging them by the length of their vowels or their stresses on the assumption that ancient Hebrew poetry was following the same rules as Greek or Latin poetry or any modern poetic art. Well—it does not!

In addition to this misconception of Hebrew poetic measure we made another mistake: we based our scanning entirely on the Masoretic vocalisation and accentuation of the texts. The Masoretes had worked out their own system, but whether that system truly represented the original pronunciation or rhythm of the language of Moses and Samuel, of Amos and Isaiah, we never questioned. The Bible with all its comments on, and explanations of, the text which had accumulated in the course of time and had been added to the original wording, had become Holy Scripture for the instruction and edification of man, and important parts of it were recited in the prayer services of the Synagogue. The Masoretes established the final shape of the text of the Bible, they fixed the pronunciation, vowels and accents, once and for all, in order to regulate the recitation of the Holy Writ. The Masoretes had their own ideas about the Hebrew language. They preferred the stress on the ultima, with some obvious exceptions such as the segolata and the pausal forms. But we have good reasons to doubt that the Masoretic tradition represents the original pronunciation and intonation. For there are other and older traditions which do not agree with the Masoretic fixation. However, it was from the Masoretic system of vocalisation and accentuation that students of Hebrew prosody drew their conclusions. The pointed Masoretic text on which we have made ourselves entirely dependent cannot provide us with a clue to the laws underlying ancient Hebrew poetic art; in fact, it has distracted us from the only possible access.

In the early forties I studied certain poetic pieces from the Book of Isaiah and I was struck by two things:

1) the regularity of the number of words or rather word-units of a sentence forming a complete and self-contained line, whether the words were short with one stress only, or long with two and even three stresses, and

2) that a line within a composition corresponded to another line of equal length also with regard to its content, that is, a sentence of a certain length was paralleled by another sentence of the same length,

so that the whole composition turned out to be one of perfect beauty and strict correspondence between outward form and inner structure.

I was amazed at this complete agreement between form and contents on the basis of such a simple device as this, and I could not imagine that nobody had ever seen this before. In the course of time I learned that the first principle, at least in its rudiments, had been discovered before in the 16th century by Rabbi AZARYAH DE ROSSI of Ferrara who had published his own ideas on the laws of Hebrew poetry in a book called *Meʾor ʿEnayim*, "The Light of the Eyes" (Mantua 1574). The principle he had found was that it was the important words and notions which formed the basic elements of Hebrew poetry, not the syllables and stresses. His discovery was favourably mentioned by the younger BUXTORF in the 17th century and by Bishop Robert LOWTH in the 18th century. BUXTORF translated substantial passages from AZARYAH's book into Latin [1]) and Bishop LOWTH gave an English version in the Preliminary Dissertation of his book on Isaiah[2]). But neither of the two, in fact nobody down to our time made any serious use of this principle. It may be that neither BUXTORF nor Bishop LOWTH were really impressed by the examples which Rabbi AZARYAH gave. He applied his method only briefly to a few of the less suitable poems such as the song of Miriam and Moses (Ex. xv), the last song of Moses (Deut. xxxii), the song of the well (Num. xxi) and the Psalm in the Book of Habakuk. It may also be that Rabbi AZARYAH was hampered by the dominating presence of the pointed Masoretic Text to go any further. So the matter was left at that until to-day. At the beginning of the 20th century Eduard SIEVERS [3]) made a final approach to Hebrew poetry on the basis of the regular change of heavy and light syllables; this method is still predominant in all modern research of Hebrew poetic art [4]).

Once we have fully grasped the principle that the basic element of ancient Hebrew poetry is the word- or thought-unit irrespective

---

[1]) *Liber Cosri*, Basel 1660: *Mantissa Dissertationum* pp. 415ff.

[2]) *De Sacra Poesi Hebraeorum*, Oxford 1753, p. 195; 2nd edition 1763, pp. 258 f.—*Isaiah. A New Translation, with a Preliminary Dissertation and Notes*, 2nd ed. London 1779, pp. xli—xlvii.

[3]) *Metrische Studien. I. Studien zur hebräischen Metrik.* Leipzig 1901.

[4]) Theodore ROBINSON is perhaps an exception in so far as he emphasized the importance of the word-unit in Hebrew poetry ("Some Principles of Hebrew Metrics", *ZAW* 54, 1936, pp. 28-43; "Basic Principles of Hebrew Poetic Form", *Festschrift Bertholet*, Tübingen 1950, pp. 438—450). Nevertheless even he remained loyal to the school of SIEVERS. Unfortunately it is impossible here to go any further into the history of the study of Hebrew poetic form.

of beats and stresses, the study of form and structure, of the relationship between form and contents, becomes really very simple and produces surprising results.

The question arises: what do we count as a unit? The answer is: everything that can be expressed by one essential word, any notion or noun, subject or object, whether it is *ben* with one or *beʿaṣṣerotekem* with three stresses, counts as one unit; any action, general or specific, that is, without or with a suffix, a pronoun, an adjective or adverb, a numeral, any essential word in the sentence represents one unit. We do not count *'et-*, the mark of the definite object, any of the particles or prepositions unless they have a suffix designating a person or an object, except the usually heavy preposition *'et* which indicates the intimate communion or togetherness [1]), the full negation *lo'* (though not *'al-*), and the conjunction *ki*, but only when it introduces the proof or logical reason, not when it opens a mere explanation [2]). On the whole one learns fairly quickly what to count as a unit and what not, but one has always to keep the function of the words in a sentence in mind.

Difficulties, of course, remain, as for instance with *kol-* which is frequently found in the MT before a noun with no particular additional meaning [3]), or with the relative particle *'ašer* which is rare in good poetry and rather belongs to prose language, but occasionally fills an important place as a substitute for a noun especially in less poetical sentences [4]). Finally there are the expressions which belong so closely together that even the Masoretes sometimes felt obliged to connect the two words by a Maqqef [5]). But one cannot rely on the Masoretes in that respect; one has to observe the logic of the sentence rather than the masoretic prescriptions which, it should be remembered, are directions for the practical recitation and do not necessarily take into account the original linguistic and logic requirements.

[1]) For instance in Is. xl 14 and twice in xlix 4.

[2]) In that case it can be conveniently translated by "namely" or sometimes even left out.

[3]) Cp. Micah iv 1f. with Is. ii 2f. where it may have been added subsequently already in ancient times as the LXX shows, possibly in order to stress the importance of the event: "all nations will come". But then the second and parallel half of the line would rather reduce the effect of this statement: "many peoples", and this is hardly likely as one would rather expect an intensification in the second clause of a parallelism of this sort.—On the other hand, *kol* has sometimes an important function to fulfil and must then be counted as a unit by itself; cf. Is. xliv 23: "the forest and every (single) tree in it".

[4]) See, for example, Is. vii 15, p. 434 f.

[5]) E.g. *ʿali-lak* which is one action and counted as one unit; see p. 439.

After having briefly stated the principles of our approach to ancient Hebrew poetry I propose to examine a small selection of poetical pieces. All I can offer in the short time allotted to the subject are merely excerpts from a much larger work which was finished about ten years ago but has never been published; this is the first occasion that the subject is discussed in public.

I should like to add that Ugaritic poetry follows much the same rules as ancient Hebrew poetry. It is based on the same principle of the word- or thought-unit, just as it widely obeys the same laws of parallelism within the line as Hebrew poetry. There is no need here to discuss these laws of parallelism, because they have been well stated by Bishop LOWTH [1]) and are well known. As for Ugaritic poetic literature the question has been dealt with by ALBRIGHT, YOUNG, and especially by GORDON in his various books on the Ugaritic language. The use of two parallel clauses in a sentence or line and the principle of the word-unit together with the close correspondence between form and structure, or rather, form and the arrangement of ideas in the composition as a whole, which again, as we shall see, creates a new parallelism apart from the one within the line, namely that of corresponding lines within the composition—these are the distinctive features in Ugaritic poetry (2nd millenium B.C.) as well as in ancient Hebrew poetry down to exilic times. With the Exile or soon after it, this ancient poetic art declined in Israel and other forms and standards of poetic structure developed, probably during or already before the Exile. These will not be the subject of the present paper.

We shall also leave out the ancient popular songs, songs which were sung by the people usually with the accompaniment of musical instruments such as the timbrel and the flute. The few songs that have come down to us in the biblical literature, for instance the Song of Miriam (Ex. xv 21), the Song of the Well (Nu. xxi 17f.), or the Song of the Defeat of Assyria (Is. xxx 31) are all very short. They form, as a rule, just one line which consists of six or at the most of 12 units. Parallelism within that line is not necessarily observed, though the lines can be subdivided in one way or another. Such lines, when sung, can be repeated again and again, and sometimes they are incorporated in longer poems such as Miriam's *Šir* of God's deed among the Egyptians or the *Šir* of God's victory over Assyria, just

[1]) *De Sacra Poesi Hebraeorum*, 1753, pp. 180ff. (ch. XIX); Ed. 1763, pp. 237ff.

as composers of modern times have incorporated folk-songs in their own *Kunstmusik*.

We omit these folksongs here as we cannot learn much from them about form and structure. They are too short. Two lines would be the minimum requirement for something that could be called a poem.

The simplest form of poetry appears in oracles. Oracles in the wider sense of the word may contain a piece of advice, a blessing or a curse, a judgement, a prophecy, or a statement about God and his will. Oracles are uttered by wise men or prophets as vehicles of divine inspiration or revelation. They can be announced as God's direct command, preceded by the words: "thus says the Lord", "the Lord has spoken," "decree of the Lord" (*ne'um YHWH*), and so on. Similar formulas are often found at the end of the oracle, occasionally also somewhere within the poem, even in the middle of a line, interrupting the sentence and transforming it into prose. In the latter case we may safely assume that the formula is not part of the original poem, because it spoils the structure of the line and of the poem as a whole. It was quite a normal thing for the editor to make such insertions when he felt it necessary to stress now and then that the oracle is the decree of God.

Most of the older oracles are in a simple form and when we translate them into any modern language, the sentences look very much like prose sentences. The early and simplest Hebrew oracles have much in common with the oracles of the *Ša'ir* or the *Kahin*, the pre-Islamic Arab poet or priest, only that there the lines usually end in a rhyme, whilst in the Hebrew oracles the important rule is that the lines are of a certain length, that is, they consist of a certain number of thought-units.

The question is: how many lines make an oracle and how many units are required for the line?

An oracle can consist of two, three, four, or five lines, rarely more. It depends on what the prophet wants, or is instructed, to say and how much he wants to say. In composing or pronouncing his oracles the prophet is comparatively free and he uses his freedom. A good example of primitive oracles are the oracles of Amos on Judah and her neighbours in chapters i and ii. The first eight oracles are fairly uniform and consist of three to five lines after an introductory line which is the same in all of them: "For three transgressions of—then follows the name: Damascus, Gaza, Tyrus, Edom, Ammon, Moab, Judah, Israel—and for four, I will not turn away the punishment".

How many units has the line of an oracle? Six units are very common, but also five, seven, and eight are quite frequent. There seems to be only one oracle—also in the Book of Amos (v 25—27)—which has nine units to each of its three lines (see p. 436).

Oracles do not, as a rule, belong to the most artistic poetry. However, we must accept them as poetry of a more primitive type, simply because they do observe the fundamental rule of some kind of regularity in the number of lines and in the number of units to the line.

A brief survey of the eight oracles in Amos i and ii will easily demonstrate this. Omitting the above mentioned introductory line to each oracle, we have first a line mentioning the transgression of which each nation is accused. The length of this line varies. After that the prophet describes the punishment which will be meted out to them; this is the actual oracle, and it is always an oracle of doom. In the following survey, the figures give the numbers of units in each line:

I.	i 3—5	4	V.	i 13—15	6
		7			6
		7			6
		7			6
II.	i 6—8	5	VI.	ii 1—3	5
		6			6
		6			6
		6			6
III.	i 9—10	8	VII.	ii 4—5	6
		6			6
					6
IV.	i 11—12	5	VIII.	ii 6—8 (ff)	6
		6			8
		6			8
					5
					5

This brief survey of a group of oracles [1]) shows us that the actual

[1]) Israel being the main target, the last oracle has many additions: first a long discourse on Israel's manifold sins of another seventeen lines which is resumed and continued in the following chapters together with a list of past punishments and the announcement of the last punishment which is to come: captivity (last verses of chapters v, vi, and vii). The additions are mostly irregular and inartistic

oracle containing the judgement, that is, what follows after the line of indictment, consists in four out of eight cases of three lines of equal length. As we shall further see, three is indeed a favourite number of lines for short poetic pieces, especially in oracles.

Let us turn now to the first two of Balaam's oracles. The lines are here not of equal length, but are, nevertheless, systematically arranged. Both oracles, as will be seen at once, are composite oracles, that is, they represent a sequence of thoughts which belong together, thus forming the complete oracle [1]).

The first, Nu. xxiii 7—10, has eight lines and is built up in the following way (the figures give again the number of units in each line):

verse 7:	7
	7
8:	5
	5
9:	5
	7
10:	7
	7

We have two lines of seven units, three of five and again two of seven with another line of seven units added to the oracle containing a reflection of Balaam on himself resulting from the oracle. Examining the oracle more closely with regard to its contents we find that the two first lines belong together, the next three, and the last two, as indicated by the division strokes; they are followed by the extra line which stands by itself.

The second oracle, Nu. xxiii 18—24, is somewhat longer; it has eleven lines. It expresses similar thoughts, and groups them according to the same structural principle, though not in the same way. We get the following picture:

verse 18:	7
19:	6
	7

in point of form and structure, with the exception of a few shorter oracles which are of considerable beauty.

[1]) The oracles of Amos against Israel (see page 429, n. 1) are largely individual oracles pronounced at different times and collected afterwards.

20:	6
21:	8
	6
22:	6
23:	6
	7
24:	6
	7

It is important to take the text of each oracle, in fact of any poetic piece, sentence by sentence. The graphic survey clearly demonstrates that the Masoretic verse division has very little to do with the division into sentences and logical sense-components of the text.

We should discuss here briefly also the most famous of Balaam's oracles which was later accepted as one of the standard Messianic prophecies in the Damascus document as well as in Early Christianity (Nu. xxiv 16f.). As it is an important prophecy also in its original setting, for it deals with the final discomfiture of Moab through Israel, we need not be surprised that Balaam says in that oracle again a few words about himself, his visionary gift and his integrity. He has to justify himself as his prophecy is not, as expected, directed against Israel; on the contrary, it is the proclamation of Israel's final victory and greatness. A literal translation may help us to recognize the true logical division of its lines:

The prophecy (*n*^{e}*ʾum*) of
a) Him who hears the decisions of God,
  who knows the knowledge of the most High,
b) Who sees the visions of the Almighty,
  who falls in trance, yet has open eyes.
c) I see it, but it will not be now,
  I behold it, but it is not yet near:
d) A star will come up from Jacob,
  a sceptre will rise from Israel;
e) He will smite the flanks of Moab
  and destroy all children of Sheth.

The oracle consists of five lines; all are of the same length of six units. The first two belong together; so do the last two lines; the middle line stands by itself and establishes the connexion between the two pairs. The word *n*^{e}*ʾum* (the "inspired" or "visionary utterance") at the beginning of the oracle serves as a kind of headline. Indicating each unit by one dash, we obtain the following graphic picture:

```
    —
a   —   —   — | —   —   —⎫
b   —   —   — | —   —   —⎭
c   —   —   — | —   —   —:
d   —   —   — | —   —   —⎫
e   —   —   — | —   —   —⎭
```

There are quite a number of poetic pieces of this type of five lines with six units each. We note here only three:

1) Num. xxi 27—29, the song of victory over the Amorites (and Moab). This is not a folksong like that of Miriam, but a *Kunstlied* sung by the "Moshelim". The first two lines and the last two form a pair each, and the middle line again stands by itself linking the two pairs together:

```
a   —   — | —   —   —   —⎫
b   —   —   — | —   —   —⎭
c   —   —   — | —   —   —
d   —   —   — | —   —   —⎫
e   —   —   — | —   —   —⎭
    (—  —)
```

The last two words (bracketed) are a comment added by a later hand and stress once more the fact that the king in question is the Amorite Sihon; but this is known already from the story itself (see verse 26), and not even a modern reader would have any doubt about the identity of the king.

2) Is. xlix 14—17, Zion's complaint and God's answer. In this poem lines two and three and lines four and five form pairs, whilst line one containing the complaint remains single:

```
a   —   — : —   — | —   —:
b   —   —   — | —   —   —⎫
c   —   —   — | —   —   —⎭
d   —   —   — | —   —   —⎫
e   —   — | —   —   —   —⎭
```

3) Is. xlvii 1 and 5, the ditty on Babylon's downfall. The two verses are, unfortunately, separated from each other in the transmitted text, but they clearly belong together and form one poem of the usual

five lines with six units each, as can be seen from the tenor of each sentence and the address repeated in each line (indicated in the diagram below by thick dashes). Vers 2, three lines of four units, and verse 3, two lines of five units, introduce further details of Babylon's humiliation in a different language, whilst verse 4, one line of six units, is an interjectional praise of the God of Israel. The graphic picture of the poem in its original form is again the same:

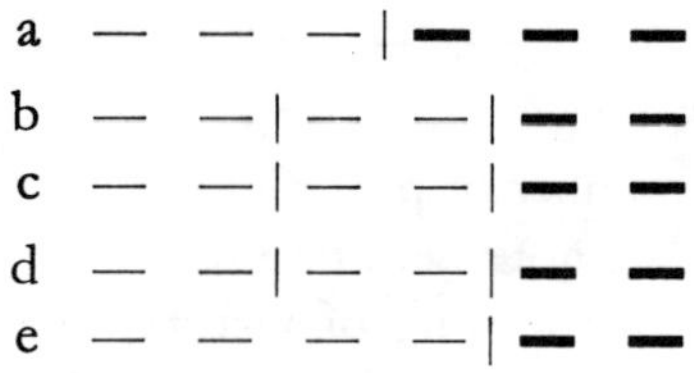

Of the last three poems 1) and 3) are songs of victory and joy, whilst 2) is a reflection on God's faithfulness which follows a song of joy over the return or imminent return of Israel from captivity.

Let us go back once more to the oracles of Balaam which bring up a question relevant to our subject: is the prophet also a poet? It is evident that we have prophecy which is clearly poetry, or to put it the other way round, we have poetry which is clearly prophecy. The story of Balaam offers interesting information on the relationship between prophecy and poetry.

Balaam was hired to utter a curse against Israel that would stick to that people until it finally came to grief. But he said things he was not expected to say: he prophesied against Moab. He obeyed the powerful God of Israel who was not his god. He was so completely under his spell that he even dropped all magic performances he used to employ in such cases (Num. xxiii 23; xxiv 1).

God reveals his will to him. The text says that he will speak to him and tell him what he is to say (xxii 20); he will put the word into his mouth (xxii 39; xxiii 5.16). We also hear that the spirit of God came over him (xxiv 2). However we do not hear the exact words which God spoke to Balaam; *dabar* can after all mean generally the kind of thing he is to say, not necessarily the exact words. Following the text closely we realize that it is Balaam who formulates and pronounces the will of God. The dictum is not described as *n*^{e}*'um YHWH*, but as *n*^{e}*'um Bil'am*. It is the *n*^{e}*'um* of a visionary, as he describes himself, of a man who falls in trance but has open eyes (xxiv 3f. and 15f.). Balaam is both a seer and a poet. He is a seer who pronounces what he has received, that is, as Balaam says himself (xxiii 20), he does not say anything of his own mind (xxiv 13). He is decidedly a visionary, but at the same time he is able to express his vision in clear and intelligible speech, in well-ordered sentences which even he who has not seen his vision can understand. He is not a mumbler or a glossolalist of whom—to use the words of the Apostle Paul—an outsider would say, he is mad.

The ancient prophet is a poet because he does not express his inspired prophecy or wisdom in ordinary prose, but in a poetic form, a form which is impressive, which will last and will be easily remembered and literally remembered. It is a form which obeys certain rules. Every sentence is well measured and confined to a line of a certain length. The length of the line depends on the thought which it is to express. Another important rule is that the lines are related to each other not only formally as regards their length and their position in the poem as a whole, but also as regards the ideas which they carry. We can imagine that there is an almost endless variety of distinct forms which a poem can have. A poem can be arranged in stanzas each consisting of two to four lines of the same or of varying lengths, but the variations must be of such a kind that the form of each stanza remains the same throughout the poem. Or the lines are not arranged in stanzas, but form one single group of lines (and thoughts) closely knit together on the basis of a symmetrical system. Or, finally, the two systems, the stanza form and the symmetrical form, can be combined in longer poetic compositions.

We will now examine a few specimens of Hebrew poetry more closely and pay special attention to the relationship between form and contents, for it is just this intimate relationship which produces the peculiar charm and outstanding beauty of ancient Hebrew poetic art. We have a considerable number of groups of 2, 3, and 4 lines which are self-contained and complete in themselves. We have mentioned groups of five lines which already suggested the existence of certain laws of correspondence between the sentences of a poem, but it is actually in the shorter poems that these laws become more obvious. We shall, therefore, begin with the simpler examples and then proceed to the more complicated poems.

An oracle of a very simple form is Is. vii 14—15. It purports to be a prophecy with a sign as announced in the headline (which remains outside the actual oracle). It consists of four lines which sound almost like prose, yet all are of the same length of eight units, and they are clearly interrelated. Its form is:

(— — — — — —:)

a — — —|— —|— — —

b — — —|— — — — —

c — — — —|— — — —

d — —|— — —|— — —

The dashes represent again the Hebrew units. The following translation may help us to see the arrangement of the contents.

a) Behold, the young woman is pregnant and will bear a son and she will call his name Immanuel.

b) He will eat butter and honey, that he may soon know to refuse the evil and choose the good.

c) For before the boy will know to refuse the evil and choose the good,

d) The land, namely that which you abhor, will be deprived of her two kings.

Lines one and two describe the sign; lines three and four interpret the meaning of the sign in its significance for the political future. "Immanuel" in line one, being a personal name, is one unit [1]). The relative *ʾ^{a}šer* forms an important part of the sentence; we have, therefore, translated it here by "namely that which," and it must be counted as a separate unit. The relative also reveals the near prose character of the language. This primitive form of Hebrew sententious speech may be compared to the *saǵʿ* in which the Arab Kahin expressed his opinions and judgements, but we do not find very many examples of such simplicity in the Hebrew Bible.

Another example of a similar type but somewhat more poetic is the oracle Is. vii 21—22:

(— — —:)

a — — — —|— —

b — — — —|— —

c — — — — — —

It consists of three lines with six units each and describes three stages:

a) A man shall feed a young cow and two sheep (not really much of a farm!);

b) And yet, from the abundance of milk he will live on butter,

c) And so will everyone who is left in the country eat butter and honey.

[1]) Some MSS have quite correctly only one word for it.

Butter and honey which also occur in the Immanuel-prophecy, or milk and honey [1]), are a reference to the ancient description of the Promised Land. This, then, is a consolation for those who will be left in the country after the disaster. There is no formal parallelism within the lines each of which is again almost prosaic, but the three lines express three thoughts in progressive order.

This is a very common device in the large family of triplets. In Is. xlvii 11 we have another oracle, this time against Babylon, with three closely interrelated lines of six units each:

a — — — | — — —
b — — — | — — —
c — — — — | — —

a) Evil will come upon you and you will not know from where it will come;
b) Mischief will fall upon you and you will not find a remedy;
c) Desolation will come upon you suddenly and take you unwares.

We also note that every line consists of two clauses.

Here are two more triplets characteristic of this group. The first is the famous passage in Amos v 25—27 which has been used with new interpretations in the Damascus document (p. VII) and in Acts ch. vii. There are three lines of nine units each, an unusual number:

a — — | — — | — — — | — — ?
b — — — | — — | — — | — — .
c — — — — | — — | — — — !

The first line is a question:

a) Have you offered me sacrifices and offerings in the desert forty years, House of Israel?

The answer to this question is not given by the House of Israel—it is obviously NO. The second line contains a statement on their defection in the land which YHWH gave them:

b) But you have borne (in procession) Sakkuth, your king, and Kaiwan, your emblems, the star of your god which you made to yourselves.

The third line declares the consequences of this act of apostasy:

c) Therefore will I send you into captivity beyond Damascus (namely to the place from which you got your alien gods, that is, Assyria), said YHWH whose name is the God of Hosts.

[1]) Milk and Butter are often used synonymously in Hebrew as well as in Ugaritic.

The language is again rather prosaic and slow-moving and there are no parallel clauses to alleviate the heaviness of the three sentences, but they describe neatly the three main stages of Israel's history.

The last example of this type we will consider is another famous saying: 1 Sam. xv 22—23a. We find it in the middle of a prose text from the Saul and Samuel cycle; it forms an essential part of the story itself. It is not an oracle in the stricter sense of the word; it is rather a precept or maxim on what God expects of man, in the present case, of Saul. Each of the three lines has seven units. The sentences are again closely inter-related and each one is beautifully constructed (note the parallel clauses!):

a — — — — | — — — ?
b — — — — | — — — !
c — — — — | — — — .

The first line puts a question:

a) Has YHWH as great a delight in burnt offerings and sacrifices as in obeying the voice of YHWH?

The second line gives the answer:

b) Behold, to obey is better than sacrifice, and to hearken than the fat of rams!

The third line produces the reason for this answer:

c) For rebellion is as the sin of witchcraft and stubbornness as iniquity and idolatry.

Summarizing our observations on this, perhaps the simplest, type of ancient Hebrew poetry, we would say that such a poem consists normally of three lines (rarely two or four or more) each of the same length. The language may still be prosaic or only slightly poetic, the sentences may be simple and may not be composed of parallel clauses, though there are some beautiful exceptions, but the lines are always intimately linked up with each other, so that it would be quite an achievement to lose a line in transmission.

The next group we will discuss are the poems which are divided into stanzas. It is a very large group. The stanza is usually short and consists of two or three, rarely of four, lines. A simple, but very good example of this kind is Is. iii 12—15. The poem is in perfect condition. It has three stanzas of two lines each and each line has six units:

1 a — — — | — — —
b — — — | — — —

2 a — — —|— — —
b — — —|— — —

3 a — — —|— — —
b — — —|— — —

The following translation will help us to see how the prophet has arranged his thoughts:

1 a) My people: they are oppressed by irresponsible men, they are ruled by women;
b) My people: your leaders are misleading (you), and they confuse the way of your paths.

2 a) YHWH is ready to plead, he stands to judge people;
b) YHWH enters into judgement with the elders and the princes of his people.

3 a) And you? You have destroyed the vineyard, the spoil of the poor is in your houses.
b) What do you mean? beating my people to pieces and grinding the faces of the poor?

The speaker is God, or the prophet as God's mouthpiece. The two lines of the first stanza are a lamentation over the people; they are parallel. The subject is God's people. In the first line, God speaks of them in the third person; in the second line he addresses them. The two lines of the second stanza are likewise parallel in form, language, and content. The subject is YHWH. The parallelism in the last stanza is also quite obvious. The subject are the leaders. They are addressed and questioned, they are accused and will be judged. We must admit that the poem follows strict rules as regards form and the distribution of its contents; it is of perfect structure and beauty.

Not all ancient poems are quite as well preserved as this one, but that is not very astounding. The Masoretes and their predecessors who handed down the text of the Bible were no fans of poetry. They had a prosaic mind and their main interest lay in the teaching of the Torah and the other Holy Scriptures. When they divided the text into verses for convenience's sake or for a better understanding of its teaching (or rather what they thought was the better understanding), they did not hesitate to cut a sentence, that is, a poetic line, right in the middle irrespective of its structure (parallelisms, etc.).

In the following example, Is. xl 9—11, we can easily detect the mistakes that had been made and can correct them. It is an exceedingly beautiful poem describing God as the Good Shepherd. Its text is well preserved, at least nothing got lost during its transmission, but it has two blemishes: a wrong division in one sentence (second line of second stanza) and a disruption in the last stanza. The poem has four stanzas of two lines each, and there are five units to the line. Each line consists of two perfect parallel clauses, and every stanza brings a new thought in progressive order. The general form of the stanza is:

— — — — —
— — — — —

The Hebrew text of the first three stanzas runs as follows:

על הר גבה עלי לך מבשרת ציון
הרימי בכח קולך מבשרת ירושלים

הרימי על תיראי אמרי לערי יהודה
הני אלהיכם הני אדני יהוה

בחזק יבוא וזרעו משלה לו
הני שכרו אתו ופעלתו לפניו

As regards the fourth stanza, we find that the first clause of the first line is in its right place, whilst the second clause is missing. The first clause is followed immediately by the full second line which again is followed by two more words. In its present state the Hebrew text of Is. xl 11 containing the fourth stanza reads as follows:

כרעה עדרו ירעה
בזרעו יקבץ טלאים ובחיקו ישא
עלות ינהל

It is evident that the last two words are the missing second clause of the first line, and the stanza should read:

כרעה עדרו ירעה עלות ינהל
בזרעו יקבץ טלאים ובחיקו ישא

The displacement must have happened very early during the transmission of the text, for the LXX has roughly the same text and has perpetuated the mistake of the transmitter or scribe.

The re-arrangement is not only required by the law of poetic form and structure, but it also displays the perfect order of the prophet's thoughts which reach their climax in the last line. God is the good shepherd who grazes his flock looking especially after the ewes that they may not come to any harm, but the newly-born lambs he takes up and carries in his arms. He who has ever watched a shepherd with his flock and seen him as he carries a lamb in his arms will realize that the prophet could not possibly describe the tender care of God for his people better than by this moving picture.

In this as in any other case where the text is disturbed, our foremost task in finding out the form of a poem, or a stanza, or line, is to take note of their structure. It is important to bear in mind that a sentence forms a line, and if it does not form a line with the required number of units, required, that is, by its place within the stanza or the whole composition, there is very likely something wrong with the transmitted text. However, such textual problems have to be handled with caution; sometimes it is better to leave the text as it is and resign. No general rules can be set up and every case must be dealt with on its own merits.

As has already been pointed out, the lines need not be all of the same length, but then we have to take the structure of the stanza or of the whole composition into account. Is. ii 2—3 is an example of a poem with two stanzas in which the lines are not of the same length:

1 a — — — 3 units
b — — — — — 5 ”
c — — — — 4 ”
d — — — — — — 6 ”

2 a — — — 3 units
b — — — — — 5 ”
c — — — — 4 ”
d — — — — — — 6 ”

The poem is well preserved except for a slight flaw. Again we notice that the Masoretes had not much sense for the integrity of a sentence: they cut the sentence of line 1d in two and attached its first half to verse 2 and connected the second with verse 3.

The poem describes a vision of the future mountain of God and its significance for the nations. The two stanzas have, as they should, absolutely the same form in number and length of lines, and the lines of the first stanza run parallel to those of the second also in regard to their content. The first stanza contains the visible event: the house of YHWH is erected on the highest mountain and the nations congregate there from all parts of the earth. The second stanza explains the meaning of the event. What do the nations come for? They come to be taught of the ways of God, for it is from Zion that the teaching will go out. It is even possible to draw a picture of what happens: in the first stanza the nations move to the mountain of God and in the second God's word goes out to them. Compare the last line of the first with that of the second stanza! There is perfect correspondence, perfect balance and harmony between the two parts of the poem both in form and structure.

We happen to have another copy of this poem in Micah iv 1—2. If only this copy had survived and not the one in Isaiah ii we should never have discovered the immaculate beauty of this poetic piece. The second stanza is the same in both copies, but the first, apart from a few minor differences which do not affect the form, has one additional word in line 1c in the text of Micah which alters the length of the line (it has here five units instead of the required four) and spoils the form of the stanza. Micah's version which for a number of reasons must be dated later than that of Isaiah, shows clearly the tendency to dissolve poetry into prose. There are many other examples which tell the same story. Why such a development should have taken place, we cannot discuss here, but there are various explanations and reasons for that. May it suffice here to state that such a development has taken place and that it certainly has affected much of Hebrew poetry in the course of its transmission. However, it is sometimes possible to establish the original form of a poem.

An interesting example in this respect is Is. xl 3—5, and the result of our investigation is not quite without theological consequences. The MT gives the following version:

2 קול קורא
8 במדבר פנו דרך יהוה ישרו בערבה מסלה לאלהינו
5 כל גיא ינשא וכל הר וגבעה ישפלו
5 והיה העקב למישור והרכסים לבקעה
6 ונגלה כבוד יהוה וראו כל בשר יחדו
3 כי פי יהוה דבר

The figures indicate the units of each line, and we must admit that the picture of the poem is not very impressive as far as form is concerned. We cannot, at first sight, really say what happened to it. It is true the second line looks a bit suspect. If we compare it with the others it is unusually long: but there is such a perfect parallelism between its two parts that it is hard to surmise that there can be anything wrong with that line. However, the LXX, or rather its Hebrew *Vorlage*, gives us a different picture. That text does not say that the way of the Lord should be prepared in the desert, and there is no equivalent for the word *baʿarabah* in the Greek translation—but, having the word *bammidbar* in the first line, it says that the voice is heard in the wilderness. The first two lines would, then, read in Hebrew:

3 קול קורא במדבר
6 פנו דרך יהוה ישרו מסלה לאלהינו

This text stresses the fact that the ancient God YHWH is a god who calls his people from the wilderness. As he once, speaking in and from the desert, delivered them from the bondage of Egypt, so again he would now bring them out of the captivity of Babylon. The idea that God calls upon Israel from the desert is very old and it was never forgotten by its prophets (Hos. ii 16f.). The Hebrew text underlying the LXX cannot, therefore, be discarded simply on the ground that it is not the traditional Masoretic text. Besides it presents a poem of a faultless regular form and a perfect disposition of its thoughts:

a — — — 3
b — — — | — — — 6
c — — | — — — 5
c — — — | — — 5
b — — — | — — — 6
a — — — 3

The sentences correspond to each other according to the length of their lines. The first and the last line, of three units each, point out that the voice crying in the wilderness comes from the mouth of YHWH. The second and last but one, with six units, contain the proclamation that the way must now be prepared for God to reveal his glory. The two middle lines of five units describe in figurative speech the change which will take place. It is by no means the people themselves who undertake the return from Babylon through the Syrian and Arabian deserts, it is God who leads them and provides for them on their way (Is. xlix 9ff.).

The old question arises once more: which of the two versions is the original and correct one, that of the MT or that of the LXX followed by the NT? This question has always been answered in favour of the MT against the "Greek" tradition. It seemed pretty clear that the early Christians had altered the text not only in the quotation in their Gospels, but also, to cover up their fraud, in the LXX, in order to adapt the Bible passage to their purpose. John the Baptist preached in the wilderness, and the people came out to hear him there. With other words: the voice of John the Baptist was the voice of God of which Isaiah spoke. The discovery of the manuscript of the Book of Isaiah in Qumran which is a thousand years older than the oldest manuscript of the Hebrew Bible and was written at least a hundred years before the compilation of the Gospels evidently settled the matter beyond any doubt. It confirmed the Masoretic text and all were agreed that the MT is correct and the LXX together with the NT have a falsified text.

We know that the early Christians did occasionally alter Scriptural passages or twisted their meaning. But we also know that the Sect of Qumran did the same. In the present case we cannot prove that it was the Early Church which altered the text, but we may, of course, suspect them to have done this in order to adapt it to the needs of its theology. We cannot prove either that the people of Qumran altered the text, though it is quite possible that they did, for they acted literally according to the text in their hand: they prepared God's way in the desert [1]).

The traditional text of the Synagogue is identical with that of Qumran, but the study of form and structure decides the question in favour of the Hebrew version underlying the LXX, accepted by the New Testament. That version may be older than that cherished in Qumran.

The piece of poetry we have just discussed is one of a fairly large group of symmetrically constructed poems. Naturally, there are no stanzas; the poem is of one piece. The symmetrical system is very simple. The first line corresponds to the last, both in length and in content, the second line to the last but one, and so forth, till we approach the middle of the poem, the axis. The axis may be formed by an individual line which stands by itself and is usually of special importance for the whole poem; or the axis is formed by an imaginary dividing line which must then be drawn between the two middle lines (as in the example we have just examined). In the first case the poem consists of an odd number of lines, three, five, seven, and so on, in the second of an even number, four, six, eight, and so forth.

A fairly simple form of this type is Is. vii 7—9, the prophecy on Damascus and Samaria. It has an introductory line of four and a concluding line also of four units; they correspond to each other.

---

[1]) 1QS VIII; the Sect understood Is. xl 4 also figuratively.

Between these are three lines of seven units each; the middle line forms the axis and contains the important prophecy:

a	לא תקום ולא תהיה	4
b	כי ראש ארם דמשק וראש דמשק רצין	7
c	ובעוד ששים וחמש שנה יחת אפרים מעם	7
b	וראש אפרים שמרון וראש שמרון בן רמליהו	7
a	אם לא תאמינו כי לא תאמנו	4

One of the most elegant pieces is Is. xxx 29—31. It is perfectly preserved and we have no trouble in ascertaining its form. It has seven lines, that means, it has again a middle line. It has the following form:

a — — — | — — — 6
b — — | — — 4
c — — — | — — 5
d — — — — | — — — 7
c — — | — — — 5
b — — | — — 4
a — — — — | — — 6

We need not write out the Hebrew text here, as it is quite easy to "scan" it according to this diagram, but we will give a translation of the poem which will more readily show the symmetry of its parallelisms than the Hebrew text.

a) This song you shall have as in the night when you sanctify yourselves for the feast,
b) And gladness of heart, as when one goes with a pipe
c) To come into the mountain of God, to the rock of Israel.
d) YHWH shall cause his glorious voice to be heard, and the lighting down of his arm to be seen,
c) With the indignation of his anger and the flame of a devouring fire,
b) Devestation and tempest and stones of hail:
a) "Through the voice of YHWH Assyria is shattered, beaten down with the rod."

It is round the middle line (d) that everything revolves: God is in his house on the mountain. From here his voice is heard, from here he acts, receiving Israel and punishing its enemy. In the first part of the poem we see Israel walking in festive procession to the mountain and rejoicing. The second part (in symmetry) shows the opposite picture: there is utter devastation, the complete overthrow of the enemy.

The last line is Israel's victory song hinted at in the first line[1] [2].

In this paper only the main principles could be discussed and illustrated by a few selected examples and I should like to conclude it with a remark of general historical interest.

It is not very long ago that Sir John MYRES showed us[3] that the composition of the Homeric poems consists of a series of subjects grouped symmetrically round a centrepiece. The same applies largely to Greek tragedy. A little later he discovered that Herodotus presented his material in much the same way and he gave us detailed tabular analyses of the histories of Herodotus[4]. MYRES maintains that this balanced arrangement of subjects which can also be found in Greek sculpture is typical for the Greeks and the Indo-Europeans.

This is not the case. The symmetrical composition is also Semitic. It is quite common in ancient Hebrew poetry, and there are very many examples in Ugaritic poetry. Naturally, we have here also, as we have seen, what MYRES calls the "progressive" or "frieze" order in which one subject follows the other progressively like the groups and episodes in a frieze (composition in stanzas).

Both arrangements, the progressive and the symmetrical order, can be combined, and we have an appreciable number of such composite poems in Ugaritic as well as in Hebrew. The most beautiful poem of this kind in Hebrew is Is. xiv 3—21, a very lively and most dramatic song over the downfall of Babylon. It is interesting to note that this poem contains quite a few reminiscences of Ugaritic mythology, just as we find in the mythological poetry of Ugarit the same combination of the two main types of poetic form.

MYRES finds both forms, the "pedimental" and the "frieze" grouping, in combination also in Greek monumental sculpture[5]. But here again we must point out that this combination of pedimental and frieze grouping in larger compositions is not an invention of the Greeks. Very probably it is a Semitic inheritance, like the alphabeth.

---

1) The introductive *ki* (in Is. xxx 31) is not to be counted as a separate unit. It could be best translated by "namely", for it shows the result of God's anger and at the same time it answers the hint to a song in the first line.

2) What the prosodists of the early 20th century have done to this beautiful poem can be seen in DUHM's commentary on *Das Buch Jesaia*, 1914, pp. 201f.

3) "Homeric Art" in *Annual of the British School of Athens*, vol. 45, 1950, especially from p. 252 onward.

4) *Herodotus, Father of History*, Oxford, 1953, especially pp. 62—134.

5) "In the sixth and fifth centuries pedimental compositions were combined in the same larger design with friezes as on the Parthenon; and in the Parthenon frieze itself the long processions converge on the pedimentally grouped deities on the east front, with the most important in the midst" (*Herodotus*, p. 63).

FORM AND STRUCTURE IN ANCIENT HEBREW POETRY (CONTINUED)

The following article is a continuation of the study on form and structure in Biblical Hebrew poetry published in this journal XIV, 4, 1964, pp. 423-445. It is not exactly its "second" part, much less its conclusion, as we can again deal only with further selections from the vast material. The majority is taken from Isaiah. The examples are of special interest as they show that there is some hope in the new approach not only to come nearer to or even to establish the original text of a poetic piece but also to gain an insight into the ways in which additions have been made and of what type they are.

On the whole the poems are well preserved within the MT, far better than the text critics of our time have surmised. Omissions are rare, but accretions of various kinds abound. The custom that words or even whole phrases have been "added to the word or taken from it" in the course of transmission, oral or literary, was well known in the Orient already in ancient times. Deut. iv 2 is a comparatively late example of a warning against such a procedure. We learn from it that making additions or omissions was an offence especially in codes of laws. But even in codes further laws were sometimes incorporated and "bylaws", explanations, comments, *Ausführungsbestimmungen*, etc. were added. In fact this was the common fate of all law codes, including the Law of Moses (in spite of the warning in Deut. iv 2).

There was, of course, greater freedom in the other branches of oral and literary tradition. As soon as collections of histories and prophetic oracles began to play their part in the instruction of the people explanations and illuminations were often felt necessary and they were inserted into the text or added to it (see p. 159, note 3). ALBRIGHT has once casually, but pertinently, remarked [1]) that the

[1]) *From the Stone Age to Christianity*. The English edition not being available, we quote from the German edition *Von der Steinzeit zum Christentum*, Sammlung Dalp, 1949, p. 69.

"oriental scribes and redactors" were more inclined to add to the text than to omit something of it.

Additions in poetical texts can often be easily recognized as such. They are usually in prose, though not always, they separate words or clauses which obviously belong together, and thus disturb the poetic form and the logical structure of the poem. The main concern of the commentator is instruction, not poetic beauty [1]).

Sometimes our findings are supported by the reading of the LXX or rather of its Hebrew *Vorlage* [2]), or, in the case of the Book Isaiah, by the Isaiah manuscript A found in Qumran, both of which are considerably older than the MT. Sometimes, however, comments have been added at such an early time that they appear already in the LXX and the Isaiah manuscript; then we have to fall back on the internal evidence as our only guide.

For the new method applied here to the study of Hebrew poetry we must refer the reader to the introductory notes in the first article [3]). The question whether certain particles are to be counted as units or not, is sometimes still difficult to decide [4]), but the reader will find further help in the notes on the pieces examined in the present article. We must consider each case on its own merit, as there are no hard and fast rules. The inquiry into what the author wants to express and to stress is always important and decides the issue.

To the selections from Isaiah we add a few specimens from the Ugaritic poetry [5]) which is roughly 750 years older than the poetry of the Second Isaiah and it has come down to us on the "original" clay-tablets. Ugaritic poetry does not by a long way reach the highly developed artistic form which the Second Isaiah employs. Still, we notice that already Ugaritic poetry observes definite laws in the structure of its lines.

It may be surprising, however, that many of the Hebrew Psalms follow similar rules. We append a few examples in order to show the direction in which further study of the formal structure of our Psalms could be undertaken.

---

[1]) ALBRIGHT, *l.c.*, p. 56.
[2]) *VT*, XIV, 1964, p. 441.
[3]) *VT*, l.c., pp. 423-426.
[4]) *VT*, l.c., p. 426.
[5]) *VT*, l.c., pp. 427 and 445

Isaiah lvi 10-12

The ditty on the lazy, greedy and drunk leaders of the nation is of a simple type. In verse 10b of the MT (line 3 of the poem) the subject of the sentence is missing; it should be either *kullam* or *hemmah*. The Isaiah text of Qumran (Is[a]) comes to our help: the missing word is *hemmah*. The MS has in the same verse *ḥozim*, a *lectio facilior* for masoretic *hozim* which is a *hapax legomenon*. The last line (8), verse 12b, is overladen in the MT; *gadol* is pleonastic and must be dropped. Indeed, the Is MS did not have it originally, but it was added by a later hand above the word *yeter*, probably when the text was compared by a scribe with another MS, evidently one of the ancestors of the MT. There has always been a tendency to "complete" biblical texts (see next note and the following example Is xl 12ff.).

It is very likely that verse 12 (lines 7 and 8) did not form part of the original poem but was added later (see the Greek versions) [1]). It takes up a new theme: one of the leaders invites the others to a drinking-bout.

The ditty, originally only verses 10 and 11, is divided into three (or if we include verse 12, into four) stanzas with two lines each, the first line (a) with five units, the second (b) with six. Lines 1, 3, 5 (five units each) deal with the leaders (*ṣopim*, *hozim*, *roʿim*) who are compared in lines 2, 4, 6 (six units each) to dogs, the last line (6) drawing the conclusion from the comparison.

Taking these emendations into consideration we obtain this text of the song:

						line	stanza	verse
	ידעו	לא	כלם	עורים	צופיו	1	1a	(10)
לנבח	יוכלו	לא	אלמים	כלבים	כלם	2	b	
	לנום	אהבי	שכבים	חזים	המה	3	2a	
שבעה	ידעו	לא	נפש	עזי	והכלבים	4	b	(11)
	הבין	ידעו	לא	רעים	והמה	5	3a	
מקצהו	לבצעו	איש	פנו	לדרכם	כלם	6	b	
	שכר	ונסבאה	יין	אקחה	אתיו	7	4a	(12)
מאד	יתר	מחר	יום	כזה	והיה	8	b	

[1]) Another example is Is. xl 7 which is missing in the LXX as well as in the Is Ms. The NT quotation 1 Peter i 24. 25a which does not contain Is. xl 7 either is identical with the text of the MS which has afterwards been "completed" by the addition of the omitted verse between the lines and on the margin by another hand.

The graphic picture of each stanza is:

a	— — — — —	5 units
b	— — — — — —	6 units

Isaiah xl 12-18

This poetic piece has been well preserved except that the MT has assimilated some substantial additions during the time of its transmission. They are easily recognizable as such. We present here the text broken up in its natural lines showing at the same time the accretions:

	Stanza	Verse
מי מדד בשעלו מים ושמים בזרת תכן	1	(12)
וכל בשלש עפר הארץ ושקל בפלס הרים		
וגבעות במאזנים		
מי תכן את רוח יהוה ואיש עצתו יודיענו	2	(13)
את מי נועץ ויבינהו וילמדהו בארח משפט		(14a)
וילמדהו דעת ודרך תבונות יודיענו		(14b)
הן גוים כמר מדלי וכשחק מאזנים נחשבו		(15)
הן איים כדק יטול		
ולבנון אין די בער וחיתו אין די עולה		(16)
כל הגוים כאין נגדו מאפס ותהו נחשבו לו	3	(17)
ואל מי תדמיון אל ומה דמות תערכו לו		(18)

A few notes on the text may be helpful. Instead of *mayim* (verse 12a), one word to be counted as one unit, Is^{a} has *mey yam*, two words which would make two units. Some scholars are impressed by the reading of the Isaiah MS and think that it has the better reading because the "sky" and the "waters of the sea" afford a more concrete parallelism. However, the parallelism of the MT, "sky" and the "water(s)" is doubtless the correct one. What the poet is thinking of is quite obviously the work of creation which is "the work of His hands" (here: *šoʿal* and *zeret*), especially the separation of "the heavens" and "the waters" (Gen. i 6-8; cf. also Ps. xix 2). We must discard the reading of the Isaiah MS. Cf. additional note on p. 180.

The earth is mentioned in the second line (verse 12b), or rather "the dust of the earth", which is a perfect parallel to "the (rock of) the mountains". Some hand has added here *g*^{e}*baʿot* as a further parallel, not to the dust of the earth but to *harim* including the synonym for *peles*. It is true, mountains and hills are a pair of words which is often used (Is ii 2; xl 4; etc.), both in prose and in poetry, but here in verse

12b the mountains have already their appropriate parallel in the dust of the earth. The last two words of verse 12 were hardly part of the original, well-designed line and we have to leave them out.

Verse 14b (five units) is a further spinning-out of the preceding clear-cut thought in 14aβ.

Verse 15a is in itself quite an interesting line and has the correct number of units required in this poem (seven), but it has no parallel line, unless we see in 15b the beginning of it with another three units missing. Besides, it should be noted that the gist of verse 15 is very tersely expressed in verse 17.

Verse 16 (a line of eight units) consists of two parts which correspond to each other, but the thought it conveys—it brings in the sacrificial cult—is not really in conformity with the character of the poem as a whole.

Verses 17 and 18 which conclude the poem are in perfect order.

I confess, I was not very happy when I noticed that the poem was interrupted by several lines of varying length, which I could not consider to be original, as they did not fit in with the rest of the poem, neither in content nor in form—until I discovered that exactly this whole piece, verses 14b-16, was *not* contained in the virgin MS of Is[a]. The scribe had copied the text from his *Vorlage* in which the 2½ verses evidently did not appear. But he left here a gap, and the space was later filled by a different hand with the missing words now to be found in our MT! The only explanation we can offer of this curious fact is that the first scribe had before him two different texts, one, probably the older, which he followed in the main and which did not contain the lines in question, and another which did. He hesitated to copy the second text, but left sufficient, or even more than sufficient, space for a possible later insertion for the addendum which in fact was, then, incorporated in his MS though not by himself [1]).

The Isaiah MS thus confirms our own findings that judging from their contents and their form these sentences could not possibly have belonged to the original poem. Unfortunately we have no such first-hand MS evidence for the redundancy of the last two words of verse 12b. The addition seems to have been made at a very early date; both the Qumran Isaiah and the LXX contain them.

We can now ascertain the form of the poem. It consists of three stanzas of two lines with seven units each.

---

[1]) It should be noted that the traditional MT also has a small open space after verse 16, although verses 17 and 18 belong quite obviously to the same paragraph.

The first two stanzas put more or less rhetorical questions to which the answer is obvious: God is the only great and powerful being. The first line of the third stanza makes a definite statement which is the basis of the last and decisive question in the last line. God is incomparable!

The following verses 19-26 serve as a comment and an answer to that question which is repeated towards the end (verse 25).

The Servant Songs

Among the cycle of the so-called Servant songs there are some which have survived in excellent condition except that they, too, were supplied with various comments which were integrated in the transmitted text. In this cycle we should include not only the "four" pieces generally known as Servant songs [1]) but also some which, though not expressly mentioning or describing the person of the Servant and his difficulties, give us a picture of his mission, his task regarding the people of Israel and his proclamation of the new *mišpaṭ*. We would suggest the following minimum list of six poems: 1) Is. xlii 1-4; 2) xlix 1-2; 3) xlix 3-6; 4) l 4-9; 5) li 4-8 consisting of three parts: 4-5, 6, 7-8; 6) lii 13 - liii. There may be a few more passages dealing with the mission of the Servant, but they have come down to us only in fragments (e.g. li 12ff.) so that we have to disregard them here. Even the passages 4) and 6) are not in a good state of preservation and it would be a very doubtful undertaking to try and reconstruct the original words as they came out of the prophet's mouth. All the other have only minor blemishes.

1) *xlii* 1-4

We take the first song first. Verse 1abα, consisting of three short sentences, is the headline apparently not only of the first song but also of the whole cycle. It contains the presentation of God's chosen Servant, the bearer of His spirit. Verse 1bβ immediately points out his important universal mission mentioned also in subsequent songs. We shall see, however, that these three words which are without a parallel line, belong somewhere else where such a short line is required. For the time being we will, therefore, separate this clause from the headline and take it over to the next group of lines and see what happens. The passage, then, runs as follows:

---

[1]) See S. Mowinckel, *He That Cometh*, 1956, pp. 187ff.

Verse	Stanza	Text	units
(1)		הן	
		עבדי אתמך בו / בחירי רצתה נפשי / נתתי רוחי עליו	
	1	משפט לגוים יוציא	3
(2)		לא יצעק ולא ישא	4
		ולא ישמע בחוץ קולו	4
(3)	2	קנה רצוץ לא ישבור	4
		ופשתה כהה לא יכבנה	4
		לאמת יוציא משפט	3
(4)	3	לא יכהה ולא ירוץ	4
		עד ישים בארץ משפט	4
		ולתורתו איים ייחלו	3

The poem consists of three stanzes each of three lines. The second and the third stanza clearly show its form: the first two lines of the stanza have four units each, the third line has only three and stands by itself. The graphic picture of the stanza is:

— — — —
— — — —
— — —

All lines with four units describe the servant and the way in which he will carry out his mission. All lines with three units (except, of course, the clauses of the headline) give an account of his mission and its impact. From the second and the third stanza it becomes clear that the three words or units of verse 1bβ should follow verse 2 and form the end-line of the first stanza where it is in its proper place. We have, thus, a well-constructed poem of exceptional beauty, if we accept the displacement of verse 1bβ.

Displacements of lines in ancient Hebrew poetry are not very common. They are far less frequent than, for instance, in pre-Islamic Arabian poetry. The reason for this is that (especially prophetic) Hebrew poetry is logically, and one might almost say rigidly, constructed. The individual lines are formally and structurally interrelated, that is, they form integral parts of a sequence of logical thoughts. Such a logical system cannot be easily brought into disorder. It is different in ancient Arabian poetry. When an Arabian poet wants to praise his horse or the maiden he loves he can begin with the eyes or the feet, with the horse's mouth or mane or the girl's lips or hair, whatever comes first to his mind. He need not observe any logical sequence simply because there is no logic in any such description. The main law he was bound to observe was that every thought should be expressed in one line and everything depended on the choice of his words and the beauty of the line. Since not even the poet himself was not obliged to maintain a prescribed order of his thoughts, we can imagine that subsequent editors of those poems may have made their own contributions to the "disarrangement" of the lines. It has been pointed out that "hardly any old-Arabian poem preserved in two different text traditions has the same order of verses" [1]).

The phenomenon is rare in Hebrew prophetic poetry, but it does occur. But whilst displacements of lines in the transmission of Arabian poems are always easily possible but not always accountable, it is comparatively easy to detect such displacements in Hebrew poetry and usually, though not always, we can even find out why a line has been displaced. This is, for instance, the case with Is. xlii 1f.

By transposing the three words which originally formed the last line of the first stanza to its beginning so that it could be easily absorbed by verse 1 when the Masoretes divided the text into verses, the "editor" achieved one thing which seemed to have been important to him, namely, to make clear to the hearer or reader right from the start what the chosen Servant was there for, what he was to do. However, he honoured the integrity of the words and left them intact [2]). By the transposition the editor spoiled the form of the stanza, but this was to him a minor concern. His main aim was instruction [3]).

---

[1]) See Carl BROCKELMANN, *Geschichte der arabischen Litteratur*, 1898, I, p. 15f. Cf. also Geo WIDENGREN, *Literary and Psychological Aspects of the Hebrew Prophets*, 1948, pp. 31f., who quotes Th. NÖLDEKE, *Beiträge zur Kenntnis der Poesie der alten Araber*, 1864, pp. VIff.

[2]) Of special interest is the reading of Is^a *umišpaṭo laggo'im yoṣi'* which makes the text situation even more obvious. The reading is clearly *mišpaṭo*, not *mišpaṭi*, as Millar BURROWS transliterates the script in his first edition of the text. That means, the scribe fell back from the first to the third person giving verse 1bß the appearance of an additional statement to the preceding three clauses; he was evidently conscious of the supplementary character of the fourth clause. M. Burrows, consciously or unconsciously, adapted the suffix of the fourth clause to the suffixes of the first three clauses: "my Servant.... he will bring my *mišpaṭ*". He corrected his mistake in the second edition.

[3]) Occasionally we meet with a complete unconcern vis-à-vis the poetic form. Displacements of lines (p. [153], n. 1) are, as we said, not very frequent. More common are insertions of explanatory words or even sentences when the editor felt obliged to make further comments or other additions for the benefit of the people. The books of the prophets were used in the service of the Synagogue long before the beginning of the Christian era.

One more remark on the preposition *'ad* in verse 4. The reader will notice that it is here not just a preposition which would not need to be counted as a unit but that it bears full emphasis (unlike the *'ad* in *'ad-matay*) and stands for the fulfilment of time. It must therefore be counted.

The first song, then, characterizes the Servant and his task in a threefold manner:

1) The Servant will not be a boisterous propagandist: yet he will bring forth universal *mišpaṭ*.

2) He will not discourage the weak and the lowly: he will bring it forth *le'emet*.

3) He will not weaken until he has established it: the world is waiting for his Torah [1]).

Isaiah xlix 1-2

The so-called "second" Servant song, xlix 1-6, has always been taken for one piece, but a more careful analysis of its contents shows that the passage consists of two poems which deal with different themes. They are also different in form. What keeps them together is the fact that both concern the same Servant.

The first of the two poems has four lines and each line has a beautiful parallelism. The text is well preserved except for the addition of one word which is out of harmony in this reflection on the Servant, namely, the third word in verse 1: *'elay*. We have to eliminate it for two reasons.

1) *'elay* appears only in the first half of the line, not in the parallel clause. Compare, for instance, Is. li 4!

2) The speaker in xlix 1 is the Servant, not God.

a) Only God can use the momentous *'ani*, the great Ego, in His pronunciamentos (cf. again Is. li 4 where the speaker is God! "my people", "my nation", "my Torah", "my *mišpaṭ*", "my righteousness", "my salvation" in verses 4-8), not man, not even the Servant on whom the spirit of God rests, for even he does not speak out of

---

1) The LXX and the NT quotations of this line have "his name" instead of "his Torah". The Hebrew text would, then, be: *welišmo 'iyyim yeyaḥelu*, "and for his name (= the revelation of his person) the nations are waiting". There is much to be said in favour of the Hebrew text underlying the LXX and the NT. The reader will find a detailed discussion of this variant reading in the article "The Conclusion of Matthew" in *ASTI* IV.

hiw own mind and for himself; he is only the executor of God's commission. The Servant could not use this "Ego".

b) How could this particular Servant say "I" and thus reveal his personal presence when he has still to remain unknown and hidden away, preserved for his future task—just this is the theme of the short poem!—and when he is described in Is xlii 2 as a person who does not shout and make a noise? The announcement could, therefore, only be made as an anyonymous announcement without the "I". Can we seriously presume that the poet himself would spoil the logic and the effect of what he wanted to express? We can only assume that the *'elay* was added by an "editor"; he was probably the same who introduced verse 5, where the speaker is the Servant, wrongly with the words: "and now speaks YHWH" (see further below).

If, as a result of these considerations, we leave out the word *'elay* (which we would otherwise have to count as a unit), we obtain a beautiful poem of immaculate form:

			Verse
units:	5	— — — — —	(1)
	7	— — — — — — —	
	7	— — — — — — —	(2)
	5	— — — — —	

We can even take one step further and note the subdivisions of the lines according to their parallelisms: 2 : 3; 3 : 4; 4 : 3; 3 : 2. The number of units in the half-lines is regularly increasing to the middle and then regularly decreasing to the end in perfect symmetry.

Isaiah xlix 3-6

This piece presents a number of textual problems. We can solve some of them. A few difficulties, however, remain, but we can at least make certain suggestions towards their solution from the point of view of logic and style, leaving it to the present reader to make his choice or to find his own solution. The main thing is to recognize the textual problems.

Like all the Servant songs this is an important piece of prophetic thought which has aroused the interest and the ingenuity of many a reader and "scholar" already before the time Isaiah was translated into Greek.

Let us begin with a general reflection. The Torah was written in clear prose and when it was read "clearly and with sense", it was "understood" (Neh. viii 8). What the prophets said who wrote poetry, was not as easily understood, or perhaps not in the sense the people were supposed to understand it. Comments were needed—at least as early as prophetic books became canonical literature or when portions from them were read in the Synagogue [1]).

The most conspicuous comments in the passage before us are made at the beginning of each of the four verses; they consist of 1, 2, or 3 words introducing, each time, the speaker. He who added these introductory formulas realized that verses 3-6 contained a dialogue. There are four such introductions: *wayyomer li* (verse 3); *waʾ*^{a}*ni ʾamarti* (v. 4); *w*^{e}*ʿattah ʾamar YHWH* (v. 5); *wayyomer* (v. 6). The first, second, and fourth formula introduce the speaker correctly, the third is definitely wrong: it introduces YHWH as speaker, but the speaker is the Servant who is engaged in a soliloquy.

One might ask, how could the commentator make such an obvious mistake? Evidently he understood the whole verse 5 as an apposition to YHWH: "And now spoke YHWH who formed me from the womb to his servant to bring......etc.", quoting in verse 6 the actual words of God which contain the new commission, but not without introducing them afresh after the long "apposition" with the formula *wayyomer*.

Later the Masoretes put a *r*^{e}*bi*^{a}*ʿ*, a disjunctive accent, at the word YHWH and connected *yoṣri* with the following word by a conjunctive accent. Evidently they sensed that the first three words of verse 5 belong together, and so do the next four. This is a very helpful hint, and we can take it a little more seriously. We should leave the introductory formula, like the others, outside the actual speech which begins, in verse 5, with *yoṣri*. The clause would then begin with a participle [2]) which must be translated: "He has made me from the womb a servant to himself (= to his purpose)"—in fact this process of preparation is still going on and must be continued until the Servant

[1]) According to Jewish tradition just before the middle of the second century B.C. This whole question cannot be discussed here.

[2]) On the use of participial sentences in Second Isaiah see Robert H. PFEIFFER, *Introduction*, p. 468, where he quotes a number of such cases. He says that the translation of Is. xl 22, "he is the one that sits", is unwarranted, but this applies also to PFEIFFER's own translation, "the one sitting", since the sentence must be conceived as a whole. The participle stands for the finite verb, "he sits" or "he is sitting"; the clause must be taken together with the following: "He sits upon the circle of the earth and (whilst) its inhabitants are (appear) like grasshoppers". The participle can refer to the past, the present, or (and) the future, as for instance in Is. xlv 7, *yoṣer ʾor*...etc.: he created, he still creates, and he will be creating in future...etc.

is revealed—"in order to bring Jacob back to him....etc." The editor has thus transformed an original, purely poetical stanza into one long prose sentence; but we are fortunate: he left the poetical parts intact.

The next difficulty is the old *crux* in verse 3: *Yisra'el* (*'ašer*). I think only those who still swear by the absolute correctness and validity of the MT in a kind of fundamentalist way would retain the word as "original". It was probably taken over from Is. xliv 21 and 23 which deal with different ideas but use very similar expressions; it is very likely that the composer of these verses used the vocabulary of xlix 3 and 5f. for his own purposes, which was a common procedure. But in the Servant song the Servant is doubtless an individual person (because of verse 6a). Later the word "Israel" must have been inserted in verse 3, perhaps not thoughtlessly, but intentionally, in order to harmonize it with passages like xlix 21-23.

Then there is the word *'aken* in verse 4b. It is not a noun, nor a verb, nor is it a vital word element within the text, as it could be easily and effectively replaced by an adversative *waw*, "and yet", "but". It need not, therefore, be counted as a unit. However we will retain it in the text given below, as it is quite possible that it served as an emphatic interjection in the recitation of the passage.

The last stumbling-block is *liheyot* in verse 6b, which makes simple prose of the poetic clause. In fact, it would, then, be the only prose sentence in the whole poem: "... and I will give you for a light to the gentiles that thou mayest be my salvation unto the end of the earth". A prose line in an otherwise well-constructed poem is hardly to be expected from a great poet. In addition, the prose line, although grammatically correct, is somewhat clumsy. Even so, a prose line makes sometimes easier reading, and to make everything as simple and as intelligible as possible is always the business of commentators. If, to achieve that end, a commentator has to insert a word or a number of words, he would do so, even at the risk of spoiling the poetic beauty. The ancient Hebrew commentator's first interest is always right teaching.

Coming back to Is. xlix 6b we note that in the two parts of the line which are separated by the masoretic disjunctive we have two pairs of distinctly parallel notions, *'or* and *yešu'ah*, *goyim* and *'ad qeṣeh ha'areṣ*. The finite verb *netattika* is, as so often in poetic lines, shared by both parts. The infinitive in 6bβ is a disturbing element as it disrupts the smooth structure of the line, although we must admit, it is very cleverly inserted [1]). Suppose, the infinitive *h*ᵉ*yot* were not there where it is now, we would not miss anything; on the contrary, we would be highly pleased by the clarity and the flowing rhythm of a line which is in perfect keeping with the high standard of the poetic form of this piece. We suggest, therefore, to omit *h*ᵉ*yot* leaving only the particle *l*ᵉ. This brings the prose line back to its poetic form which is, as we shall see, the form required by the structure of the poem as a whole.

The text of the poem is, then, as follows. We add to it a list of those words of the traditional text which we are obliged to omit.

text	units	stanza	verse
עבדי[1] אתה[2] בך אתפאר	4	1	(3)
לריק[3] יגעתי לתהו והבל כחי כליתי	6		(4)
אכן			
משפטי את יהוה ופעלתי את אלהי	6		
יצרי[4] מבטן לעבד לו	4	2	(5)
לשובב יעקב אליו וישראל לו יאסף	6		
ואכבד בעיני יהוה ואלהי היה עזי	6		
נקל[5] מהיותך לי עבד	4	3	(6)
להקים את שבטי יעקב ונצורי ישראל להשיב	6		
ונתתיך לאור גוים ל[6]ישועתי עד קצה הארץ	6		

1 ויאמר לי
2 ישראל אשר
3 ואני אמרתי
4 ועתה אמר יהוה
5 ויאמר
6 היות

The poem has three stanzes; their form is similar to that of the first Servant song:

a — — — —
b 1 — — — — — —
b 2 — — — — — —

The first and short line of each stanza has four units and deals exclusively with the unique relationship between God and His Servant. The other two and longer lines with six units each tell us about the

[1]) No study of insertions (words or groups of words) and of the way in which they have been effected has ever been made. One of the cleverest manipulations is that of the Targumist on Is. liii 5.

life of the Servant in connexion with his task. This is very artistically done. The second line of each stanza describes his past and unsuccessful labour (1 b 1), his immediate task (2 b 1) and his future and greater task (3 b 1). The last line points out that his task and success lies entirely in the hands of God (1 b 2), that he will be glorified in the eyes of Him who is his strength (2 b 2), for he is now appointed to be the light and the salvation of the world (3 b 2). We see that all the three stanzas, line by line, are perfectly parallel to each other not only in form but also with regard to their subject matter (again very much like the first Servant song).

All that now remains to be said is a qualification of the statement we made above, namely, that the poem represents a dialogue between the Servant and his Lord. Looking at the poem once more, it is rather more likely that not only verses 4 and 5 are a soliloquy, but that the whole poem represents a reflection of the Servant on his destiny which begins (verse 3) and ends (verse 6) with a direct word of God to him and which he now repeats to himself, whereas he deals with God's carlier commission (verse 5) more indirectly. The poem is complete and perfect, and the author had no need to furnish his thoughts with inserted comments.

Isaiah l 4-9 *and lii* 13 - *liii*..

The text of Is. l 4-9 is very much disturbed. It contains repetitions or resumptions of a line, and there are insertions, but there seem to be also omissions. I would not dare to analyse the structure of the poem much less to reconstruct its form. All we can say is that this poem was also composed in strophic form with lines of five and possibly also of six units, but how many lines there were to the stanza we cannot say. Well preserved lines with five units are in verse 6 (two lines), verse 7 (after *'al-ken*, one line), and verse 8 (two lines beginning with *mi*).

The last Servant song, lii 13 - liii, is in an even worse condition, and all that we have said about Is. l 4-9 applies also to this song. It seems, however, that the length of the lines at the beginning of this poem was seven units (lii 13 - liii 1), then lines with six units predominate but they are mixed with lines of five (verses 4-6) and seven units (verses 7-9)—if we accept the present state of the text! Some lines are prose, though perhaps poetic prose. The original poem may have been considerably amplified at an early time, espe-especially in its middle part and at the end.

Isaiah li 4-8

The song Is. li 4-8, on the other hand, presents hardly any difficulties at all. It is the glorification of God's Torah which is parallelled to *mišpaṭ*, *ṣedeq* (*ṣ*ᵉ*daqah*) and *yešaʿ* (*y*ᵉ*šuʿah*); with other words, this passage mentions all the aspects of God's salvation. It consists of two main parts of four lines each, verses 4-5 and 7-8, separated by a centre-section, verse 6. Let us deal with verse 6 first. Its three lines have each six units. They declare the transitoriness of heaven and earth in contra-distinction to God's *y*ᵉ*šuʿah* and *ṣ*ᵉ*daqah* (which are here synonymous with his *torah* and *mišpaṭ* [1]).

Just before the *ʾatnaḥ* of verse 6 are four words inserted by an eager commentator adding another parallel, *w*ᵉ*yoš*ᵉ*beha k*ᵉ*mo-ken y*ᵉ*mutun*, meaning: the earth will pass away and so will also its inhabitants. That sounds quite natural, but this parallel is nevertheless definitely out of place here. The commentator overstepped the logic of the original idea. The poet's object was to announce the actualisation of God's *mišpaṭ* among the nations (verse 5) which will last for ever (all generations, verse 8). The poet would hardly have reduced his message of hope to nothing by the pitiful thought that "the inhabitants of the earth will likewise die out". But maybe we can excuse the commentator for his zeal; perhaps he was thinking of the goyim if we generalize the thought in verse 8a, whilst Israel as the *ʿam ʿolam* will live for ever.

There is a strong possibility that the two sentences of verse 5 have changed places, namely, that 5b should come before 5a. We would suggest two reasons for such a change: 1) 5a is the object and final realisation of the hope expressed in 5b, and 2) verse 5 would then run parallel to verse 4. But although such an exchange of lines is not common in Hebrew poetry, it may have occurred in the course of transmission, for this is a case where it could happen, because the two lines (statements) are so close to each other.

The word *ki* occurs three times: in verses 4 and 6, where it should not be counted, as it has no significance of its own, and in verse 8, where it must be counted as a unit, for it introduces the reasons for the preceding argument.

---

[1]) Is. li 6 (understood in its context) is a favourite passage of Jesus: Mat. v 18; Luke xvi 17; xxi 33(!). Unfortunately it is not referred to by Nestle, neither on the margin nor in the *index locorum V.T.*

The form of the whole piece can be established as follows:

verse	stanza	units	
(4)	1	6	— — — — — —
		7	— — — — — — —
(5b)		5	— — — — —
(5a)		7	— — — — — — —
(6)	intermediate	6	— — — — — —
		6	— — — — — —
		6	— — — — — —
(7)	2	7	— — — — — — —
		5	— — — — —
(8)		7	— — — — — — —
		6	— — — — — —

If we accept the change of places in verse 5, the two main parts of the poem (stanzas 1 and 2) are in symmetry with each other, with the three intermediate lines as middle piece; if not, we must accept what appears to be a blemish.

Isaiah v 1-5

The text of the song of the vineyard is in good condition so that it is not necessary to reproduce it here, but a few remarks on certain words will be helpful.

The particle *-naʾ* in verse 1 (not in Is^{a}), verse 3 (in Is^{a} *nah* forming part of the verb),and verse 5 is no unit in itself, as it does not add anything to the cohortative and the imp. emph. The *ʾet ʾašer* in verse 5 represents the object and must be counted. The word *ʿattah* at the beginning of verse 3 is a purely rhetorical addition for the listener or reader so as to draw his attention to a new point, but nothing is lost if we drop it. We found a similar example of a redundant *ʿattah* in Is. xlix 5 (see above). The second *ʿattah* in verse 5 is of an entirely different nature; it is original and forms an important part of the line.

Keeping these observations in mind and dividing the poem into its natural lines, we can easily establish the form of the song:

verse	line	stanza	units	
(1)	1	1	5	— — — — —
	2		6	— — — — — —
(2)	3		4	— — — —
	4		6	— — — — — —
	5		5	— — — — —

(3)				—
	6	2	8	— — — — — — — —
(4)	7		7	— — — — — — —
	8		6	— — — — — —
(5)	9		7	— — — — — — —
	10		8	— — — — — — — —

The poem has two stanzas each dealing with its own theme. Each has five lines of unequal lengths, but they are arranged in perfect symmetry. The first and last lines of both stanzas (that is, lines 1 and 5; 6 and 10) are the decisive ones in the whole poem. The three middle lines in the first stanza (lines 2-4) describe the labour in the vineyard, those in the second stanza (7-9) contain the counsel that is taken over the lost labour; the middle parts are parallel to each other. The last line of the poem brings the verdict. It announces the destruction of the vineyard, its return to uncultivated or desert land. This is the end of the vineyard. Verses 6 and 7 are not part of the original poem. Verse 6 is merely a further illumination of the poem's last line (verse 5b), but we cannot say that this amplification is very logical; for after the vineyard has already become a *mirmas* it does not matter really whether God lets the clouds rain upon it or not, as, being a *mirmas*, it will produce only weeds anyway. Verse 7 is the explanation of the parable of the vineyard to make sure that everyone understands its moral. These additional lines are poetical prose (they contain parallelisms within the sentence, but they are of irregular lengths and cannot be adjusted to any system).

Isaiah xiv 3-23

The last poetic piece from Isaiah we propose to examine is the triumphal song on the fall of Babylon. It is one of the longest poems that have come down to us from the post-exilic period. It is of a peculiarly composite nature and consists of no less than eight parts, each presenting a dramatic scene. In that respect it is quite unique. Moreover it is one of the best preserved poems of the whole biblical literature; not a line, not even a word is missing. It is one of the most instructive examples of ancient Hebrew poetry.

However, two things have happened to it during its transmission. Four lines, namely verses 16 and 17 have been displaced. Their obvious and natural place is after verse 9 (see further below). Disarrangements are rare in this type of poetry which requires a logical sequence of thoughts and scenes, but they do happen now and then.

Then, there is a clause of eight words in verse 19, *l*^{e}*buš ḥ*^{a}*rugim m*^{e}*ṭoʿaney ḥereb*, *yor*^{e}*dey ʾel-ʾabney-bor;* this separates the two simple parallelisms *k*^{e}*neṣer nitʿab* and *k*^{e}*peger mubas* which clearly belong together. The inserted sentence is evidently meant as an "embellishment" (*eine weitere Ausmalung*) with a reference to the word *bor* in verse 15, but it breaks up the smooth flow of the poetic line. The picture it contains is not a very happy one; it does not fit in with either of the two parallel expressions, "like a rejected shoot thrown away, like some carcass which is trodden down". Besides nobody would walk over stones, if he can help it. A pit covered with stones is almost a proper grave. The original text (without the inserted clause) points out that the corpse of the King of Babylon is simply thrown away to be trampled under foot, that is, that he is not going to have any grave at all.

The last two verses, 22 and 23, are a divine oracle. That this is the case has been specially stressed by some ancient commentator who inserted no less than three times the words *n*^{e}*ʾum YHWH* (*ṣ*^{e}*baʾot*), so as to make quite sure that Babylon is wiped out for ever and will never rise again, for this is God's decision. These insertions are quite superfluous, as the poet left no doubt that God Himself is speaking here; His promise is given in two well-measured parallel lines of perfect rhythm.

A few further notes on the particles may follow here:

1) *kol* in verse 7 is a unit by itself. The poet means to say: the "whole" earth without exception is quiet.

2) There is no particular stress on the first *kol* in verse 18 and it is not counted as a unit, but the second in *kullam* is.

3) *gam* in verse 8 must be counted, as it does not just stand for "and", "also", "in addition"; it has a special emphasis: "even" the cypresses and the cedars suffer no longer. The same applies to *gam* in verse 10: "even you", King of Babylon, have been made equal to ourselves.

4) *ki* in verse 20 is evidently not particularly stressed and not to be counted as a unit (see further below).

The text, divided into its natural parts and logical lines, runs as follows:

	units	parts	verse
והיה ביום הניח יהוה לך	5	I	(3)
מעצבך ומרגזך ומן העבדה הקשה אשר עבד בך	6		

(4)		6	ונשאת המשל הזה על מלך בבל ואמרת
		5	איך שבת נגש שבתה מדהבה
(5)	IIa	6	שבר יהוה מטה רשעים שבט משלים
(6)		6	מכה עמים בעברה מכת בלתי סרה
		6	רדה באף גוים מרדף בלי חשך
(7)	IIb	6	נחה שקטה כל הארץ פצחו רנה
(8)		6	גם ברושים שמחו לך ארזי לבנון
		6	מאז שכבת לא יעלה הכרת עלינו
(9)	IIIa	6	שאול מתחת רגזה לך לקראת בואך
		5	עורר לך רפאים כל עתודי ארץ
		4	הקים מכסאותם כל מלכי גוים
(16)	intermediate	5	ראיך אליך ישגיחו אליך יתבוננו
	IIIb	6	הזה האיש מרגיז הארץ מרעיש ממלכות
(17)		5	שם תבל כמדבר ועריו הרס
		4	אסיריו לא פתח ביתה
(10)	IV	4	כלם יענו ויאמרו אליך
		6	גם אתה חלית כמונו אלינו נמשלת
(11)		5	הורד שאול גאונך המית נבליך
		5	תחתיך יצע רמה ומכסיך תולעה
(12)		6	איך נפלת משמים הילל בן שחר
		4	נגדעת לארץ חולש על גוים
(13)	V	5	ואתה אמרת בלבבך השמים אעלה
		5	ממעל לכוכבי אל ארים כסאי
		5	ואשב בהר מועד בירכתי צפון
(14)		5	אעלה על במתי עב אדמה לעליון
(15)		5	אך אל שאול תורד אל ירכתי בור
(18)	VI	7	כל מלכי גוים כלם שכבו בכבוד איש בביתו
(19)		7	ואתה השלכת מקברך כנצר נתעב[1] כפגר מובס
(20)	VII	4	לא תחד אתם בקבורה
		4	כי ארצך שחת עמך הרגת
		5	לא יקרא לעולם זרע מרעים
(21)		5	הכינו לבניו מטבח בעון אבתם
		4	בל יקמו וירשו ארץ
		4	ומלאו פני תבל ערים
(22)	VIII	8	וקמתי עליהם[2] והכרתי לבבל שם ושאר ונין ונכד[3]
(23)		8	ושמתיה למורש קפד ואגמי מים וטאטאתיה במטאטא השמד[4]

Omitted: [1] לבש הרגים מטעני חרב יורדי אל אבני בור

[2] נאם יהוה צבאות

[3] נאם יהוה

[4] נאם יהוה צבאות

Part I (verses 3 and 4) consists of four lines: 5 - 6 - 6 - 5 (symmetrical structure). Note the close correspondence between the first and the last line; the day of rest has come, the oppressor has ceased.

Part II (verses 5 to 8) has six lines with six units each. It can be subdivided into two stanzas; a) God has broken the evil sceptre which governed the nations and b) the whole earth is quiet now, even the trees which the King of Babylon felled for his palaces and cities are at rest.

Part III (verses 9, 16, and 17) describes the scene in the underworld. All the dead rulers rise from their seats to receive the mighty King (verse 9), he arrives, they look at him in amazement asking (verse 16a): Is this the man who made the earth tremble.... (verses 16b and 17)?

There are seven lines in this part. The middle line (5 units) stands by itself and divides the scene into two equal parts: a) the excitement in the underworld at the appearance of the King of Babylon and b) the questions they put to each other. Each of these two pictures has three lines of differing length in this order: 6 - 5 - 4. The unrest and the amazement in the underworld could hardly be better expressed than by such unequal lines, yet the form of the two stanzas is the same and shows that they belong together. Compare this with the preceding part which describes the rest and quiet in six well-proportioned lines!

Part IV (verses 10-12), six lines with the units 4 - 6 - 5 - 5 - 6 - 4 (symmetrical) begins with the words: "And they all will answer and say to you....". This is the answer to the questions raised in verses 16 and 17 which have, logically, to come before verse 10. We have rearranged the text accordingly.

Part V, (verses 13-15), five lines of equal length (five units each), continues the satire showing the irony of the fate of the Babylonian king, his immense boast ending in his utter humiliation.

Part VI (verses 18 and 19) is short and has only two lines of seven units each: the kings of the nations all have their houses (graves), but the King of Babylon has none.

Part VII (verses 20 and 21) has six lines with the following order of units: 4 - 4 - 5 - 5 - 4 - 4 (symmetrical). The first two lines (4 - 4) declare that he will not be buried with them that have their burying-place and nobody will know where his remains lie; after all, he has destroyed his land and killed his people. The next two lines (5 - 5) express the wish that no descendents shall be named for ever and any that are left shall be slaughtered because of the guilt of their fathers so that (the last two lines, 4 - 4) they may never inherit the earth and fill it with their cities.

Part VIII (verses 22 and 23) with two lines, eight units to each, contains the final oracle of God which confirms the utter destruction of Babylon, its inhabitants and its land. The sentences are long and heavy, as it befits a weighty oracle of God.

There is much that can be said about this unique poem, unique in its contents and its form, but we must leave any further discussion to the expositors. The knowledge of its form and structure, the logical sequence of its scenes and thoughts can here be of some help. In more recent years it has been repeatedly pointed out that certain ideas and terms in this passage are taken over from Ugaritic mythology. To this we must add that the form of this poem comes likewise close to the form in which Ugaritic legends and ritual texts were composed. As at least some myths were undoubtedly recited or performed in Ugarit, it is quite possible that the Hebrew poem on the fall of Babylon served a similar purpose. Verse 4a says: "you will take up this *mašal* about the King of Babylon" [1]). Each scene or speech is composed in a different but fixed form and it must be admitted that this is the most appropriate form for any lively recitation.

Some Ugaritic Examples

We will now proceed to examine a few specimens from the Ugaritic mythological literature which is hundreds of years older than its Hebrew counterpart. The myths have come down to us on original clay tablets. That means that the texts have not suffered by their transmission from generation to generation, unlike Hebrew poetry which has later been used in the religious instruction of the people. This, certainly, is a considerable advantage. The Ugaritic texts do not abound in additions like Hebrew texts which have been edited and re-edited in the course of time, but scribal errors and omissions occur now and then which is evidenced by parallel texts.

We shall see that Ugaritic poetry already observed the same general principles in its composition as Hebrew poetry, but its artistic beauty is definitely on a lower level than, for instance, the poem in Is. xiv.

---

[1]) The *mašal* here is not just a "proverb" or a popular ditty, but quite a lengthy dramatic poem. It is more like the ἱερὸς λόγος of the Greeks who imitated τὰ μυθολογούμενα by speech and gestures.

We choose first a short poem of four lines which was recited seven times at the beginning of the fertility rite in Ugarit. The reader will find a full discussion in *ASTI* III, 1964, pp. 147ff. Here we are concerned only with its form and structure. The text is (Gordon, UM, 1955, p. 144, no. 52, lines 8-11):

	units:
mt wšr yṯb	3
bdh ḫṭ ṯkl bdh ḫṭ ulmn	6
yzbrnn zbrm gpn yṣmdnn ṣmdm gpn	6
yšql šdmth km gpn	3

km (like Hebrew *ke* or *kemo*) is not counted as a unit.

Translation:

Mot — and — Šar sits,
In his hand the staff of bereavement
— in his hand the staff of widowhood.
They pruned him as one prunes the vine
— they bound him as one binds the vine,
He is felled in his field like a vine.

The poem is symmetrically built both in form and contents. Lines 1 and 4 (with three units each) and lines 2 and 3 (six units each) are parallel to each other.

The next passage is taken from the *Krt* text. It occurs twice [1]: lines (137)-(153) (Gordon, *UM*, p. 185b) and lines (281)-(300) (Gordon, *UM*, p. 187a). The second passage is in a better state of preservation.

		units
	(281) *wyʿn Krt Tʿ*	3
A:	(282) *lm ank ksp* (283) *wyrq ḫrṣ* (284) *yd mqmh*	7
	wʿbd (285) *ʿlm ṯlṯ sswm*	4
	(286) *mrkbt btrbṣ* [2] (287) *bn amt*	4
	pd in (288) *bbty ttn*	4
	tn (289) *ly mṯt Ḥry* (290) *nʿmt šbḥ* [3] *bkrk*	7
B:	(291) *dknʿm* [4] *ʿnt* (292) *nʿmh km tsm* (293) *ʿṯtrt tsmh*	6
	(294) *dʿqh ib iqni* (295) *ʿpʿph sp ṯrml* [5]	6

---

[1] We disregard the very fragmentary lines 44-56 (ten lines missing) which contain part of the vision.

[2] *btrbṣt* in line 141.

[3] *špḥ* in line 144.

[4] *dk nʿm* in line 145.

[5] After this line the first version (lines 148f.) has a further line (one word missing) of the same length (six units): *tḥgrn*... *(b-d)m ašlw bṣp ʿnh*.

(296) *dbḥlmy il ytn* (297) *bšrty ab adm* 6
(298) *wld špḥ lkrt* (299) *wǵlm lʿbd* (300) *il* 6
ttbʿ mlakm lyṯb 3

The nine lines of A and B are only a small section of a long poem, a kind of Odyssee, consisting of several hundred lines, but they show clearly how the author arranged his material systematically in well-ordered lines of varying but fixed lengths. The portion selected from the legend is complete in itself. It contains the message of King Krt to King Pbl. Krt has been bereaved of his relatives and his progeny and he asks Pbl for his daughter as wife.

And Krt of T' answered:

A: What use have I for silver (money) and minted gold in her stead,
A life-long slave, three horses,
A chariot from the stable of the son of a maid?
But that which is not in my house, give!
Give me the lady Ḥry, the well-bred, your first-born,

B: Whose goodness is like the goodness of Anat,
whose beauty is like the beauty of Astarte,
Whose eyebrows are (as beautiful as) inlaid lapis-lazuli,
whose eyes (as) a bowl of alabaster (?),
About whom in my dream Il gave (= announced),
in my vision, the Father of Man:
An offspring shall be born to Krt,
a scion to the Servant of Il.

The piece can be easily divided into two parts, A and B. The first and the last line of A have each seven units, and they correspond to each other also in their contents. Krt does not want her value in money, he wants the beautiful girl herself. The three middle lines of A, four units each, tell us that he is not interested in any barter value either, a slave, horses, a chariot, he has got all that. He needs what he as *not* got in his house. This leads up to the last line of A: he wants Ḥry. The next group of four lines with six units each give a description of her charms [1]); it is of such a woman as she appeared to him in a vision that Il promised him a male descendant.

The tale of the poem, of which we have reproduced here only a small section, progresses slowly and with repetitions stage by stage, picture by picture, or speech by speech, whilst each theme is dealt

---

[1]) See G. GERLEMAN's article "Die Bildsprache des Hohenliedes" in *ASTI* I, 1962, pp. 24ff., for this type of description of female beauty.

with in a definite set of well-balanced lines of appropriate lengths. The law of parallelism is as well observed as in Hebrew poetry not only between the half-clauses of a line, but also among the lines themselves, or, if they do not run parallel one after the other, they correspond to each other symmetrically.

As this system of laws is fairly strictly observed in Ugaritic poetry, it can help us sometimes over textual difficulties. The present text is an example. The first line of A has at the end the expression *yd mqmh* which occurs in the story several times [1]). At least five—if not more—different meanings of the expression have been suggested. H. L. Ginsberg (*ANET*, 1950, p. 144a) translates it: "friendship by covenant", but he does not say, why; C. H. Gordon (*UL*, 1949, p. 73): "a share of her estate"; G. R. Driver (*Canaanite Myths and Legends*, 1955, p. 33a): "a share of his estate"; John Gray (*Krt Text*, 1955, p. 13): "in token of her value"; J. Aistleitner (*WUS*, 1963, p. 278): "Gold, soviel als vorrätig". Whom shalt we trust? Ginsberg's translation is sheer fancy. Driver thinks the *h* in *mqmh* is the suffix 3rd pers. masc. and connects it with King Pbl; Aistleitner thinks the same, but connects this suffix with gold. Should it not, then, also refer to silver? Gordon and Gray hold that the suffix refers to the beautiful young lady, and this is certainly correct considering the correspondence between the first and the last line of part A. Gordon takes *mqm* in the sense of late Aramaic *m^eqama'*, "estate", "acquired goods" (he is probably followed by Driver). However, two things are quite clear: 1) that King Pbl does not want to give his daughter away, at least not to King Krt, and 2) that King Krt would not be satisfied with anything in exchange of this priceless woman. This the message of Krt must express, and there should be no difficulty in translating the expression *yd mqmh*. *Yd*, "hand", has in most (not only Semitic) languages a wide prepositional use [2]). *Mqm* is originally "place", "stead". The whole expression can only mean "instead of her", "in her stead" (Hebr.: *bimqomah*). Gray's translation comes nearest to it.

The two examples from Ugaritic texts we have just discussed are most instructive. We could now examine further specimens, but we would not gain a deeper general insight into the composition of Ugaritic poetry: an extended discussion would probably interest only

---

[1]) Lines 54, 127, 139, (251), (270), 284.

[2]) Cf. also Gordon, *UM*, p. 83 under 10.17.

the Ugaritic expert. We are still in the beginning of the study of Ugaritic poetry, and we would be well advised if we chose only those passages for investigation which are well preserved.

The writer himself is still not absolutely certain about the counting of a number of particles as independent units. The Ugaritic scribes used word-dividers, short, little wedges between the words, but as they were applied rather arbitrarily, the word-divider is no help to us.

We are also still uncertain about the negation *l* = *la*ʿ (Hebrew *lo*ʾ which is always counted as a unit, whilst ʾ*al*- is not). The Ugaritic *la*ʾ is usually written together with its verb, sometimes it is attached to the preceding relative *d* and separated from the verb.

The preposition ʿ*m* is another problem. Ugaritic has not the "heavy" Hebrew preposition ʾ*et* (which always represents a unit even when it is not connected with a suffix), but ʿ*m* takes its place (as well that of Hebrew ʿ*im* which is not counted). We can draw our conclusions only from texts which are complete, and we still have not got a sufficient number for the study of these particular problems.

An excellent text for the study of form and structure in Ugaritic poetry is a passage from the Baʿal and ʿAnat cycle III (GORDON, *UM*, p. 188a). We can group the first lines (from line 2 onward) in the following way: 4 - 4 - 4 - 4; 3 - 4 - 3; 6 - 6; 6 - 4 - 3 - 4 - 6; 4 (single); etc. But there are also quite a few other suitable texts.

Three Psalms

We will now append a few notes on the Psalms. Many of them have what seems to us an "irregular" form. They often have beautiful lines, but we find that they are not always so well coordinated, at least not in the way in which the prophetic poet handled his material. We have the impression that "lines" were the most important thing for the psalmist, a beautiful thought which could be expressed in one or a few lines; but that thought was not always strictly related to the preceding or following thought, though a certain sequence of thoughts was observed. Sometimes, lines and the thoughts which they expressed could be repeated in the same psalm as a kind of refrain, or they could be reused in other psalms in the same or in a slightly different form.

Psalms are a class of poetry of their own. They cannot be compared to the prophetic oracles which excel in conciseness and pithiness, much less to the type of poems in the Second Isaiah which, no doubt, represent the climax of poetic art in Israel. Already at a very early time the Psalms, or many of them, had their place in worship. They were made for recitation. Oracles, on the other hand, were not composed for liturgical use, although they later found a place in the service of the Synagogue. Originally they conveyed a direct message to the people, their leaders, or their king.

The Psalmist had considerably more freedom in composing his song than any other poet. There was no need for him to be as terse as the composer of direct divine messages. He could amplify his thoughts, he could repeat them and extend them to lengthy litanies of praise, thanksgiving, or supplication. But in spite of this greater freedom there are quite a number of Psalms in which we can detect certain rules, though not those strict rules of well-measured stanzas or symmetrical poems. The rules which the psalmists observed in their compositions are practically the same as those employed by the Ugaritic poets for their myths and rituals which, as we have already pointed out, are much less refined in the disposition of their material than the poetic pieces of the Hebrew prophets. It should not be forgotten that the Psalms, like the Ugaritic myths and rituals, were designed to be recited in divine service.

If we knew a little more about ancient "psalmody", we would most likely also have a better insight into the composition of psalms. Unfortunately we know next to nothing about it. It seems, however, that the psalmists made an extensive use of introductions. They are different in nature from the "introductory" or explanatory formulas inserted in a number of prophetic pieces by "commentators" (cf., e.g., the poems from Is. xiv or xlix). They are not inserted subsequently, after the composition of the psalm, but they are original and begin the sentence. In *no case* can they be omitted, for they form an integral part of the sentence. It makes the sentence often look like a prose sentence, and this has confused some scholars who have suggested that many of the Hebrew psalms are prose psalms. This is not the case. We must recognize these initial words as original and acknowledge their purpose in psalmody as a genuine introduction to the line that follows immediately afterwards. They are absolutely necessary and we must, therefore, allow them a "line" to themselves, however short that line may be. The result is surprising: the Psalm reveals its poetic character.

Psalm i is an excellent example which can demonstrate this.

verse		units
(1)	— —	2
	— — — —	4

	— — — —	4	
	— — — —	4	
		—	
(2)	— — — —	4	
	— — — —	4	
		—	
(3)	— — — — — :	5	
		—	
	— — —	3	
	— — —	3	
	— — —	3	
		—	
(4)	— — —!	3	
		—	
	— — — —	4	
		—	
(5)	— :	1	
		—	
	— — — —	4	7
	— — —	3	
	— — — —	4	7
	— — —	3	

We have marked the natural sections of this psalm by short strokes in the column indicating the number of units so that the structure of the psalm can be more easily discerned and appreciated. We regret that we cannot agree with Father Sebastian BULLOUGH who recently [1]) advocated the prose character of Psalm i. We admit, however, and the reader will share this opinion, that the psalm does not exhibit the same artistic refinement as the poetry of Isaiah, neither in form nor in structure. Psalms represent a different type of poetry.

Psalm xxiv has a similar arrangement of lines.

(1)	— —	headline
	— — — — — —	6
(2)	— — — — — —	6
		—
(3)	— — — — ?	4
	— — — — ?	4

[1]) In a paper read at a meeting of the S.O.T.S. in London, January 1965.

(4) — — — — ! 4

— — — — 4 } 7
— — — 3

(5) — — — — 4 } 7
— — — 3

(6) — — — — — — (—) 6

(7) — — — — — — : 6
— — — ! 3

(8) — — — — ? 4
— — — — — — ! 6

(9) — — — — — — : 6
— — — ! 3

(10) — — — — — ? 5
— — — — — ! (-) 5

Verse 7 is repeated in verse 9. Verse 10 is an intensification of verse 8.

Psalm xcviii is slightly more difficult, and we have to take the different stresses on certain words into account. The *ki* in verse 1 introduces the reason why a new song must be sung. We would, therefore, give it a full unit. The preposition *lipney* in verse 6 stands for *l^{e}*; compare the construction in verses 4 and 5! The two first words of verse 9 belong to verse 8. The preposition must be counted here as it has a different value. The jubilation in verses 4-7 refers to all living beings on earth and in the sea: they sing *to* the Lord; in verse 8 the rivers and mountains sing *before* the lord!

(1) —
— — — — — — — 7
— — — — — 5
(2) — — — — — — — 7

(3) — — — — — 5
— — — — — 5

(4) — — — — — — 6

(5)	— — — — — —	6
(6)	— — — — — —	6
(7)	— — — — — —	6
		—
(8)	— — — — — — — —	8
(9)	— — — — — — — —	8

We are still in the early stages of our investigation, but it is hoped that the new approach to the study of ancient Hebrew "prosody" which has been outlined in these two articles may help towards a deeper understanding of the poetry of ancient Israel.

Additional Note (Is. xl 12a):

The LXX replaced the Hebrew creation motif by the three Greek "elements": water, heaven, and earth, taking "the (dust of the) earth" over from verse 12b. As the Hebrew text underlying the LXX contained already the two words *ug*^{e}*baʿot b*^{e}*moʾẓ*^{e}*nayim* (see the discussion on this amplification) the LXX translators, having disposed of "the dust of the earth", found in the two words a convenient parallelism for the "mountains". They translated *g*^{e}*baʿot* with νάπαι, "wooded hills", with the emphasis on the trees (!), as a νάπη can also be a wooded "glen" (Waldschlucht).

FORM AND STRUCTURE OF ISAIAH 58 *)

I

In the MT the whole chapter of Is. 58 is laid out in one paragraph, whilst the Qumran manuscript Is[a] has correctly divided it into two paragraphs by beginning a new line with verse 13. Indeed, the chapter deals with two different subjects: verses 1-12, the Day of Fasting, and verses 13-14, the Sabbath. In the first and longer paragraph, the Qumran manuscript has also a few subdivisions which are indicated by small gaps (*s^e^ṯumoṯ*) after verses 4, 5bα, 7, 8, 9a, 11 [1]). Some of these reveal a good sense for the division of the subject matter. Evidently, these subdivisions were later dropped or not recognized by the Masoretes.

The following study of Is. 58 concerns itself especially with the first part of the chapter, verses 1-12, but a short discussion of the last verses will conclude it.

The text of the Isaiah manuscript is already more or less the same as the text of the Masoretes [2]). Common to both is also the omission of a half-line, i.e., four words required by the law of parallelism after the first four words of verse 6. As so often, the transmitted text contains a number of insertions in various places. It seems that all of them were already found in the manuscript from which the scribe of Is[a] made his copy. There is, finally, a further addition at the end of the paragraph: part of verse 11 and verse 12. Verse 10a is obviously displaced; it should follow immediately after verse 7.

The first part, verses 1-12, consists of two distinct poems, verses 1-2 and 3-11a. They are different in form and structure; but both deal with the Day of Fasting, although fasting is not expressly mentioned in the first poem. In its present state the first poem forms a kind of introduction to the second poem. This is due to its am-

*) This article is a further contribution to the study of form and structure in ancient Hebrew poetry. The two first parts appeared in *VT* XIV (1964), 4, pp. 423-444 and XVI (1966), 2, pp. 152-180, where the reader will also find a brief discussion of the principles on which this new approach is based.

plification in verse 2 (now rather long) which adapts it to the second poem. The result is that verses 1-12 appear to be of one piece. This must have happened at a very early time, certainly before the Qumran scribe copied the text, for the addition appears already in his manuscript, and he did not leave a dividing gap between verses 2 and 3. Most likely he found the addition and adaptation already in his *Vorlage*. Even the Hebrew text underlying the LXX considers the first two verses of Is. 58 as part of the following, but the translators must have found the transition in the Hebrew text a bit too abrupt and felt obliged to insert here the word λέγοντες which obviously makes for a better understanding of the traditional text. There is no equivalent for it in the Hebrew text.

II

The first poem which is fully preserved in verses 1 and 2 is originally self-contained. Its adaptation to the contents of the second and much longer poem was effected by the insertion of one line of seven units: *k^egoy ʾ^ašer ṣ^eḏaqah ʿaśah umišpat ʾ^elohaw loʾ ʿaẓaḇ*. The word *ʾ^ašer* transforms this line which is poetic in its structure (with parallelism, 4 + 3, common to lines of seven units) into prose. The four lines which are left have only six units each [3]). We can subdivide it into two stanzas consisting of two lines each. Thus we obtain a poem of perfect form and structure, for the two stanzas deal with two different though interrelated aspects or parts of the divine message.

units							stanza	verse
6	קולך	הרם	כשופר	אל תחשך	בגרון	קרא	1	(1)
6	חטאתם	יעקב	ולבית	פשעם	לעמי	והגד		
6	יחפצון*	דרכי	ודעת	ידרשון	יום יום	אותי	2	(2)
6	יחפצון	אלהים	קרבת	צדק	משפטי	ישאלוני		

*) we omit: כגוי אשר צדקה עשה ומשפט אלהיו לא עזב

The poem contains the divine commission to a "preacher" for the Fast Day. It begins with the summons: *q^eraʾ* (= cry, preach, proclaim, admonish), much in the same way as Is. 40, 6f. which also brings a short sermon to be addressed to the people (cf. also Jona 1, 2; 3, 2; Zech. 1, 14.17).

In the first stanza (58, 1) God asks the preacher to cry out, to raise his voice like a *šofar* and tell "my (=God's) people" their sins. The *šofar* is mentioned here not only as a figure to describe the force of the outcry, it has a special function also as the instrument which announces the nearness of God [4]) and the appropriate time for the people to consider their sins and to do repentance. The main day for the blowing of the *šofar* is the New Year's Day, but it is also blown already throughout the month of Elul preceding the New Year's Day. The time from the 1st Elul to Yom Kippur (40 days) is traditionally the time of repentance, particularly the last ten days of this period from New Year's Day to the Day of Atonement, at the end of which the *šofar* can be heard for the last time [5]). It should also be noted that Isaiah's admonition (55,6): "Seek the Lord while he is near" has since early Rabbinic times been applied to these ten days of repentance and penance (bRH 18a).

This knowledge helps us to evaluate the contents of the second stanza of our poem which gives us the gist of the actual message for the Fast Day. What does God require of the people after they have confessed their sins? What kind of life should they live? The answer does not consist of a lengthy enumeration of good deeds they should now do, not even a fast on a particular day is mentioned; they should rather deepen and intensify their relationship with God in their daily lives: "Me shall they seek daily and strive to gain the knowledge of my ways, me shall they ask about the ordinances of a righteous life and have pleasure in (a life in) the nearness of God". No modern Yom Kippur preacher could deliver a better and more "modern" sermon. The message was, indeed, entirely new. Fasting, ashes, sack-cloth are of no avail before God, but a continual (= *yom yom*) life in God's nearness [6]).

The insertion *kegoy..... ʿazab* spoils the relevancy of this admonition completely and it reduces the clear and simple interpretation of God's will to the people to a mere conversation between God and the preacher about the people. The directness of God's proclamation of God's will is lost. Not only is the inserted sentence a prose sentence, but it transforms the whole verse 2 into a longish prose construction. True, the parallelism is still preserved in the individual lines now forming the various clauses, but parallelisms alone do not yet make real Hebrew poetry. They are sometimes used also in prose sentences, and then we speak, rightly or wrongly, of poetic prose. The decisive feature of good Hebrew poetry is the structure of the whole, the arrangement of the contents in well-constructed pithy lines of appropriate lengths as well as the inter-relationship between these lines with respect to contents and length. This can be clearly seen in many poems which have not been "revised" by a second hand [7]). Insertions (additions to the text, comments of various kinds to explain a word or a sentence, to emphasize a particular teaching or even to introduce new ideas) are hardly ever made arbitrarily. It is, therefore, not enough to state that certain words are an addition and that they should be left out from the traditional text, but we should also, as far as possible, investigate into the function of the addition and find out what was in the commentator's mind, how the addition affects the text and whether we may not sometimes draw certain conclusions regarding the change of the religious climate since the time when the original poem was composed. This would be the subject of a further special study.

As regards the insertion in Is. 58, 2 we can already make the following observations. It should be noted that the inserted clause has its verbs in the perfect, whilst the original poem uses the imperative in stanza 1 and the imperfect in stanza 2 which expresses the iussive mood. This is perfectly logical: stanza 1 contains the straightforward commission to the preacher, in stanza 2 God tells him what the people are required to do.

The inserted clause affects also the first line of the second stanza and includes it in the new long sentence which comprises the whole of verse 2. In the MT this verse begins with a *waw*: *we'oti*. This *waw* cannot be understood as the simple copulative conjunction "and"; that would not make any sense. Indeed all translaters of the MT have given it an adversative or concessive meaning (AV and RSV: "yet"; the modern Swedish version: "väl"; MENGE: "zwar"; Luther follows the Vulgate). The *waw* in this sense fulfils an important function in the MT: it links verse 2a with the inserted clause which follows immediately afterwards. This *waw*, however, is a later addition. We do not yet find it in the Is MS and in the LXX (and the Vulgate). The simple *'oti* represents the earlier reading. In fact, the *waw* would be out of place in the original poem.

As we have seen, the second stanza does not recommend fasting on a particular day of the year as penance for sins and does not even mention it, but an altogether new way of life throughout the year. This is just what the people of the time do not realize, for the astonished question in verse 3 shows that they deem material fasting a sufficient remedy, which it is not (see verse 5). Verse 2 in its original shorter form is, indeed, a sermon on the only real repentance by a complete change of life which alone is valid before God, but of which the people do not seem to have any knowledge. In its present form (with the insertion), however, it would suggest that the people knew already what God required of them, which makes the sermon superfluous.

III

The subject of the second and longer poem in ch. 58 is an exposition of what God considers to be a real and genuine "fast". It is in the form of an answer to the question which the people put to God (verse 3a; first line of the first stanza): "Why do we fast and you do not look, why do we humble ourselves and you do not take any notice?"

The whole poem is fully preserved with the exception of a half-line which got lost. On the other hand, as is so often the case, this poem also collected a number of additional lines in the course of its transmission. Such additions do not make it easier for us to establish the structure of a poem. Sometimes the LXX can be of help in discovering the original wording of a line [8]), sometimes the Qumran MS Is[a] supplies a missing word [9]) or indicates a later addition [10]), but frequently we are left in the lurch by both of them, as in the present case, where insertions had been made in pre-Qumran and pre-LXX times. Then we must avail ourselves of other methods.

There is one stanza in the poem which is made up of three perfect lines with inner parallelisms. These three lines are sharply outlined against their context and quite obviously belong together. After a description of the people's idea of fasting (verse 4) God asks the people (verse 5): Is that what you call a fast? Following this, he tells them what he considers a genuine fast (verse 6).

Breaking up verse 5 into its natural lines we get the following picture of the structure of this stanza:

line 1:	— — — — — — — —	8 units
line 2:	— — — — — —	6 units
line 3:	— — — — — —	6 units

With this picture in mind we can discern three more stanzas. Verse 6 follows exactly the same pattern, only that the second part of the first line required by parallelism (four more units) is wanting. Verses 3 and 4 contain the first stanza. Verse 3a gives the first line of eight units which introduces the subject of the poem. It contains the self-righteous question: *lammah ṣamnu*..., "why (actually:

what for) do we fast", and you do not acknowledge it? God gives a pertinent answer to this impertinent question (verse 4, beginning with the second word): "For to quarrel and to fight you fast, to smite with evil fist; you do not fast for letting your voice be heard on high". These are the second and third lines with six units. It should be noted that all the four clauses of these two lines begin with the particle *l^e^* corresponding to the *l^e^* in *lammah*. A similar repetition of the interrogative particle *h^a^* will be found at the beginning of all three lines of the second stanza (resumed at the beginning of the first line of the third stanza to introduce the new theme). These repetitions are a highly artistic device which make God's questions and answers ironic and terse.

The thought contained in 3bα is not the interpolator's own idea; it is taken over from verse 13 where it is in its correct place.

The simple and direct answer which God gave to the people's question (3a) evidently seemed too harsh and abrupt. The "editor" of the text found it therefore necessary to tone it down a little, since to him there was nothing wrong with fasting. He introduced a sentence beginning with an assuageing and friendly *hen*: "Look here, on the day of your fast you follow your private business and afflict all your workers". The line serves as a gradual introduction to the heavier reproaches in verse 4 which are taken up once more by the obliging *hen*: "Look here (friends)!" Verse 4 contains the lines 2 and 3 of the first stanza; each has six units. That means that *hen* is redundant; it is not part of the original line; it is the editor's addition. He thus succeeded in integrating his own sentence (3b) also formally and syntactically into the text, as the two demonstrative particles *hen* have at the same time a coordinating function [11]).

Stanzas 3 and 4 begin both with the (demonstrative) particle *h^a^lo'*, partly resuming the (interrogative) particles *h^a^* in the three lines of stanza 2 thus introducing, in perfect formal beauty, God's answer concerning the right kind of fast.

Stanza 3 will be found in verse 6 with four words missing in the first line, stanza 4 in verse 7 which, however, contains only the first line with eight units and the second with six. The third line which should continue or conclude the thought of the second line and also have six units, is not lost but was cut off and shifted to another place. It is preserved in verse 10a. We should not forget that the editorial work of a book like that of Isaiah followed other principles than those required by a purely literary edition of ancient Hebrew poetry:

the book was edited for the instruction of the people with comparatively little interest in the poetic form [12]). This accounts for a number of displacements of lines in Hebrew poetical texts, although they are not too frequent. In the present case, there are not only further lines which have been inserted in the text, but the original lines have also been rearranged as it seemed fit to the editor in order to integrate the additional material.

Then there are two more stanzas, 5 and 6, belonging to the original poem. They form the conclusion of the poem; they are a kind of epilogue. These last two stanzas differ in form from the first four which indicates a change of subject matter [13]). Whilst the first four deal exclusively with the fast, first as actually performed (stanzas 1 and 2) and secondly as required (stanzas 3 and 4), the epilogue contains the promise of the reward for the fulfilment of a fast desired by God. The form of these two stanzas is:

line 1: — — — — — — — 7 units
line 2: — — — — — — 6 units

Both stanzas show the same artistic device: they begin with the adverb *'az*, "(only) then", in order to stress the actualization of the promise.

Verse 8 contains the first of the final stanzas complete. The Qumran MS Is[a] has a little blank space before and after this verse. They are placed correctly and help us to isolate this stanza and establish its form. The last stanza is made up of verse 9a and 11a which should follow 9a.

We must now examine the lines and words which are left over: 9b, 10b, 11b together with the last two words of 11a, and verse 12.

Verse 9b begins with a lonely *'im*, not a very poetical beginning for a line in the context of a poem which otherwise abounds in the repetition of a particle at the beginning of its lines! Further, in the MT 9b forms one verse with 9a; that means that the conjunction *'im* attaches 9b to 9a which begins with *'az*. One should expect the clause with *'im* to precede the clause with *'az* [14]). But here the protasis follows the apodosis, which is most unusual, if it occurs at all.

We can adduce a third observation in support of our conclusion, but before we do that, we have first to sort out the various clauses which follow verse 9a.

We suggested that verse 8 contains the first of the two final stanzas. If we accept its form, the second final stanza would consist of 9a and 11a. Both stanzas begin, then, with *'az*! They are the conclusion to the whole poem and, in particular, the answer to the introductory question in verse 3a, in so far as both stanzas announce the reward for a genuine fast as desired by God and described in verses 6, 7, and 10a (stanzas 3 and 4 of the poem).

Verse 9b merely mentions three further individual sins which man commits against his fellow-man. The first of these has already been well expressed in verse 6; the second and third are just ordinary sins. "Pointing with the finger" and "speaking evil" are surely bad things which should not be done. Desisting from these sins would, however, not yet constitute a "fast" (see the mandatory demands in stanzas 3 and 4). Verse 9b reveals itself as an amplification of the original text.

It is interesting to note that Is[a] has after 9a, just before the *'im*, a clear open space which the scribe most likely found already in his *Vorlage* from which he copied. This points to two things: 1) the sentence in 9a finishes here; 2) the discussion is taken up anew in 9b. The Qumran MS differs here from the MT in its judgement on the structure of verse 9. According to the MS verse 10a (which had been cut off from its context in verse 7) is made dependent on the same *'im*. The protasis would then consist of the three clauses contained in verses 9b and 10a, and the concluding apodosis would comprise the various periods from verse 10b to 12 [15]). This would make one unusually long sentence (9b-12) which includes poetical lines (verses 10a and 11a) belonging to the original poem, but as regards the whole complex sentence, we must admit, it is of an unpoetic, i.e. irregular, structure. Verse 10b is also an additional line (only five units); it repeats, rather less beautifully, what has already been said in verse 8a.

To the line in 11a which concludes the original poem most appropriately (the theme is fasting!) two more words are attached: The strengthening of the bones could not be missed! The result is then described (11b) in an allegorical picture: "you will be like a watered garden, (nay) like a source of water", to which a qualification is added in prose (note the *'ašer*): "the waters of which will not fail".

Verse 12 is a further addition and deals with a new and different subject. It contains the promise for a better time for the nation: the descendents will rebuild the ruins, etc. However, there may be a slight possibility of including the two lines in the poem (see further below on p. 78f).

The graphic picture of the lines and sentences of verses 9b-12 is as follows:

(9b)	— — — — — — — —	8 units
(10)	— — — — — —	6 units *)
	— — — — —	5 units
(11)	— — — — — —	6 units *)
	— —	2 units
	— — — — — — — —	8 units
(12)	— — — — — — — —	8 units
	— — — — — — —	7 units

*) These two lines belong to the original poem.

The form of this portion is unpoetic; it corresponds in no way to the beautiful and well-constructed poem contained in the verses 3-11a.

We can now reproduce the text of the poem Is. 58, 3-11a in its original form which discloses its beautiful structure:

	units	stanza	verse
למה צמנו ולא ראית ענינו נפשנו ולא תדע [1]	8	1	(3)
לריב ומצה תצומו ולהכות באגרף רשע	6		(4)
לא תצומו כיום להשמיע במרום קולכם	6		
הכזה יהיה צום אבחרהו יום ענות אדם נפשו	8	2	(5)
הלכף כאגמון ראשו ושק ואפר יציע	6		
הלזה תקרא צום ויום רצון ליהוה	6		
הלוא זה צום אבחרהו — — — — [2]	8	3	(6)
פתח חרצבות רשע התר אגדות מוטה	6		
ושלח רצוצים חפשים וכל [3] מוטה תנתקו	6		
הלוא פרס לרעב לחמך ועניים מרודים תביא בית	8	4	(7)
כי תראה ערם וכסיתו ומבשרך לא תתעלם	6		
ותפק לרעב נפשך ונפש נענה תשביע	6		(10a)

[1] omitting verse 3b הן ······ הן

[2] four units, required by the law of parallelism, are missing. Evidently they were already lost in the Hebrew *Vorlage* of the LXX. The Greek translaters sensed that something was missing here and filled the lacuna with the two words λεγει κυριος. The corresponding Hebrew emendation, *ne*ʾ*um* ʾ*adonai YHWH*, suggested by Kittel in his *BH*, should therefore be dropped.

[3] *kol* must be counted as a unit; see *VT* XIV, p. 426, end of note 3.

	units	stanza	verse
אז יבקע כשמר אורך וארכתך מהרה תצמח	7	5	(8)
והלך לפניך צדקך כבוד יהוה יאספך	6		
אז תקרא ויהוה יענה תשוע ויאמר הנני [4]	7	6	(9a)
ונחך יהוה תמיד והשביע בצחצחות נפשך [5]	6		(11a)

[4] omitting 9b, 10b, the last two words of 11a; 10a has its place in stanza 4.
[5] omitting 11b.

The poem on the fast was probably composed sometime during the Exile or in early post-exilic times. No date can be given. It is more than likely that it was known to the author of Zech. ch. 7 and 8 (note the question in 7, 3). The reference in 7, 7 to the "former prophets" need not necessarily apply to Is. 58. It is true Zech. 7, 8ff. and 8, 16f. contain similar thoughts, but they are reminders of the warnings and rebukes of the older prophets like Hosea, First Isaiah, and others (cf. also Jer. 36), whilst Isaiah 58, 3ff. is a renewal of the demands of God.

Zechariah mentions several fast days: in the fifth month (7, 3), in the fifth and the seventh (7, 5), in the fourth, fifth, seventh, and tenth (8, 19). We are inclined to think that the author of Is. 58, 3-11a had the Day of Atonement (the fast in the seventh month) in mind because of the emphasis on the significance of quite a different type of fast for the individual and a new relationship with his neighbour before God (see also note 17)

It should, however, be noted that the additional verse 12 which mentions the rebuilding of the ruins seems to refer the fast to the day or days of mourning over the destruction of Jerusalem. We pointed out (see above p. 00) that verse 12 brings in an entirely new idea which does not play any role in the preceding poem with its predominently ethico-religious concern. It is not mentioned before, but introduced rather abruptly and supercedes the promises contained in stanzas 5 and 6 appropriately beginning with *'az*. Although both lines of verse 12 consist of parallel clauses, they are irregular in length and do not confirm to the rigid formal structure of the poem. Nevertheless, verse 12 may have been intended as an additional epilogue with the special stress on the restoration of the city or cities of Judah (similar to the treatment which the fast received in Zechariah 7 and 8). It may very well be that the author of Is. 58, 12 was a contemporary of the author of Zech. 7 and 8, for both of them were concerned about the restoration of the land.

But be this as it may, the poem on the fast is undoubtedly one of the most highly finished ancient Hebrew compositions, and we are very fortunate that it has come down to us practically intact.

IV

The last two verses of ch. 58 do not deal any more with the fast, but with the observance of the Sabbath. Whilst the masoretic tradition of the text does not appear to note the change of the subject, the Qumran MS of Is[a] indicates the fact by beginning here a new paragraph. The two verses have preserved complete a poem of perfect form, but as regards it structure it does not reach the artistic beauty of Is. 58, 3-11a or the other poems of the book of Isaiah we discussed in the two earlier articles.

The poem consists of five lines with the following number of units: 7 - 6 - 7 - 6 - 7.

						units	verse
ביום קדשי	חפצך	עשות	רגלך	משבת	אם תשיב	7	(13)
מכבד	יהוה	לקדוש	ענג	לשבת	וקראת	6	
ודבר דבר	חפצך	ממצוא	דרכיך	מעשות	וכבדתו	7	
ארץ	על במתי	והרכבתיך	על יהוה	תתענג	אז	6	(14)
יהוה דבר	כי פי	אביך	יעקב	נחלת	והאכלתיך	7	

It is not unlikely that the author of this poem followed the example of stanzas 5 and 6 of the preceding poem which has also lines of 7 and 6 units, only that his composition has a symmetrical form; in the disposition of the contents, however, i.e., in its structure, the poem is not symmetrically built [15]). This also shows its inferior artistic quality. In its last half-line (14b) which is not parallel to the first half-line (14b), it re-applies the formula contained in the last line of the perfectly symmetrical poem Is. 40, 3-5, in which it corresponds to the first line (3 units) [16]).

Nevertheless, Is. 58, 13f. is an original poem and most perfectly preserved, with no additions or insertions. It should be noted that it begins with *'im* and an imperf. 3. pers. sing., exactly like verse 9b which begins a new sub-paragraph in the Is. MS. As we had to declare verse 9b (together with 10b and the latter part of 11) an addition by some editor, we recognize now that the *'im* with the imperf. by which he opens the section 9b-12 is an attempt at a formal assimilation to the following paragraph 13f. with the effect that the last paragraph of the chapter comes closer to the preceding section.

We also note in verse 13 the two expressions *ʿaśoṯ ḥapaṣeḵa* and *mimmeṣo' ḥepṣeḵa* which suit their purpose excellently in a discourse on Sabbath observance. Undoubtedly the two expressions are here in their original setting. But it so happens that the only other day on which "no work at all" was to be done is the Yom Kippur [17]). It is therefore not surprising that the editor of Is. 58 saw that something is missing in the context of the discourse on the fast; the injunction for the Sabbath was, therefore, inserted in verse 3b, which we already found to be an addition to the poem which actually deals with the fast only. This use of words or thoughts from the last poem (58, 13f.) is another proof of the secondary nature of some passages in 58, 3-12 which we recognized as interpolations.

We learn from this discussion that the three parts of Is. 58 have been well adapted to each other by later hands. We need not wonder, therefore, that in the final (masoretic) edition of the text the chapter forms one single paragraph.

---

1) Millar BURROWS has ignored all of them in his transliteration, except the one after 5bα.

2) There are some minor differences; see EISSFELDT's list in KITTEL's *BH*. Sometimes the MT represents the better reading, sometimes the MS. One case will be discussed further below (see note 3).

3) *yom yom* = "daily" (verse 2aα) is one notion and must be counted as one unit. With Is MS we omit the first *waw* in verse 2 (see further below).

4) See *HEC* (*Hebräer-Essener-Christen*) pp. 356ff.

5) Orthodox Jews in Jerusalem also blow the shofar on other days of the year when, according to their opinion, a great sin has been committed in Israel.

6) Similarly, for Jeremia (9, 24f.) circumcision of the flesh counts for nothing, but circumcision of the heart is the important thing.

7) See the examples in the earlier articles referred to in the footnote on page 69.

8) E.g. Is. 40, 3: see *VT* XIV (1964), pp. 441ff.

9) E.g. Is. 56, 10: see *VT* XVI (1966), p. 154.

10) E.g. Is. 40, 14b-16: see *VT* XVI (1966), p. 155.

11) There are various ways of incorporating further material (words, or clauses, or sentences) in the original text. No study on this textual problem yet exists.

12) See our observations in *VT* XVI (1966), pp. 153. A fuller study will appear in a later issue of this Annual.

13) A remarkable example of this change of subjects (or scenes) and change of form is Is. 14, 3-23; see *VT* XVI (1966), pp. 171.

14) Many examples: Is. 58, 13f.; Job 9, 30f.; 11, 13-15; 22, 23 and 26; Prov. 2, 3-5; etc. *'az* in Is. 58,.8 follows after *ki* in verse 7 (cf. Job 3, 3). There is no reference to this grammatical point in *GK*, neither in BROCKELMANN's *Syntax*.

15) Cp., for instance, Is. 30, 29-31; 40, 3-5; 49, 1-2; 51, 4-8; also 5, 1-5; see the two earlier articles mentioned in note 7.

16) See *VT* XIV, pp. 441f.

[17]) Lev. 23 gives a full account of the feast days as well as of Shabbat and Yom Kippur. There are two different rules about work on these days. The rule which applies to the feast days is: "You shall do no laborious work (*kol mᵉleḵeṯ ‘ᵃḇoḏah lo’ ṯa‘ᵃśu*)". The formulation of the rule for Shabbat and Yom Kippur is shorter which makes the rule much stricter: "You shall do no work at all (*kol mᵉla’ḵah lo’ ṯa‘ᵃśu*)".

Maśkîl

1. The verb *śkl* is used in the Bible exclusively in the *hiphil*, although a single exception does appear in the *qal* (1 Sam. 18:30) which Ehrlich replaced, rightly or wrongly, by the *hiphil* participle. The most common tense in which the verb appears is the participle, which is often used as a noun. The only biblical derivative from the root *śkl* is *śēkẹl*; all others, such as *śkly*, *śklywt*, and *śklnwt*, are later forms.

The Bible translations often render the verb by "succeed," "be successful," or "prosper," but we should not forget that the fundamental sense of the root embraces the intellectual and spiritual faculties, such as perspicacity, perception, discernment, understanding, insight, and, finally, knowledge and wisdom. If applied to life and action, the outcome will be success and victory, carrying something through, achieving one's aim, for which the Bible has the more common and perhaps more appropriate verb *ṣlḥ* (usually in the *hiphil*, though a few passages in which the verb appears in the *qal* have as the subject the—especially prophetic—spirit of God which overcomes and takes possession of a person).

2. Like the derivatives from the roots *byn*, *ḥkm*, and *yd'*, the words *maśkîl* and *śēkẹl* can be used in the profane sense of human thought, when thought is a result of learning and experience, of quick intellectual grasp or good education, as the following examples show: 1 Sam. 25:3; 1 Chr. 26:14; Job 22:2; 34:35; Dan. 1:4,17; 8:25; Gen. 3:6 (by eating a forbidden fruit).

The book of Proverbs contains many sayings of worldly wisdom expressed by any of the *hiphil* forms from the root *śkl* or by the noun *śēkẹl* (synonymous with *bînāh*, *da'at*, and *ḥokmāh*), but we must not overlook the fact that the whole collection, taken from various sources of the wisdom literature of the time, is a Jewish book and became canonical inasmuch as all wisdom comes from God and aims again at the right knowledge of God. He who aspires to that right understanding, who thinks and acts in the consciousness of his dependence on God is the only true *maśkîl*. Whoever put the selection of wise sayings together or edited the book did not conceal the intention and the meaning of this collection from the listener and the reader. The introduction of the book, Prov. 1:1-7, each verse of which is important, makes his intentions abundantly clear right from the beginning. The alignment with God is emphasized throughout the book in various ways (cf., e.g., 3:4-7; 9:10; 13:15; 15:24; 16:20,22; 30: 5-6). A *maśkẹlẹt* wife is from God (19:14); she who fears God deserves praise (31:30; cf. 1:7; 3:7; 9:10).

3. If we investigate the passages in which forms of the root *śkl* play a prominent part, it strikes us that the overwhelming majority are reflections on the knowledge of God, His miracles and deeds in creation and history, His supreme power over all mankind, His will and His pleasure that man should obey His word and the Torah He had given, and walk accordingly, and that man should continually seek the Lord, should recognize, acknowledge, and pro-

claim His supreme sovereignty, and sing His praise.

God should be the center of the thought of the true *maśkîl*. God looks down from heaven on the sons of man to see if there is a *maśkîl*, one who seeks God and does good; the answer is negative (Ps. 14:1-3; 53:1-3). Not even the shepherds of the people have sought God(and have consequently acted unwisely) (Jer. 10:21). Man must seek God and must search Him out in order to know Him who delights in kindness, justice, and righteousness (9:23). Israel had no insight (*bînāh*); had they been wise and understanding (*yaśkîlû*) they would have considered (*yābînû*) the outcome (Deut. 32:28f.; Ps. 106:7) and realized (*l^e haśkîl*) His faithfulness (Dan. 9:13). God will do wonders again that they may see and know, that they may consider and comprehend (*yaśkîlû*) the hand (power) of God (Isa. 41:20).

4. Man does not consider the ways of God (*lō' hiśkîlû*, Job 34:27), but God will bring them to do that consideration and they will fear Him (Ps. 2:10f.; 64:10). The Psalmist promises to give heed to a blameless way of life (*'askîlāh b^e dęręk tāmîm*) and asks God when He will come to him. In another Psalm, he (or God himself?) will give instruction about the way in which man should walk (*'aśkîl^e kā w^e 'ōr^e kā b^e dęręk zû tēlēk*, 32:8). Again the Psalmist asks the fools among the people when they will be wise (*mātay taśkîlû*); when they shall acknowledge that God teaches man *da'at* by His Torah (94:8-12). God makes man wiser than his adversaries by the commandments of the Torah, more enlightened (*hiśkaltî*) by pondering over God's testimonies than his other teachers (119:97-99).

Israel was to keep the words of the Covenant, God's testimonies in the Torah of Moses, and follow them that they might act wisely and succeed (*l^e ma'an taśkîlû*) in everything they do (Deut. 29:8), wherever they go (Josh. 1:7; 1 Kgs. 2:3), for God will then be with them (Josh. 1:9). The Torah is their *ḥokmāh* and their *bînāh* (Deut. 4:6).

The *maśkîl* who foresees the coming evil should be silent, since he realizes that God Himself is bringing it about in order to punish the people, who did not seek Him and did not do what was good in His eyes that they might live (Amos 5:13; cf. 5:4,6,14f.; cf. Lev. 18:5).

5. David conceived (*hiśkîl*) the plan of the temple building after God's personal direction and design (1 Chr. 28:19). God sends a messenger to enlighten Daniel and explain to him the mysteries which he by himself cannot understand (Dan. 9:22, *yāsā'tî l^e haśkîlkā bînāh*; 25, *w^e tēda' w^e taśkēl*). David prays that God may give Solomon *śękęl* and *bînāh* to keep his Torah for only if Solomon keeps the laws will he succeed (*taṣlî^a ḥ*) (1 Chr. 22:12f.; 2 Chr. 2:11). It is also in God's good hand to send an *'îš śękęl* (Ezra 8:18) and shepherds after His heart who will lead the people with knowledge and understanding (*dē'āh w^e haśkēl*, Jer. 3:15); He will raise out of David's line a righteous branch who will rule wisely (*w^e hiśkîl*) and establish right and justice (23:5). The king will be wise and successful (*yaśkîl*) as long as he keeps the commandments of Moses and God is with him (2 Kgs. 18:7), whilst the enemies will not prevail in any respect (*lō' hiśkîlû*, Jer. 20:11).

6. It is only natural that Deutero-Isaiah firmly believes that the Servant of the Lord *yaśkîl* (Isa. 52:13), which the modern translations usually render "shall prosper" (RSV, NEB)—though not as a hero in the battle against the enemy or as an international politician. The older English version (AV) seems to have come nearer to the original intention of the author by rendering the word "shall deal prudently," which did not, however, satisfy modern scholars. The LXX had simply *sunesei* (Vulgate: *intelliget*). The statements about the Servant are introduced with the words that God has chosen him and supports him, that He has pleasure in him and will give His spirit on him (42:1), for his task is to establish (God's)

justice on earth and be a light to the nations. His success rests on this precondition from which it cannot be divorced.

7. Those who make their own gods do not know nor comprehend (the real God), for their eyes and hearts are prevented from seeing and understanding (*mērᵉ'ôt. . .mēhaśkîl*, Isa. 44:18). According to Job, it is God Himself who keeps the heart away from all ability of understanding (*śekel*, Job 17:4). In other words: it is in God alone that insight and understanding have their origin.

8. We have now to discuss the word *maśkîl* in the headings of the Psalms, where it occurs thirteen times.[1] Many attempts have been made at an explanation of this phenomenon, but none of them seems to come to a satisfactory conclusion. The headings are younger than the Psalms themselves. They probably date from pre-Maccabaean times.[2] Unfortunately, as they are "almost certainly not original," the NEB omitted them throughout. It is evident that the term *maśkîl* which designates a person who pleases God, is used here in a different way. It seems to connote a special type of Psalm, and the question now is what type of Psalm was selected to deserve this name, for not even ten percent of the Psalms were given this distinction. We have no doubt about the root meaning: "having or giving insight, showing or giving wisdom." What kind of insight or wisdom?

9. Mowinckel defines *maśkîl* as "die religiös-moralische Einsicht," "a supranormal wisdom and insight."[3] As such a song was the cultic vehicle of "a supranormal power," it was particularly "effective" in influencing or mollifying God, and Mowinckel, therefore, sees in a *maśkîl*-Psalm an "efficacious song." This explanation, at least in its first part, is quite plausible and may come near the truth, but it still leaves us in uncertainty about the significance or intended meaning of the term in the Psalm titles. We must not wonder, therefore, that the introductions to the Old Testament[4] do not hesitate to declare that the technical sense of the word remains obscure.[5]

1 Ps. 32; 42; 44f.; 52-55; 74; 78; 88f.; 142. Ps. 45 is an exceptional case, for though it is also called *maśkîl*, the word is immediately followed by another description: *šîr yᵉdîdôt* 'love-song' or 'wedding-song', as if *maśkîl* did not fit the contents and character of the Psalm; but perhaps it does, for it is quite obvious that this song was allegorically interpreted, like the Song of Songs (see the distinct allusions in Midrash *Tehillim*).

2 John F. A. Sawyer, "An Analysis of the Context and Meaning of the Psalm-Headings," *Transactions of the Glasgow University Oriental Society* 22 (1970), 26.

3 S. Mowinckel, *Die technischen Termini in den Psalmenüberschriften*, Psalmenstudien 4 (1923), 5-7; idem, *The Psalms in Israel's Worship* (1962), 2:94, 209; H. H. Rowley, *Worship in Ancient Israel* (1967), 210.

4 E.g., R. H. Pfeiffer, *Introduction*, 2nd ed. (1948), 642; O. Eissfeldt, *Introduction* (1965), 453.

5 Rowley, *Worship*, 211, n. 12, mentions some older efforts to explain the Psalm headings besides C. W. Ahlström's attempt in his *Psalm 89* (1959), 21f. Ahlström thinks that the term denoted a psalm used in the "renewal rites." (See Mowinckel's criticism in *JSS* 5 (1960), 295f.). A more recent view is offered by Sawyer, *Analysis*, 26-38, who suggests that the ancient term may originally have had nothing to do with Old Testament Hebrew *maśkîl* 'wise'. However, another root *śkl* has so far not been found. He reminds us also that "like *miktām*, *maśkîl* was taken as an epithet of David by Aquila and Symmachus" (p. 33). It is doubtful whether the two Greek translators were on the right track, for there are *maśkîl*-Psalms which were ascribed to others than David. Very likely they did not know what to do with the word *maśkîl* in the headings.

10. We may ask how the ancients understood the term. It is always interesting to see how the people of the immediate postbiblical times, who were so much nearer to the Scriptures, interpreted the texts; their views are often illuminating.

The LXX translates it regularly with *sunesios* or with *eis sunesin* (only Ps. 41, 43, 44), which would mean: "of or for wisdom," "leading to wise thinking and living," "for instruction," but, again, we are left uncertain about the kind or essence of that wisdom or intelligence.[6]

11. We do not hear much from the Rabbis about how they understood the term *maśkîl* in the Psalm headings. The question, it seems, is broached only once. From Midrash *Tehillim* on Ps. 32:1 where the term occurs for the first time in a heading, we gather that they took *maśkîl* to connote a person such as David and explained this interpretation with Prov. 15:24 (with the help of Ps. 34:6 and Dan. 4:31, as opposed to Num. 16:37 and Ps. 55:24): The path of life is upward for the *maśkîl*. They are the sons of man who look upward, *šęniśtaklû l^{e}ma$^{'a}$lāh*. A modern scholar would hardly agree with this kind of exegesis; nevertheless, it is the upshot of the Rabbis' train of thought. To them *maśkîl* indicates a way of life: looking up to God—and (with respect to Ps. 32:1), God will forgive his transgression.

12. The Targumist, on the other hand, identifies the word with *śēkel*, but he qualifies it throughout as *śiklā' ṭābā*, which is literally 'good wisdom', 'right understanding', 'commendable intelligence', etc.—except in one place, Ps. 78, where that understanding is called *śiklā' d^{e}rû^{a}ḥ qudšā'* 'wisdom of (in, from, through) the Holy Spirit'.

We should note that already the Hebrew equivalent of *śiklā' ṭābā'*, *śēkęl ṭôb* (which occurs in Ps. 111:10; Prov. 3:4; 13:15; 2 Chr. 30:22) is always understood as a quality or way of life pleasing God. *Yir'at YHWH* as *rē'šît ḥokmāh* is *śēkęl ṭôb* to all who act accordingly (Ps. 111:10). It brings favor with God and man (Prov. 3:4) and is the opposite of the way of the faithless (13:15). On the passage in Chronicles, see below. *Ṭôbat śēkęl*, said of Abigail, is not necessarily *śēkęl ṭôb*.

The Aramaic heading of Ps. 78 points to the right attitude in man's walk of life and anticipates the teaching of the Qumran sectarians of the Holy Spirit as guiding power.[7]

13. If we ask ourselves, what are the subjects of the *maśkîl* -Psalms, we find that they express man's repentance and God's forgiveness, prayers for help and salvation, recognition of God's greatness, thirsting and searching for God, teaching the Way, trusting in God, and especially praises for his wonderful deeds.

There are other Psalms which express similar ideas—for instance, the group of the Hallel-Psalms—but only a few Psalms have received the title *maśkîl*. These are Psalms which proclaim God's unique power, declare man's utter dependence on him, and teach man that he must acknowledge this fact and adjust his life according to this insight.

6 The Vulgate follows closely the LXX: *intellectus, ad intellectum, pro maeleth intelligentiae* (Ps. 52).

7 It would be rewarding to examine Ps. 78 more in detail, for not only does its representation of Israel's past, its disbelief and continuous revolt remind us of the Sectarian portrait of Israel's history (as reviewed, for instance, in the first part of the Damascus Document), but also its vocabulary figures in the language of Qumran, to mention but a few: *bāśār hēmāh; bagg^{e}dū; lō' bāṭ^{e}ḥû; y^{e}kazz^{e}bû; lō' hę'ęmînû ęt 'ēl; b^{e}niplā'ôt; lō' šām^{e}rū 'ęt b^{e}rît.*

14. The word *maśkîl* appears in a similar sense already once within the context of a song or praise of God's powerful reign (Ps. 47:8): ". . .sing to our King; for the King of all the earth is God, sing a *maśkîl*," that is, a proclamation of God's exclusive kingship which is at the same time a profession of faith and of loyalty.

It has often been pointed out[8] that 2 Chr. 30:22 may help us in an understanding of the term in this context. The chronicler records that the *maśkîlîm* were a group of Levitic temple singers (note the foregoing verse 21!). We must remember that *mitwaddîm* (in verse 22) is resonant also with confession and repentance. This specification is followed by the three words *śēkęl ṭôb laYHWH*, usually paraphrased (RSV, NEB): "who had shown good skill or true understanding in the service of the Lord." This translation does not do justice to the text, which says a little more, namely: "with great ardour, with special devotion to the Lord" (King Hezekiah had talked intimately with them, "to their heart").

2 Chr. 30:22, understood in this way, may indeed be of some help in finding the meaning of *maśkîl* Ps. 47:8. The Targum translates the line *zammᵉrû maśkîl* as follows: *šabbaḥû qodomôy bᵉśiklā' ṭābā'*. *Maskîl* is taken here not as a connotation of some particular kind of Psalm, but the translator adverbializes the Hebrew expression: "Sing praises before Him with all devotion."

15. Nehemiah relates that the public reading of God's Torah by the Levites was done *mᵉpōrāš wᵉśôm śēkęl*, "clearly and with the right understanding (emphasis) and the people grasped the meaning while it was read" (Neh. 8:8). The elders and leaders of the people together with the priests and the Levites assembled with Ezra in order to study carefully the words of the Torah, *lᵉhaśkîl 'ęt dibrê hatôrāh*, 8:13). They did it in earnest and in the right spirit. We also learn from the book of Nehemiah in the great prayer of repentance, when all the people had been called together for the highest praise of the eternal God (9:5f.), that it is he who "has given his good spirit to enlighten them" (*lᵉhaśkîlām*, 9:20). This is an important statement.

Though we do find in the fourth benediction of the Shmoneh-Esreh a clear confession that God bestowed on man *dē'āh bînāh wᵉhaśkēl*, the Rabbis had not much room for any continued activity of the holy spirit after the prophets Haggai, Zechariah, and Malachi[9]; but it played a considerable part in contemporary heretic circles, not only among the various Essenic groups but also among the early Christians.

16. The last and latest passages of the Old Testament which mention persons called *maśkîlîm* need special attention. We find them in the last two chapters of the book of Daniel (11:33, 35; 12:3, 10). Who are these *maśkîlîm*? They are distinct in quality and character from the common people (the *rabbîm*). They are endowed with deep insight and understanding of God's acts, especially of the coming mysterious happenings until the approaching of the end. Of course we can call them 'wise', but the translation of *maśkîlê 'ām* (11:33), "those among the people who are wise" (RSV), or "the wise leaders of the nation" (NEB), is certainly insufficient; the older translation "they that understand among the people" (AV) was slightly better. They belong to the *yôdᵉ'ê 'ęlōhāyw*, to that section of the people who know their

8 Cf. Gesenius-Buhl, *Handwörterbuch* (1915), s.v. *maśkîl.*
9 H. Kosmala, *Hebräer-Essener-Christen* (Leiden, 1959), 263f.

God (11:32); they will not sit still but become *maśkîlê 'ām* who will enlighten the *rabbîm* led astray by the *marši'ê b^{e}rît.* They will suffer hardships and death. The divine purpose of the misery which will come over them is to purify some of them, refine them and make them white until the time of the appointed end (verse 35). When the time of trouble is over, the nation will be saved, that is, every one whose name is written in the book (12:1f.). The *maśkîlîm*—including here all those who have been enlightened—will comprehend (verse 10).

We see that the meaning of *maśkîl* in the sense of 'teacher' or 'instructor' is already fully developed and in use in the last two chapters of the book of Daniel. The *maśkîl* who has *da'at 'elōhîm*, not just knowledge of God, but the deeper "Erkenntnis" of God, knows the mysteries of his wonderful deeds, knows that the *qēṣ (a'ḥarît yômayyā')*,[10] with its punishment and reward, is coming, and therefore gives heed to the perfect way before God.

17. It is in this sense that the word *maśkîl* became a technical term in the Scriptures of Qumran, singling out the teacher who not only instructs the members and the novices of the sect in the knowledge of God and His ways with man but also teaches them the way of life which God wants them to persue that they may escape the oncoming judgment.[11]

We may expect that the *maśkîl* has attained insight and wisdom, but the simple translation 'wise man' says too little and can be misleading as regards his standing and function within the community.

18. The tasks of the *maśkîl* are clearly laid out in the Manual of Discipline (S) and the Damascus Document (D). S III,13-IV,26, the catechism, is a short guidebook on the fundamental teachings concerning the requirements of that day; it is addressed to the *maśkîl* and is meant to be a help for his instruction. It is his obligation *l^{e}hābîn ûl^{e}lammēd* (those who are predestined among the children of man to become and be) the Sons of Light (S III,13; IV,22; X,26-XI,2), *l^{e}hā'îr* man's heart (IV, 2), *l^{e}hôkî^{a}ḥ* they that have chosen the Way in the knowledge of truth and righteous justice (IX, 17f.; cf. D XII, 20ff.), *l^{e}hanḥôtām* in *dē'āh* (S IX, 18) in one word *l^{e}haśkîlām* in the community in the mysteries of God's wonderful truth (IX, 18f.; cf. XI, 1 and D XIII, 7f.) and in the perfection of the Way (S IV, 22).

19. The *maśkîl* is a teacher strictly within the community; he is not a missionary. He must not argue or mix with those of the Pit; his teaching is arcane discipline and he must not reveal it to the evildoers, to those outside the community (S IX,16f.; cf. Amos 5:13!).

20. It goes without saying that the teaching must be accompanied and proved by an exemplary life. Who, then, could become a teacher? It was not enough to have the necessary mental and spiritual qualifications for his teaching office, he must also have distinguished himself by a perfect way of life.

There is a remarkable passage in the Epistle of James which may well have served as a warning against some who were aspiring to the office of a teacher.[12] James says on this point:

10 About these terms see Kosmala, "At the End of the Days," *ASTI* 2 (1963), 27-37.

11 Attention to this fact and the complete dependence on the teaching of the Bible on *maśkîl* was drawn already in the writer's, *Hebräer*, 284. Three years later, Naphtali Wieder came to the same conclusion in his book, *The Judaean Scrolls and Karaism* (London, 1962), 104, 110-12.

12 Much of the thought as well as of the terminology of Qumran has been taken up by early (Jewish) Christianity. We cannot enlarge on this subject here. The reader is referred to the ample material collected in the writer's *Hebraer*, which consists of studies in the proto-history of early Christianity.

"Let not many of you become teachers (*didaskaloi*, there is no adequate Greek translation of the Hebrew term), for you know that we who teach shall be judged with greater strictness. For we all make many mistakes; and if any one makes no mistakes in what he says, he is a perfect man . . . ." (3:1f.). "Who among you is wise (*sophos* = *ḥākam*) and understanding (*epistemon* = *maśkîl*[13])? By his good life let him show his works in the humility of wisdom (*en prauteti sophias* = *'anwat hokmāh*) . . . ." 3:13f.). This kind of wisdom is not "earthly wisdom" (3:15), it is "wisdom from above" (3:17).

The *maśkîl* of Qumran was bound to teach and answer in *'anāwāh* (S XI,1). He is endowed with *rûaḥ 'anāwāh* and with *śēkel ûbînāh weḥokmat gebûrāh*, that is, with understanding, insight, and wisdom of (divine!) power (S IV,2f.).[14]

For this type of teacher none of the biblical concepts was so well suited as the term *maśkîl*, none other was so intimately correlated with fear of God and divine wisdom that it could become an adequate name for the bearer of "supra-natural" wisdom.

21. The last sectarian group which adopted this term were the Karaites,[15] but the word was now applied to the whole group[16] in concordance with the passages in Dan. 11 and 12 where the word occurred only in the plural and finally (12:10) included all enlightened men whether they were official teachers or not. As *maśkîlê 'am* (11:33), the Karaites considered themselves the teachers of Israel, which had gone astray, and they regarded it as their task to bring Israel back to the "true way of the Torah."

13 Cf. LXX to Neh. 8:8, 13; Dan. 1:4; 5:11.

14 Cf. Dan. 2:20, 23: *ḥokmeta' ûgebûretā'dî lēh hî'*; Mic. 3:8.

15 Wieder, *Judaean Scrolls*, 104-20; Leon Nemoy, *Karaite Anthology* (New Haven, 1952), 39, 330.

16 Anan, the founder of the sect, was called *rō'š hammaśkîlîm* by his adherents.

A. Dupont-Sommer, *Les écrits esséniens découverts près de la Mer Morte*. Paris, Payot, 1959. 446 pp. Price 3.000 fr.

This book represents the *summa* of Professor Dupont-Sommer's work on the Dead Sea Scrolls. We are grateful for this monumental one-volume edition. There are few scholars who have made such important contributions as he to our knowledge of the Sect in the Judaean Desert, its identification, its history and chronology, as well as its constitution and theology. The ideas and arguments which he put forward already at an early stage of the discussion, first in his *Aperçus préliminaires* (1950) and two years later in his *Nouveaux aperçus* still very largely hold their ground. It may be said that opinion is becoming more and more consolidated behind them in spite of the opposition of some other scholars who have advocated different views. Right from the beginning—although he was not the very first to make this suggestion—Dupont-Sommer identified the Sect of Qumran with the Essenes of Josephus, Philo and Plinius. This view, has now found its expression also in the title of his book. He propounds it once more in the second chapter, after having given in the first a translation of all the older historical records of the Essenes. In ch. XII he investigates into the historical background of the Essenes of Qumran and their enemies (the *Kittim* and the Wicked Priest). Ch. XIII deals with the anonymous founder, prophet and leader of the congregation, the Teacher of Righteousness.

The greater part of the volume (chs. III-XI, pp. 83-348) consists of the translations of all the non-Biblical literature of the Sect—excepting those writings which are too mutilated for any coherent translation and all the minor fragments. It is now the most substantial collection of translated texts in French, in fact in any language, and supersedes Albert Vincent's edition (1955). In addition to the Manual of Discipline, the Damascus Document, and the Habakkuk Commentary, it contains not only the complete translation of the Thanksgiving Hymns and the War Scroll, but also the Genesis Apocryphon and many of the longer fragments of the exegetical, apocalyptical, and liturgical writings, so far as the texts were published before the end of 1958. One may, however, regret that some of the longer fragments of the Hymns, such as I-V, have not been included. Some of Dupont-Sommer's translations have already appeared elsewhere but have been revised for the present volume. The translation of the Hymns is a reprint from his *Livre des hymnes* (1957). Philological notes have been omitted from the present edition, which like his former two books of *Aperçus* addresses itself also to the less erudite public. The translations are literal unlike those of Th. H. Gaster (*Dead Sea Scriptures*, 1956), but nevertheless lucid and make, like the rest of his book, easy reading even for the foreigner. Each document or group of documents is preceded by an introduction. The introduction to the Biblical commentaries contains a short but excellent explanation of *pešer*, the text interpretation peculiar to the Essenes and early Christians. We also note the correct explanation of the word *midraš* (pp. 323f.), used once in the so-called Florilegium.

It is not possible here to discuss Dupont-Sommer's translations in full.

He himself modestly admits that they still remain provisional. The last pages of his *avant-propos* are worthy of a true scholar. Quoting a famous French scientist he confesses that knowledge advances "par ratures successives", by scrapping preconceived or favourite ideas. A few observations may therefore be permitted here in passing. As far as the Manual of Discipline is concerned, DUPONT-SOMMER seems to have been guided by BROWNLEE's translation, which was one of the first (1951) and still is, because of its many references, a very useful edition, but many of its renderings will have to be abandoned. The *maśkil* of S III, 13 is certainly more than just a "wise man" (*homme entendu, intelligent*). The term appears already fully developped in the book of Daniel and denotes finally an instructor or teacher (ix 13, 22; xi 33; xii 3), whose various tasks are then described in detail in the Sectarian literature (cf. S IX, 12-21). *Šlwm* in S III, 15 is hardly *šālom*, but rather *šillum*, first suggested, it seems, by HABERMANN (1952), who however did not give any reasons for his reading. The Biblical reference is Hos. ix 7, where we find both expressions: *pᵉquddah* and *šillum*. The meaning of the Sectarian text is: the *maśkil* is to instruct them "with regard to the visitation of their afflictions together with (*'im*) the appointed times of their retribution" (cf. Hebr. xi 6: God is a μισθαποδότης). The same applies to *šlwm* in H I, 17 (not considered by HABERMANN). In other places he has definitely improved upon BROWNLEE's renderings, for instance in S V, 11 f. He has also replaced the faulty translation of the editors of the Genesis Apocryphon "bad (pestilential) wind", adopted by BARDTKE, DEL MEDICO, and others, by "evil spirit". The mistake was already noticed (in *IEJ* 1957, p. 107) by D. FLUSSER, the New Testament scholar of the Hebrew University.

That there is a close relationship between early Christianity and Essenism can no longer be denied in spite of the opposition of those who lay all stress on the differences between the two theologies. Here also DUPONT-SOMMER was one of the first to point out some of the relevant problems. He deals with them once more in ch. XIV of his present book. The progress in this field of study is necessarily slow, not because Christian scholars are stunned by the similarities in thought and expression and afraid that Christianity might suffer loss from its uniqueness and originality, as some journalists suspected, but simply because our Hebraists and Old Testament scholars are rarely sufficiently familiar with the New Testament and therefore unable to draw conclusions from a comparative study. Apart from a few books of a more general nature for the wider public only studies of details have so far appeared. Of the collection of fourteen articles edited by K. STENDAHL in 1957 all but three were available already before the end of the year 1955, which saw the publication of important new texts DUPONT-SOMMER concludes his own chapter (which is occupied mainly with John the Baptist, Jesus, and the Teacher of Righteousness, and leaves aside the theological concepts and problems of the New Testament epistles) with an appropriate quotation from a short comparative study of the same year 1957, by R. P. DANIELOU: "The discoveries of Qumran solve a considerable number of New Testament problems which exegesis has been unable to solve, . . . and very likely the number of problems solved will increase."

On the other hand it is now safe to say that a careful comparative study of the New Testament will also shed new light on many ambiguous or obscure passages in the Qumran documents. Is the *geber* of H III, 9 "the Messiah" or "the new creature"? Is the *geber* of S IV, 20 "everyone" and must we here, as also DUPONT-SOMMER does, adopt YADIN's reading, or rather alteration, of the text, that "the bodily building of everyman" will be refined, an idea not to be found elsewhere in the Scrolls or in the New Testament, or had we not better follow the Old Testament trend, developed in the New Testament epistles, that God will purify and separate a new people from the rest of mankind unto himself? And is *miqdaš 'adam* (Florilegium I, 6) a "sanctuary made with the hands of man", or is it, in agreement with New Testament thought and in concordance with the Sectarian texts, a "human sanctuary" which God had in mind to build for himself, that they might offer him in it works of the law? These are only a few suggestions, but there are many more. Much careful study remains to be done, and we may refer here to DUPONT-SOMMER's own words: "It is highly desirable that all possible tracks are explored, and that in all freedom."

A number of appendices are added to the book. In these, with the exception of the first which deals with the two copper scrolls found in cave III, he discusses and refutes various theories about the origin of the Qumran Sect, which has been identified with Qaraites (S. ZEITLIN), with Hebrew Christians (J. L. TEICHER), with Zealots (C. ROTH), and with a Pharisaic group (CH. RABIN). These brief chapters are models of critical reviews. The last one is concerned with the two "unnecessary" books of DEL MEDICO who considers the Essenes to be a myth. One of his books has been translated into English, but nobody knows why.

The book which deserves a translation into English and other languages is the present one by DUPONT-SOMMER.

Hans Walter Huppenbauer, *Der Mensch zwischen zwei Welten. Der Dualismus der Texte von Qumran (Höhle I) und der Damaskusfragmente. Ein Beitrag zur Vorgeschichte des Evangeliums.* Abhandlungen zur Theologie des Alten und Neuen Testaments, 34. Zürich, Zwingli Verlag, 1959. 132 pp. Price DM 19.—.

The dualistic thought of the Sect of Qumran has been early recognized as the most peculiar trait of its theology. The book before us is a presentation of the problem (p. 13) "with a view to its importance for NT studies" (p. 7), although the author does not follow this line into the early Christian writings. In the first five chapters he gives an exposition of the dualism in each of the five larger documents. A further chapter is devoted to the longer fragments, whilst the last contains the summary of these studies. In the first chapter on the Manual of Discipline and related fragments (S, Sa, Sb), by far the longest, he surveys the various well-known opposites truth (righteousness)—perversion and light—darkness, which are the basic elements of the teaching in the catechism (S III, 13-IV, 26).

Whether it is possible to speak of a dualism God — Man (pp. 40 f., 67 ff.) may be questioned. The author introduces here a special type of dualism which he calls "metaphysical dualism" (pp. 10, 68, 104). Naturally there is a difference between God and Man, but the descriptive appositions ("weak" Man — "holy" God) are sufficient to show that Man and God are no genuine opposites which are hostile to each other and can never be united, such as light and darkness or righteousness and perversion (cf. here the clear definition of Paul in 2 Cor vi 14. See also the author's own remark in note 447). God has a definite purpose with Man (s. pp. 68 f., 102 below): Man can and must be raised from his inferior state and can attain to celestial glory in a life to come. This, however, is possible only if he belongs to those who are chosen and called (p. 107). The fight of God against his enemies in the end of the days (p. 72 f.) is, therefore, not the fight against "weak" Man, but the judgement God passes on "all Belial" (H III, 27 f.). Although this eschatological fight will be fought by "the heros of heaven" (III, 35 f.), we also know from the War-Scroll that this army will include the chosen from Israel. "Flesh", therefore, denotes sometimes not "weak" Man, but the nations over which Israel will rule one day (p. 87). The decisive line of division must be drawn between light (truth, righteousness) and darkness (perversion), and as Man can belong to either of the two camps the dividing line goes actually right through mankind (s.a. the author's own note 455). This division has its origin already in the act of creation (cf. H I, 7-9; IV, 38 f.; XV, 12-17; also S III, 18 ff.; IV, 16 ff.; Dam II, 7, 13, 15) or even (according to H XV, 14) in God's mind b e f o r e the creation. It is the *praedestinatio duplex* of Man which is the basic problem of the dualism of Qumran especially with regard to the human side. The author mentions it twice expressly (note 438 and pp. 111 f.) and alludes to it briefly when speaking of God's providence (pp. 60 f.; 64, 67, 74, 88, 95, 99), but does not, unfortunately, investigate into it. On one occassion he maintains that evil cannot come directly from God (p. 97), on another he admits that God is the creator of everything including the principle of evil, which is permitted to work among men for an appointed time (cf. pp. 95, 98, 99).

The author is surprised at finding that "just where the thought of the Sect culminates in an extreme monotheism, it becomes dualistic" (pp. 97 f.) or that the Sectarian dualism is "immer wieder durchbrochen" (p. 111). Following Nötscher very closely he concludes (p. 112), that the dualism of the Sect is not an absolute but a "relative dualism" "always with ethics as the main concern". Nötscher's formula was: "it is a relative, ethical dualism whose beginning and end are dependent on God" (*Terminologie*, p. 83, not fully quoted by Huppenbauer). So our author's findings do not go beyond Nötscher's statement. Two pages later the author says in his final remarks: "It is evident that the dualistic elements in the faith of the

Sect stand in the service of other theological tenets"—but these are rather his personal reflexions, not necessarily those of the Sect.

The dualism of the Sect is certainly a vexed problem which cannot be easily divorced from the question of its origin. Our author decided to leave this question alone (p. 13). K. G. KUHN and DUPONT-SOMMER tried to trace the Qumran dualism back to the dualism of the Iranian religion, whilst K. SCHUBERT prefers Stoicism as its source. Others, like G. MOLIN and to some extent H. WILDBERGER, have drawn our attention to certain statements in the OT on God as the God of light, older beliefs which may underlie the Qumran dualism, but suppose that the Biblical ideas have been influenced by Iranian conceptions. HUPPENBAUER seems to favour this latter view (s. his note 20) but makes no attempt to solve the riddle.

It is not very likely that a Jewish sect for which the Scriptures mean everything should go and borrow fundamental ideas directly from pagan religions or philosophies instead of accepting the Biblical traditions about the God of Israel. Yet the similarity with Iranian conceptions cannot be denied. Setting out from these two observations we have only one possible solution, and the key to it is Is. xlv 7 ff. This important passage has already been overlooked by S. AALEN in his monumental study. HUPPENBAUER quotes it (p. 97, not registered in his index), but only in order to deny the acceptability of its teaching! The passage follows immediately after the introduction of Cyrus as the Shepherd and Annointed One of God (Is. xliv 25-xlv 6), who, using him as his tool (xliv 28, xlv 13), will bring the false religion of the Babylonians to nought (xliv 25, xlv 16, 20). Cyrus was the representative of a new and distinctly different religion of light defeating darkness. But if Cyrus is the tool in the hand of God who has made everything (xliv 24, xlv 12; etc.) and who is the sole God over all the nations from the East to the West (xlv 5 f., 20-24), then God must also be the creator and lord of the two forces light and darkness (xlv 7). That these two opposites represent not only physical elements but stand as symbols for principles is evident from the parallel line: "who makes peace and creates evil". The Hebrew root *šlm* also implies "completeness" and "perfectness". Some translators have rendered *šalom* here, not unduly, by "welfare" and "salvation" (adopted also by HUPPENBAUER: "*Heil*"), and we can indeed place it, as the Second Isaiah does (verse 8), beside the other blessings of God, *ṣedeq* and *ješaʿ*. Two things must not be forgotten: (1) that the God of Israel and fire have very early been correlated and that fire gives light (Ex xiii 21) just as light can become fire (Is x 17); (2) that light and darkness are natural symbols for good and evil and were as such in use evidently before any Iranian influence can be ascertained (Is. v 20; Amos v 18, 20). The equalization of light and darkness with good and bad, true and false religion cannot, however, be assigned with certainty to the time before the rise of the Iranians (Is. xlii 16 f.; their identification with wisdom and foolishness is even later, Eccl. ii 13 f.).

It was no difficult step for the Second Isaiah to accept the Iranian dualism as form and symbol and to integrate it into his own religion. Light, that goes without saying, could only be with the true God, beside whom there was no one else (xlv 5 a, 6 b; etc.). Man, his creation, could not resist him or call him to account (9 and 10). The God of Israel knows alone what is going to be and he alone must be asked about it (11), for he is the "hidden hand" (15) behind everything. The prophetic speaker saluted Cyrus as the Chosen One of God trusting that the conqueror would understand his calling and recognize and acknowledge the power of the God of Israel, the dispenser of "the treasures of darkness" (Babylonia; cf. xlii 16 f.), whom he had not known before as the true God of the universe (xlv 2-5 and 6). The Second Isaiah professes absolute monotheism but makes use—and one must say, ingeniously—of a form derived from the dualistic Iranian system without, however, taking over its actual contents. In the simple formula of verse 7 the Iranian religion—in whatever variety it may have presented itself to the Second Isaiah—appears completely transformed, digested and merged in the strictly monotheistic faith of Israel.

It is possible that the Sect when they conceived the dualistic view of men and their respective spirits went directly back to the basic dictum Is. xlv 7. But it is also possible that the dualistic tradition coming from the Second Isaiah saw its revival already before the Sect developped its theology. Traces of such a revival can be seen in the book of Daniel which, in its first part (chs. i-vi), also deals with the oncoming downfall of Babylon (!). It shows the God of Heaven (Daniel's God) as the highest God (ii 37 f., 47, iii 28, iv 31 f. with a literal quotation from Is. xlv 9), who must be asked (Dan ii 22 a, cf. Is xlv 15; Dan ii 28 a, 29); for he knows what is in the darkness and the light dwells with him (22 b). This last sentence refers in the first place to God's revealing power, but being at the same time the concluding statement it presupposes a general reflexion on the God in whose power are both, light and darkness. Even the missionary element from Is. xlv 4-6, 20, 22 is not missing, only that in the visionary book of Daniel the mission is immediately successfull (ii 47, iii 28 f., 33, iv 22 b-23, 31 f., 34, vi 26 f.; cf. also the so-called Prayer of Nabonid from Cave IV). From more recent finds in Qumran we know that the book of Daniel was in favour with the Sect and that other pseudo-Danielic literature was in existence.

The dependence of the teaching of Qumran on Is. xlv is hardly to be doubted, all the more so as the dualism of Is. xlv 7 must be described with the same words as the Qumranian dualism: it is "relative" dualism.

THE HOUSE OF DAVID, from the Fall of the Kingdom of Judah to the Fall of the Second Commonwealth and After, by JACOB LIVER. The Magnes Press, Jerusalem, 1959. Pp. XIV + 168. (In Hebrew, with an English summary).

The book is divided into two parts. In the first, the author presents an investigation into the biblical records of the Davidic dynasty (especially 1 Chron. 3) and the later traditions on the Davidic descent of families or individual persons as found outside the Bible in the Jewish literature of the pre-Christian era, the New Testament and elsewhere. He comes to the conclusion that there is nothing in the literary sources outside the Bible that can be relied upon, with perhaps one exception: namely, that the Babylonian Exilarchs were "somehow genealogically related to the Davidic family but such a relationship is unproved." The author therefore feels justified in speaking of the early total decline of the Davidic family, about the beginning of the fourth century B.C.E.

In the second part of the book, he tries to explain how this complete decline was brought about and how, after many generations, the idea of a Messianic King of the House of David came again to the fore. Concurrent with the conclusion reached in his study of the genealogical trees and family traditions, he emphasizes that the hope for a Davidic Messiah was never connected with the presence of a family or persons claiming Davidic descent. This statement is on the whole correct, although one is not quite satisfied with the author's treatment of the post-biblical evidence regarding the existence of families of Davidic descent during the time of the Second Temple and after. Some of these traditions, he thinks, may have been fabricated *ad hoc;* others he brushes away as untrustworthy and irrelevant. A record by a Christian writer, preserved by Eusebius, on the burning of genealogical books by King Herod is dismissed on the ground that "no confirmation can be found in Jewish sources" (p. 35, note 40). This record should have been examined on its merits, for it at least shows that genealogical books existed. Joachim Jeremias, who had previously collected the post-biblical material bearing on the problem (see *Jerusalem zur Zeit Jesu,* 1923 ff., 2nd edition 1958, part II B. pp. 145-174), after careful examination of this passage, comes to the conclusion that it is inadmissible to regard the whole story as a fable. Considering that the preservation of genealogical books played such an important role during and after the establishment of the Jewish commonwealth, it is difficult to believe that this custom was dropped afterwards. How much stress was laid on the registration of descent is, for instance, to be seen from the Damascus document. Surely not all genealogical trees were spurious. That family traditions, especially among families of noble descent, are as far as possible kept alive (even where there are no written records) is a universal fact; also that such traditions are usually respected by others unless there is reason for suspicion or intent to defame. The problem of genealogies during the time of the Second Temple and after, needs a far more cautious treatment than it has received in the present work.

The author also discusses (pp. 32-36) the genealogical trees of Jesus (Matthew 1 and Luke 3) and the second century records (mentioned by Eusebius) on the Davidic origin of the descendants of the family of Jesus. The two New Testament genealogies are indeed a vexed problem and much has been written on it by Christian scholars. In pursuance of his general thesis that traditions on Davidic parentage are extremely doubtful, the author attaches much importance to the discourse of Jesus about himself: "The Messiah cannot be of Davidic descent, which, by implication, means that Jesus himself does not descend from the House of David." He quotes Joseph Klausner in favour of his view; but on consulting the last (German) edition of Klausner's work on *Jesus of Nazareth* (Jerusalem, 1952, p. 440, note 47), we find that even he is far more cautious and warns against the rash conclusion "that Jesus was not a son of David."

In spite of the author's hypercritical attitude to historical records, and his somewhat superior manner in treating the work of other scholars, the book is a notable contribution to the discussion of the Davidic problem, and it is to be regretted that it will remain unknown to scholars who do not read Hebrew.